TWENTIETH CENTURY VIEWS

The aim of this series is to present the best in contemporary critical opinion on major authors, providing a twentieth century perspective on their
changing status in an era of profound revaluation.

Maynard Mack, *Series Editor*
Yale University

STEINBECK

A COLLECTION OF CRITICAL ESSAYS

Edited by
Robert Murray Davis

Prentice-Hall, Inc. *Englewood Cliffs, N.J.*

© 1972 by Prentice-Hall, Inc., Englewood Cliffs, New Jersey. A SPECTRUM BOOK. All rights reserved. No part of this book may be reproduced in any form or by any means without permission in writing from the publisher. ISBN: C 0-13-846659-9; P 0-13-846642-4. *Library of Congress Catalog Card Number 75-178763.* Printed in the United States of America.

10 9 8 7

PRENTICE-HALL INTERNATIONAL, INC. (*London*)
PRENTICE-HALL OF AUSTRALIA, PTY. LTD. (*Sydney*)
PRENTICE-HALL OF CANADA, LTD. (*Toronto*)
PRENTICE-HALL OF INDIA PRIVATE LIMITED (*New Delhi*)
PRENTICE-HALL OF JAPAN, INC. (*Tokyo*)

Contents

v

To M. C. Davis

Introduction

by Robert Murray Davis

The most striking feature of John Steinbeck's current reputation is that his audience would rather read than praise him. Except for *Bombs Away*, his well-intentioned contribution to the war effort in 1942, all of his books are readily available in paperback editions both in this country and England. Translations of his work continue to proliferate: in 1968 alone, according to *Index Translationum*, forty-four titles were issued in twelve languages. These numbers are small; the major works and most of the minor ones had long since been translated. Millions have seen movie versions of *The Grapes of Wrath, Tortilla Flat, East of Eden, The Pearl, The Wayward Bus, The Moon is Down, The Red Pony*, and *Of Mice and Men*. In 1968, the year of his death, three television shows were based on his work, and two years later an opera based on *Of Mice and Men* was performed in Seattle. And, in what should have been the crowning point of his career, he was awarded the Nobel Prize for Literature in 1962.

The extent and nature of this popularity have had almost wholly negative effects on his critical reputation. Arthur Mizener asked, "Does a Moral Vision of the Thirties Deserve a Nobel Prize?" and decided that it did not, attributing the award to the relative crudity of European readings of American writers and to the politics of literary prizes.[1] He voiced most eloquently the general reaction of the literary establishment. Six years later, Harry T. Moore, author of the first book on Steinbeck (1939), publicly repented of his youthful enthusiasm in the "Epilogue" of the second edition of *The Novels of John Steinbeck: A First Critical Study*.[2] Once Steinbeck seemed promising, Moore said, but "Over the years he has become the idol of book clubs and movie audiences, and of a vast uninstructed reading public. Literary experts of high standing have either ignored Steinbeck or, in critical books

---

[1] *New York Times Book Review*, December 9, 1962, pp. 4, 43–45.
[2] (New York: Kennikat Press, 1968).

and journals of limited circulation, have exposed his defects" (p. 98). Moore is essentially correct about critical trends. Although *Modern Fiction Studies* devoted a special issue to his work in 1965, it began with Peter Lisca's "Steinbeck's Image of Man and His Decline as a Writer" and included Warren French's admission that the recovery he had hoped for on the evidence of the story "How Mr. Hogan Robbed a Bank" had failed to materialize in *The Winter of Our Discontent*. Since then, a number of articles on Steinbeck and even a *Steinbeck Quarterly* have appeared; but the most prestigious journals, *American Literature* and *PMLA*, gave space only to negative or qualified discussion of *Tortilla Flat*, and even the *Quarterly* has expressed reservations about some of Steinbeck's novels.

Steinbeck's fall from critical and academic favor can in part be explained by shifts in literary fashion. The late 1930s, which marked the high point of his reputation, favored sympathetic pictures of the dispossessed (many of his novels can be and were fitted into this category) and applauded broad and optimistic statements about The People, preferably couched in pseudoepic form. Carl Sandburg, Archibald MacLeish, the Benét brothers, and a host of lesser-known writers sought to combine the social muse with the epic strain, passed through a period of public favor, and have for the most part sunk beneath critical consideration.[3] Insofar as Steinbeck shared or seemed to share their views and methods, he has come to seem dated. A bit later, during the flush of patriotism that followed Pearl Harbor and the uncertainties of the first year of World War II, The People gave place to "the little people," the virtuous, peaceful, and colorless cross between peasant and petit bourgeois by and for whom, in the accounts of war correspondents, the war was being fought. A great many erstwhile rebels—real ones like Nancy Cunard and fictional ones like Evelyn Waugh's Basil Seal—discovered that rebellion was no longer possible and fell reluctantly into line. Writers who had always felt the tug of social responsibility subordinated their talents to the "War Effort."

Anyone compelled to seek the causes of Steinbeck's decline as a writer—and the flaws were latent even in his work of the 1930s—can point to the war. Earlier, his work happened to accord with fashion; with the outbreak of war, he began to write in a particular fashion and by his own account to omit uncomfortable truths in order to foster

---

[3] See Barker Fairley, "John Steinbeck and the Coming Literature," *Sewanee Review*, L (April–June 1942), 145–61.

popular American illusions.[4] It would be melodramatic to say that this breach of integrity finished him as a writer—*Cannery Row* and *The Wayward Bus* came later, and he was passing through a climacteric that included a divorce and remarriage and a move from California to New York. However, his first two really bad books were direct contributions to the war effort. *Bombs Away* is a disaster, full of hearty patriotism, bluff egalitarianism crossed with elitism (". . . the cadets were drawn from a cross-section background of America but they are the top part of the cross-section"), and admiration for killer instinct. The typical air gunner, for example, closely resembles the vicious Curly in *Of Mice and Men*, but Steinbeck praises him. Steinbeck the biologist could label as subspecies German Aryans "and the dark Aryans of Italy and the yellow Aryans of Japan."[5] *The Moon is Down* is better than *Bombs Away*, but it too is full of patriotic platitudes, and its characters are flat and pompous.

Thereafter, Steinbeck made only two attempts to deal with contemporary life in his fiction, in *The Wayward Bus* and *The Winter of Our Discontent*, moving for the most part into allegory, pastoral, fantasy, and historical panorama. Most of these later books were popular, but reviewers who expected another *Grapes of Wrath* or *Of Mice and Men* were disappointed, and those who help reputations rather than sales were for the most part hostile. Furthermore, Steinbeck's attempt to state positive values ran afoul of the bias towards the existential questioning of values. Besides falling out of fashion, he had fallen out of touch. His nonfiction books reveal his distaste for the course American life had taken; and in *Travels With Charley*, published a year after his last novel, he admitted that "I did not know my own country. . . . I had not felt the country for twenty-five years. I was writing of something I did not know about, and it seems to me that in a so-called writer this is criminal."[6] If he ever rediscovered the country, he did not write about it in a novel. Perhaps he did not need to: critics damned or forgot him and the public continued to buy his books, early and late.

[4] See the Introduction to *Once There Was a War* (New York: The Viking Press, Inc., 1958), pp. xi–xviii.

[5] The war mania affected other writers. Hemingway, for example, decided that the final solution to the German problem was blanket castration (Introduction to *Men at War* [New York: Crown Publishers, 1942], p. xxiv).

[6] *Travels with Charley in Search of America* (New York: The Viking Press, Inc., 1962), p. 5.

II

Confronted by the divergence between critical and popular taste, one may be tempted to ignore the problem, to damn either or both extremes, or to relegate Steinbeck's stories to "uninstructed readers" and introductory literature courses where they can prepare students to read more complex and mature work. Or one may attempt to discover the causes of Steinbeck's popularity to see if the crowd has gone right, or partly right, and to discriminate between novels that will fade from notice and those, if any, that may become a permanent part of our literature. The last course is most rewarding, for it not only attempts to do justice to Steinbeck's work, it also raises important questions about popular fiction and about nonrealistic fictional modes, such as allegory and fable, that are returning to literary and popular favor.

It is easy to condemn the popular writer. However, a work can be popular either because it panders to the audience's prejudices and egoism, or because, as Sir Philip Sidney and Joseph Addison pointed out, it appeals to and satisfies common, basic needs and drives. One must concede that a good deal of Steinbeck's work falls into the former category, that it is "Midcult" in Dwight Macdonald's description: "Technically . . . advanced enough to impress the middlebrows without worrying them" and "In content . . . 'central' and 'universal,' in that line of hollowly portentous art which the French call *pompier* after the glittering, golden beplumed helmets of their firemen." [7] When, for example, structural patterns in Steinbeck's novels are clear, they are almost blindingly obvious: the Exodus analogy in *The Grapes of Wrath,* combined with interchapters whose function is always quite clear; the centrifugal-centripetal movements in *Tortilla Flat*; the foreshadowings of the deaths of Curley's wife and of Lennie in *Of Mice and Men*; the various "songs" in *The Pearl*. When the patterns are more obscure, as in *Cannery Row* and *The Pastures of Heaven* and in some episodes of *Tortilla Flat,* they are sufficiently buried so as not to bother the reader who is content to amuse himself with the individual episodes.

Furthermore, the Midcult reader, who "aspires towards Universality above all," finds many passages in Steinbeck to suit his taste. In fact, Steinbeck shared that taste and was puzzled by criticism of it: "I have noticed," he wrote in the journal he kept while writing *East of Eden,*

[7] *Against the American Grain* (New York: Random House, Inc., 1962), p. 40.

"so many of the reviews of my work show a fear and a hatred of ideas and speculations. It seems to be true that people can only take parables fully clothed with flesh. Any attempt to correlate in terms of thought is frightening." [8] The fact that he was serious and sincere—qualities whose double edge most readers never perceive—reassured his audience; the fact that most of the ideas were obvious, even platitudinous, close enough to what most readers feel they ought to think and vague enough to provide comfortably large loopholes, endeared him to that audience. For example, his credo in *East of Eden,* quoted by R. W. B. Lewis (see the last essay in this collection) as evidence that Steinbeck could regain his former power, is serious, high-minded, and banal. Less orthodox sentiments are presented in thoroughly American terms: he attacks the banks and corporations; he criticizes the dehumanizing tendency of capitalist and collectivist alike; he criticizes the narrowness and lack of charity of conventional, respectable people; he asserts the claims of masculine ease and companionship against respectable, female-dominated society. At his worst, he asserts that it is "the duty of the writer to lift up, to extend, to encourage." [9]

The description of Steinbeck as conventional thinker contradicts Edmund Wilson's view of his "biological realism" as a consistent philosophy and Steinbeck's own assertion that he viewed the world from a scientific, "nonteleological" viewpoint.[10] Had Steinbeck consistently applied "is" thinking rather than "why" thinking, he would have been forced to abandon his role as social critic, which he regarded as central to any writer's purpose. Had he confined "is" thinking to his nonfiction, he would have lost some of the range and detachment he obviously required for his authorial stance. His attempts to avoid either logical extreme led him into some basic confusion. In *The Grapes of Wrath,* for example, the preacher Casy is nonteleological in asserting that "There ain't no sin and there ain't no virtue. There's just stuff people do," but he goes on to say that "Some of the things folks do is nice, and some ain't nice, but that's as far as any man got a right to say"—which raises more issues than it resolves. "Nice and not nice" is an unsatisfactory substitute for more rigorous categories, not only for the Christian like Graham Greene, who bases *Brighton Rock* on much the same kind of polarized value systems, but also for

[8] *Journal of a Novel: The East of Eden Letters* (New York: The Viking Press, Inc., 1969), pp. 166–67.

[9] *Ibid.,* p. 115.

[10] *Classics and Commercials* (New York: Vintage Books, 1962), p. 45.

the existentialist. Steinbeck's system, subjective and vaguely social at once, does not allow for tragedy or for real conflict because he is unable to make clear distinctions. At best, this attitude results in the mellow tolerance of *To a God Unknown*; at worst, it leads to the bland toleration of human foibles in *The Short Reign of Pippin IV*, where an old man echoes Casy with "There's just people—just what people do." Such an attitude will support the extravagant comedies of James Branch Cabell and Aubrey Menen, but it cannot deal with serious or even very complex issues when anything much is at stake. And there are other confusions. Steinbeck advocates humane treatment of the Joads and the other migrants because inhumane treatment will lead to destruction, but he blurs the argument that the "haves" should act from self-interest by adding Ma's assertion that the people will endure because they are toughened by hardship. If the soft inhabitants are inevitably to be replaced by the hungry immigrants, then presumably no ameliorative efforts will be availing. Or if man has choice and therefore direction of his fate, "nice and not nice" are inadequate to judge his behavior in terms of the basic law of survival. Of course, Steinbeck's major concern in *The Grapes of Wrath* is to arouse sympathy for the Joads and their fellows and to convert that sympathy into action; therefore, ideas and theories are used, as they were in his other novels, primarily as rhetorical devices chosen to suit a local situation, not the novel as a whole. Thus, at the beginning of *East of Eden* he is trying to make Cathy Ames seem horrifying, and he posits the theory that she is a moral monster, totally set apart from humanity. Later in the novel he strives for universality and asserts that there is perhaps a bit of the monster in all of us. Edmund Wilson was wrong; Steinbeck was far less tough-minded than Aldous Huxley, whose distressed migrant in *After Many a Summer Dies the Swan* is, however unwittingly, responsible for his own plight in ways that Steinbeck can never quite admit of the Joads. Huxley may not have had a first-rate mind or have been a better novelist than Steinbeck, but he knew what thinking meant, and Steinbeck never really did.

Although the inability to handle generalizations crippled Steinbeck as a discursive writer—of his nonfiction books, only *The Sea of Cortez* is anything but embarrassing—it may be that inconsistency is not a fatal handicap to a novelist. In fact, F. Scott Fitzgerald insisted that holding contradictory ideas at the same time was the mark of a first-rate mind. However, Steinbeck was rarely able to yoke opposites. Instead, he embraced one simplicity, whether of idea or character, at a time. For example, the police officer is a minor but recurring figure in Steinbeck's novels, and he is presented in either of two ways: as remote, brutal, faceless oppressor, or as benevolent, wise, and tolerant guardian of his flock. Never is there any complexity. Steinbeck offers what seems to be an explanation in "A Primer on the 30's": "There's a lot of people that when they get scared they get mean, and the scareder they get the meaner they get. A cop with the situation in hand don't need no night stick or gun." [11] But what about the good cop who loses control? The mediocre officer who muddles along? They never appear in Steinbeck's work. Thus, while his characters and his generalizations tell us something—many scared people are mean—they tell us less than some readers are willing to accept, or at least to accept over and over again.

This passion for simplicity, together with his belief in something like the Elizabethan microcosm-macrocosm theory, accounts for Steinbeck's inclination, more frequently indulged as he grew older, to allegorize, generalize, and typify not merely in stating themes or sketching characters but in formulating the central fables of his novels. Both rationale and method were stated clearly in his preface to *The Forgotten Village*:

> Our story centered on one family in one small village. We wished our audience to know this family very well, and incidentally to like it, as we did. Then, from association with this little personalized group, the larger conclusion concerning the racial group could be drawn with something like participation. Birth and death, joy and sorrow, are constants, experiences common to the whole species. If one participates first in these constants, one is able to go from them to the variables of customs, practices, *mores,* taboos, and foreign social patterns.[12]

Steinbeck's critics have been so pleased to discover this key to his method that they have ignored its overtones. It is obviously the statement of an incorrigible generalizer for whom "the tide pool stretches both ways, digs back to electrons and leaps space into the universe and fights out of the moment into non-conceptual time." [13] In making this leap, of course, he may forget all about the tide pool and the individual creatures therein; and in the disastrous documentary, *Bombs Away,* and in his novels, the person is sometimes lost in the message. This is most notoriously true of *Burning Bright,* where the characters change from acrobats to farmers to seamen without doing violence to anything

[11] *Esquire,* LIII (June 1960), 92.
[12] *The Forgotten Village* (New York: The Viking Press, Inc., 1941), p. [5].
[13] *Sea of Cortez* (New York: The Viking Press, Inc., 1941), p. 85.

but probability and language. In his best work, including *The Grapes of Wrath,* he is able to offset this generalizing tendency with a genuine interest in and concern for his central characters—in fact, to clothe his parables with flesh.

Even so, one almost always has the feeling that Steinbeck is detached from his characters and that, as T. K. Whipple pointed out, he is able "to take the sting out of reality and yet leave it all there except the sting." [14] This frequently allows readers to relax, to suspend or overturn quotidian judgments, to give vent to suppressed feelings in not very revolutionary fashion, and to identify with and yet remain detached from his characters. It is comforting to give an easy yes or no, more difficult, as Leslie Fiedler maintains, to say the hard "No! In Thunder." Steinbeck sometimes tried, as in *Cannery Row,* to give the public a "poisoned creampuff," but as with Shaw they licked off the cream and left the poison.[15] At his most earnest, Steinbeck resembles another Edwardian, John Galsworthy, who offered not real conflicts or dilemmas but "tests for right feelings"—perhaps an even better definition than Dwight Macdonald's for the Midcult artist.[16]

III

Yet even the critic most fervent in support of high art and its audience should pause to ask if Steinbeck's popularity over thirty-five years and twenty-seven books may not spring from qualities lasting in the work and perceptive in the audience—if, as Pope says, the lines of judgment are drawn more or less distinctly, but the same in all men. This consideration leads to a more or less neutral ground of literary discussion rarely touched upon, the question, not of self-gratifying or flattering qualities discussed earlier, but of the *interesting,* of that which is capable of engaging and holding our attention. Judged in this light, Steinbeck has obviously engaged his audience and endured longer than contemporaries of greater political or literary orthodoxy, and among the reasons he has done so are his forms and the world he creates within those forms.

[14] *Study Out the Land* (Berkeley and Los Angeles: University of California Press, 1943), p. 105.

[15] Antonia Seixas, "John Steinbeck and the Non-Teleological Bus," in *Steinbeck and His Critics,* ed. E. W. Tedlock, Jr., and C. V. Wicker (Albuquerque: University of New Mexico Press, 1957), p. 276.

[16] Samuel Hynes, *The Edwardian Turn of Mind* (Princeton: Princeton University Press, 1968), p. 84.

Steinbeck asserted that the writer must "set down his time as nearly as he can understand it" and must serve as "the watch-dog of society . . . to satirize its silliness, to attack its injustices, to stigmatize its faults";[17] in the 1930s and again in 1960 he did research in the field to improve his control of material; and several of his books can justly be called social novels.[18] A closer examination of the whole body of Steinbeck's work, however, shows that he was not often a realist in method and never wholly realistic in mode. Instead, he consciously employed what Robert Scholes and Robert Kellogg call *fictional,* as opposed to *empirical* forms, and fictional forms, based on "allegiance to the ideal," may be either romantic, to delight, or didactic, to instruct.[19] Seen in this perspective, Steinbeck's preference for allegory, pastoral, and fable is not an attempt to escape from reality but to create a world which exists within the work. One need not look far to discover that most reviewers and critics reject nonmimetic fictional modes; Philip Rahv's assertion that allegory is an inferior mode is typical.[20] More recently, critics like Stanley Alexander and Lawrence William Jones have argued the case for these forms and, what is more, have begun to make discriminations between effective and ineffective use of them. And Robert Scholes has argued in *The Fabulators* that these modes are again becoming dominant in the most exciting contemporary fiction.[21] Whatever the arguments of the critics, it is obvious that readers at all levels like traditional tales that draw upon "the harvest of symbols in our minds" and that remind us of fears and drives common to all men.[22] Steinbeck was sometimes guilty of using the method with too great facility, as in *East of Eden,* where he tried to reduce all human stories to one story, but he did not always abuse it. In *The Pearl,* for example, he focuses on the efforts of Kino to keep the pearl and upon his resignation of his dream at the end. Warren French and others have criticized the tale for its lack of realism, but to ask questions about Kino's future status—what will come of his

[17] *A Russian Journal* (New York: The Viking Press, Inc., 1948), pp. 27, 164. It is noteworthy that after these statements, Steinbeck turned away from the contemporary scene in his fiction.
[18] See Warren French, *The Social Novel at the End of an Era* (Carbondale, Ill.: Southern Illinois University Press, 1966).
[19] *The Nature of Narrative* (New York: Oxford University Press, 1966), pp. 13–14.
[20] See "Fiction and the Criticism of Fiction" in *The Myth and the Powerhouse* (New York: Farrar, Straus & Giroux, Inc., 1965).
[21] (New York: Oxford University Press, 1967).
[22] *Sea of Cortez,* p. 34.

killing his pursuers or whether he will be able to resume his former
place in society—is to ignore the story's mode and purpose. More
sophisticated critics are able to judge a nonrealistic work in literary
rather than in sociological or psychological terms; readers less sophisticated than French are able to accept the story in terms of its generic
premises without being conscious of genre.

The fictional world which Steinbeck creates within these nonempiri-
cal frameworks is, paradoxically, interesting to his readers because it
includes actions and sensations they recognize and which few other
writers give them. At the same time, this world exists at a remove from
immediacy—not simply the stingless reality described by Whipple but
in something like a pastoral landscape. To some extent, the past is
pastoral: the revival of Trollope during World War II and the phe-
nomenal success of *The Forsyte Saga* as upper-middle-brow television
soap opera demonstrate that the social criticism of one age tends to
become nostalgia-fodder in the next. Yet, simplified though it is, the
world that Steinbeck creates is based in reality. His tendency to focus
on a small, manageable cast of characters—often, as Harry Moore
noted, in a valley—reflects the topography and demography of an
earlier America as well as of California.[23] Furthermore, the values of
Steinbeck's world are based on social realities of a world that has almost disappeared. Essentially, it is a world in which standards can be
readily formulated and achievement readily judged; where competence
is measured in terms of the handyman or the generalist; where events
move slowly or at least time is not fully scheduled; where angst does
not exist; where the incomprehensible is readily accepted as mystery;
where people in frequent contact with more vulgar facts of life lack
at least some genteel squeamishness and perhaps some theoretical bru-
tality; where men recognize but are not obsessed by class distinctions
or separated by specialization. In *The Pastures of Heaven*, for example,
John Whiteside is the valley's aristocrat, a Harvard man who reads
classical history for pleasure, but he sees nothing incongruous in working alongside his neighbors and his men. In *East of Eden*, Samuel
Hamilton can deliver a baby, drill a well, administer a salutary beating,
and discuss philosophy without embarrassment. On a simpler level,
Slim is "the prince of the ranch" in *Of Mice and Men* because of his

---

[23] Freeman Champney's description of California in this collection contributes a
valuable perspective on Steinbeck's work, but it lacks Nathanael West's premonition
that California might have the cream rather than the pick of America's madmen
and the contemporary feeling in some quarters that California sets the trend for
the country as a whole.

competence and calmness, and Juan Chicoy of *The Wayward Bus,* in contrast to Mr. Pritchard, can not only drive a car but fix it; and though Steinbeck does not show him doing it, he could probably kill and cook a cow.

Steinbeck does show many people doing things. Like Hemingway and like the authors of recent books dealing with golf, baseball, and surgery—but unlike most modern novelists—he was interested in people working, going methodically and competently through a process. A monkey wrench inspired him as a fly rod did Hemingway. One gets the feeling that the characters like to work and that Steinbeck values them for it. As we become more specialized, these processes become mysterious to us, and we come to value more highly those who can do them and describe them to us. Furthermore, we have always admired and sought to emulate people who could do many things, especially things with their hands, and do them naturally and without fuss. My mother's father, for example, could trade a horse advantageously, fix his car, drill and thread the seat for an oil plug, convert a carriage shed into a house, do all but the most complex veterinary's tasks, write guest articles for small-town newspapers, serve in two state legislatures, read voraciously, swear profusely and imaginatively, and, for recreational purposes, lie copiously and brilliantly. My father has been, among other things, a brakeman, a butcher, an oil field roustabout, and a salesman or trader of most movable objects. They and many like them share a place in American mythology with, at one extreme, Mark Twain's King and Duke, ready to turn a hand at anything, and at the other, Benjamin Franklin and Orr of *Catch–22.* And, of course, Doc and Mac of *Cannery Row,* Mac of *In Dubious Battle,* a host of other Steinbeck characters, and the users of the *Whole Earth Catalog.*

One of the engaging qualities of Steinbeck's attitude towards work is his matter-of-fact acceptance of it, combined with a sense of natural piety and ritual. For Hemingway, work is either specialized and divorced from its ends or it is presented as something outside the normal course of events. Essentially, it is a tourist's or camper's attitude. For Steinbeck, it is what one does in order to live. Unlike Hemingway, he never elevates process into a mystique, but he has a strong sense of natural rhythms and laws that must be observed in work. Gay and Mack accept as "Magic" a broken needle-valve in *Cannery Row;* the paisanos of *Tortilla Flat* have a delicate sense of the laws of discourse, which is their only work; Juan Chicoy barks a knuckle (like Tom Joad, mingling blood and oil) and observes "it's good luck. . . . You

can't finish a job without blood. That's what my old man used to say"
—one of the most ancient rituals identifying man with his work and
with the mysterious forces which seem to govern it.

IV

In order to endure, however, a writer must give us more than traditional form, coherent and pleasing fictional worlds, and concrete tex-
tures. What distinguishes Steinbeck from a Louis Bromfield or Bess
Streeter Aldrich or Booth Tarkington is not simply talent but the
ability to embody in his work a deeply felt personal mythos that is
more than theme or belief.[24] It need not be positive, uplifting,
nay-saying in Thunder or otherwise, or even conscious, but when it is
not present we become painfully aware that, as Joseph Wood Krutch
says, Steinbeck has not "recreated a myth" but merely "moralized a
tale." [25]

Steinbeck's mythos centers on one of the grandest generalizations of
all: "What we have wanted always is an *unchangeable,* and we have
found that only a compass point, a thought, an individual ideal, does
not change. . . ." [26] To a nonteleological thinker, abstractions, absolutes, and final causes are illusions; but Blake Nevius has argued that
Steinbeck "both cherishes and rejects" illusions and portrays characters who, "Although they are victimized by their illusions, which are
ultimately powerless in the face of reality . . . through them . . . have
realized whatever beauty, grace, and meaning life holds for them." [27]
This oversimplifies, but it does point to the central role of illusion in
Steinbeck's work. Basically, Steinbeck seems to think that illusions derive from the instinct for survival and the instinct for reproduction, in
that order the two basic laws of life. Thus man, as individual and as
species, must change and adapt; but change denies or seems to deny
absolutes, and men fear change, as do Muley Graves in *The Grapes of
Wrath* and the sterile woman who creates the changeless garden in
"The White Quail." Other characters recognize and seek to survive
by mastering change and manipulating other people: Henry Morgan

---

[24] See Harry T. Moore, "John Steinbeck: A Memorial Statement," *Steinbeck Newsletter,* II (Spring 1969), 23.
[25] "John Steinbeck's Dramatic Tale of Three Generations," *New York Herald
Tribune Book Review,* September 21, 1952, p. 1.
[26] *Sea of Cortez,* p. 37.
[27] "Steinbeck: One Aspect," in *Steinbeck and His Critics,* pp. 197–98.

in Steinbeck's first novel and Ethan Allan Hawley in his last devote their lives to the illusions of power, only to find that greatness demands single-mindedness, that only children are single-minded, and that children are not happy. In his more scientific moments, as in *The Moon Is Down* and *In Dubious Battle*, Steinbeck seemed to believe that the leader was simply a specialized cell of the collective animal or that he led because he happened to be going in the direction that the group chose. Early in *The Grapes of Wrath*, Tom Joad gives what seems to be the perfect nonteleogical response to Casy's "I got the call to lead the people, an' no place to lead 'em": "What the hell you want to lead 'em someplace for? Jus' lead 'em." In more humanistic moments, Steinbeck emphasized not so much the idea of leadership as that of greatness. Whether active or contemplative, the unusual man is lonely: Joseph Wayne in *To a God Unknown* feels set apart by his father's blessing; Danny in *Tortilla Flat* is set apart by his property; Doc in *Cannery Row* is set apart by his knowledge and his detachment. The clearest statement of this side of the theme comes in *East of Eden*: the man who tells the truth will be punished, and greatness is a burden. "On one side you have warmth and companionship and sweet understanding, and on the other—cold, lonely greatness."

Except for Jim Casy and perhaps the matured Tom Joad, Steinbeck does not portray the leader with full sympathy. Either he is self-deluding about the sources and objects of his drives, like Henry Morgan, or he is objective and brutal like Mac of *In Dubious Battle*. However, Steinbeck's sympathies are extended toward those who combine illusions about survival and procreation in the dynastic impulse. Richard Whiteside attempts to found a dynasty in the final story of *The Pastures of Heaven*; Joseph Wayne is the patriarch who reestablishes his clan in *To a God Unknown*; Adam Trask seeks to found a new paradise in *East of Eden*. The dynastic drive is obviously an attempt to harness and defeat change. Wayne observes, "The first grave. Now we're getting somewhere. Houses and children and graves, that's home. . . . Those are the things to hold a man down." On a lower level, Lennie and George, the Joads, the boys at the Palace Flophouse, and even the paisanos feel the pull of a place of one's own.

The pattern of exodus and settlement is found, of course, in Scripture and in American history, and Steinbeck used conscious parallels from both in his fiction; but the impulse towards that pattern must have come from within, a reflection of his own family's movement, always from New England to the Salinas Valley, always from narrow-

ness to the promise of plenty, always a defeat of the dream because of
the infidelity of wife or child or nature. These characters are not, like
Morgan, satirized because they are illusioned; instead, they are presented as men who trusted and were in a sense betrayed and are therefore figures not of tragedy, but of pathos.

Nevertheless, these men are illusioned, and therefore responsible for
the dream and for its defeat. Steinbeck most deeply sympathized with
two contrasting types of men: those who could with open eyes pursue
dreams to their logical conclusion, like Joseph Wayne, and those like
Juan Chicoy who were able to go beyond illusion to accept reality, or
like Samuel Hamilton were able to recognize and accept their own
mediocrity. Most of all, he sympathized with those who went beyond
the illusions even of survival and of reproduction, who dispensed with
"this shock-absorber, hope" and recognized their place in the larger
scheme, who did not generalize but felt the wholeness of nature.[28] At
his best, Steinbeck is able to communicate this emotion, which is not
humanistic or humane or even scientific.[29] The old hermit in *To a
God Unknown*, speaking of his nightly sacrifices to the sun, expresses
the emotion most directly: he kills the animals "because it makes me
glad," and at a certain moment, when "My life will reach a calm level
place," he "will go over the edge of the world with the sun. . . . In
every man this thing is hidden. It tries to get out, but a man's fears
distort it." Similarly, Doc in *Cannery Row*, having seen the dead girl
in the tide-pool, hears "a high thin piercingly sweet flute carrying a
melody he could never remember," and at the end of the novel recites,
from the last stanza of *Black Marigolds*, "Just for a small and a forgotten time / I have had full in my eyes from off my girl / The whitest
pouring of eternal light. . . ." And the novel closes with a description
of the rattlesnakes staring into space. However, Doc does not quote the
stanza's last line, which Steinbeck leaves implicit: "The heavy knife.
As to a gala day." [30] Only death frees man from change, and only those
who are aware of the rhythms of life can penetrate this secret and accept it. This, then, is the most important cause of Steinbeck's detachment and apparently baseless optimism: man will be defeated by
change, but he can overcome the fear of defeat by understanding and
acceptance.

[28] *Sea of Cortez*, p. 86.
[29] See the essays by Woodburn O. Ross in *Steinbeck and His Critics*, especially
"John Steinbeck: Naturalism's Priest."
[30] In *East of Eden* carnations are called the Nails of Love, marigolds the Nails of
Death.

Of course, Steinbeck did not always take himself seriously or at least did not always have the promptings of his private mythos, which R. W. B. Lewis calls his daemon. All of Steinbeck's critics agree that much of his work cannot endure, is indeed stillborn. Except for *The Sea of Cortez*, his nonfiction is mediocre to dreadful; almost everything written after 1947 is seriously flawed, primarily in the strained quality of the prose. However, many of his books still live, in the sense that they are read, discussed, and reprinted, and at least some of them may last beyond this admittedly marginal existence. *The Pearl* will continue to be read only if the audience can be persuaded to accept it as a fable, and this seems more possible than it did ten years ago. *Cannery Row* has a modest but increasing reputation. *Tortilla Flat* has been attacked, but it may have qualities which can survive these assaults. Many of the short stories, especially "The Chrysanthemums," "Flight," *The Red Pony*, and perhaps "The Snake," "The White Quail," and some of the stories in *The Pastures of Heaven*, still retain their freshness despite repeated antholigizings; and even if Steinbeck does not deserve to rank with Chekhov as a writer of short stories, Chekhov must be invoked as a standard.[31] *Of Mice and Men, The Grapes of Wrath*, and *In Dubious Battle* seem to be secure, though the second may come to seem dated and the last, least-known of Steinbeck's major works, may rise in critical esteem and claim wider attention. However, it is neglected only by comparison; *To a God Unknown* and *The Wayward Bus* are generally scorned. Both have flaws, but the first evokes the natural world and man's kinship to it with a freshness that Steinbeck was seldom to surpass, and it conveys with a quirky, engaging, and slightly overblown style Steinbeck's most characteristic themes. The second evokes, with fascinated loathing, the grimy, sugary, and second-hand quality of postwar, pre-Holiday Inn America. Both deal with men who consciously enter traps—the one of ritual, the other of responsibility—and read in this way, they could be revalued. For now, they can serve as a touchstone for critics: anyone who purports to be a spokesman for Steinbeck but who summarily rejects both novels is not to be trusted because he cannot see the qualities that may enable Steinbeck's work to endure.

The essential Steinbeck, the Steinbeck who can be read and studied with pleasure and profit, gives us more than a picture, more even than "a moral vision," of the thirties—though these would be neither dis-

---

[31] See Robert Penn Warren, "A Fine Anthology of Steinbeck's Writings," *New York Times Book Review*, August 22, 1943, p. 6.

creditable nor unimportant. He not only writes about, he *conveys* and therefore causes us to reexperience and revalue things that are important to us: a feeling for the integrity and rhythm of common experience; an awareness of man's shattering of or flowing with natural patterns; an acceptance, with what Edmund Wilson called an "unpanicky scrutiny of life," [32] of man's potentialities and of the dignity possible within his limitations. A Norwegian admirer has compared his stories to the sagas, in which gods and heroes "battled endlessly for ascendancy, one over the other, but of course there were no final victories, as there cannot be with gods, or nature, or man . . . because these things have a way of renewing themselves." [33] In Steinbeck's best work, this vision and the method chosen to convey it support and justify each other.

V

The foregoing discussion has treated Steinbeck as a whole; yet argue as we may that a coherent vision and a body of work are essential for a serious writer, it is not Dickens we read, but *Bleak House,* not Wordsworth, but "Tintern Abbey," not Pope, but "An Epistle to Dr. Arbuthnot." Inspired by individual works, we search out others, and generalizations about an author's world or even about his technique seem irrelevant to anyone who has not first been captivated by a single story or poem. These principles, or truisms, have governed the choice of essays for this volume. Articles which merely explicate, which find parallels and patterns, are useful primarily to the specialist; others demand more genuinely critical approaches which ask why and to what effect the materials have been chosen. More useful in their time but now largely of historical interest are the essays which supported or denounced Steinbeck, not to further moral or political ideas, but to show the ways in which he was related to his literary and intellectual predecessors and in which he embodied those ideas in fiction.

Both types of analysis are concerned more with what Steinbeck wrote than the way in which he wrote it, and while the second helps us to form judgments, the critical consensus about Steinbeck's thought and the relative merits of his novels is clear enough that attention can be more fruitfully devoted to his positive achievement as an artist. There-

[32] *Classics and Commercials,* p. 45.
[33] Quoted in Lester J. Marks, "John Ernst Steinbeck: 1902–1968," *Steinbeck Newsletter,* II (Spring 1969), 21–22.

fore, eight of the essays reprinted here deal with individual novels generally considered to be his best from viewpoints which seem to yield the best results: structural, mythic, generic, psychological, historical. The essays by Joseph Fontenrose and George Bluestone consider sympathetically but not uncritically two important aspects of Steinbeck's career: his nonteleological thought and his relation to the motion pictures that have popularized his fiction. The remaining essays, by Freeman Champney and R. W. B. Lewis, are more general attempts to summarize and judge. Both are limited by temporal context: our understanding of California, of intellectualism and anti-intellectualism, of faith in man, and of America are not what they were in 1947 or 1958. Yet if Steinbeck is to endure, his novels will continue to manifest qualities that transcend their own limitations and those of their critics; and periodic revaluations of the novels will lead, again and again, to attempts to summarize and judge—to account for Steinbeck's appeal to and value for new generations of readers.

John Steinbeck, Californian

by Freeman Champney

John Steinbeck is one of the few American writers who can be discussed in both past and present. He has done important work for fifteen years or so and he is still developing and experimenting. So much criticism and analysis of his work have been published that writing any more seems a little silly—we have several times as many passable literary critics now as we have halfway good creators. But most of the critics are Easterners and have discussed Steinbeck's books with little or no knowledge of the country in which he grew up and which he writes about. Even a casual direct contact with this country and its people suggests that this background is the most important thing to know about Steinbeck and that it explains much of his writing better than any amount of remote analysis. It also explains things about the East by comparison and contrast.

The Salinas Valley roughly parallels the coast, thirty miles or so inland, for most of its length of about a hundred and twenty miles. It is one of the smaller of California's central valleys, which run up and down the state between mountain ranges. The enclosing hills have the steep slopes and the barren, rounded crests which have evoked so many anatomical comparisons. During much of the year they are brown and dry, turning green during the rainy winter. The river, the highway, and the Southern Pacific Railroad chase each other down the valley floor. The river itself, like most California rivers, is normally sandy, brush-choked, and nearly dry but carries a great volume of floodwater when the big rains come. At the lower end of the valley the flat bottom-land is cut into great fields of lettuce, broccoli, alfalfa, sugar beets, and other truck crops. Cattle are raised on the slopes of the hills. Salinas

"John Steinbeck, Californian" by Freeman Champney. From *The Antioch Review*, VII (September 1947), 345–62. Copyright © 1947 by The Antioch Review, Inc. Reprinted by permission of the publisher.

(where Steinbeck was born and raised) is about ten miles inland from the river's mouth in Monterey Bay. It is the county seat and the trading and shipping center for the lower part of the valley. It looks a little more metropolitan than the raw valley towns but not much more.

Cattle-raising has been a valley occupation since the days of the missions but the intensive cultivation of vegetables—especially lettuce, which takes up more than 50,000 acres—has outranked it in importance for some time. But the nostalgic glamor of the cowhand days is clung to. You see fifty lean men in sombreros, tight jeans, and riding boots for every visible horse. Once a year Salinas stages "California's Biggest Rodeo" and cashes in handsomely on its nostalgia.

Lettuce, however, is the big industry of the valley, and its growing, packing, and shipping follow the highly capitalized pattern of California agriculture that Carey McWilliams has accurately called "Factories in the Field." In 1936 a strike by lettuce packing shed workers was crushed at a cost of around a quarter of a million dollars. Civil liberties, local government, and normal judicial processes were all suspended during the strike and Salinas was governed by a general staff directed by the Associated Farmers and the big lettuce growers and shippers. The local police were bossed by a reserve army officer imported for the job, and at the height of the strike all male residents of Salinas between 18 and 45 were mobilized under penalty of arrest, were deputized and armed. Beatings, tear gas attacks, wholesale arrests, threats to lynch San Francisco newspapermen if they didn't leave town, and machine guns and barbed wire all figured in the month-long struggle which finally broke the strike and destroyed the union.

So much for John Steinbeck's birthplace, where he lived his first nineteen years. From Salinas it is about fifteen miles through a pass in the Santa Lucia Range to the Monterey Peninsula. This fantastic area contains some of the most picturesque country in the world and an assortment of humanity almost as bizarre and much less permanent. Monterey itself is tough and raucous. Its harbor shelters the purse-seiners of the sardine fleet; farther west the shore is solid with the processing plants (Cannery Row) that receive the catch. The fishermen and cannery workers are Italian, Portuguese, Japanese, a few Chinese, and the paisanos of *Tortilla Flat*. Nearby is the army post of Fort Ord and the main business section along Alvarado Street is thick with ratty-looking bars. Sardine fishing and the canneries are highly speculative, feast-or-famine affairs. Beyond this variable economic base, Monterey

has its honkeytonks for the military and a considerable volume of tourist business (they come to see the fishing boats and the historic adobes
and absorb the legends of the rancho and mission days).

Just west of Cannery Row is the city of Pacific Grove. Its recent
history stems from the days when it was a Methodist camp-meeting
ground, complete with a fence, and duly locked against the sinful
world at curfew. Today it has become rather nondescript middle-class
—a haven for retired Middlewesterners of the staider sorts and a respectable residential town. Its moralistic past lingers on in convenants
in real estate deeds forever prohibiting the sale of liquor, and in books
in the public library from which the profanity has been scratched with
a righteous nail file (apparently; maybe it was a hat pin or a corset
stay). Public night life in Pacific Grove is limited to a few dreary milk-
shake dens and occasional prowling teenagers trying to make noises
like juvenile delinquents.

Across the wooded ridge of the Peninsula is Carmel-by-the-Sea.
Originally an artists-and-writers colony, Carmel has become a fashionable center for all sorts of people with cultural pretensions and a sur-
plus of money. It is quaint and arty and individualistic and grimly
"unspoiled." Down the coast from Carmel is the craggy and desolate
Big Sur country (once Robinson Jeffers' special literary domain). Most
of the shore line between Pacific Grove and Carmel, and most of the
wooded hills behind it, are part of the Del Monte Properties—an ex-
clusive real estate development purveying summer homes and de luxe
lodge accommodations to the financial aristocracy of California.

The Monterey Peninsula has a lively bohemian-artist-writer class.
The ones with money live in Carmel. The others, in the hills above
Monterey, in the Big Sur country, or anywhere else where rents are low
and the folkways relaxed. The mild climate makes a minimum of
clothes and housing quite tolerable. The shifting population, the resort atmosphere, and the lack of strenuous industry all give a certain
glamor and acceptability to the bohemian life. It even has a certain
economic importance as part of the tourist bait.

One other environmental feature should be mentioned: the Bay
swarms with marine life. Even a casual observer of the tide pools gets
some of the feeling for biological diversity, fecundity, and struggle
which has played so important a part in Steinbeck's thinking.

II

John Steinbeck grew up in Salinas and after four years at Stanford University he lived at various times in Carmel and Pacific Grove and kept a fishing boat in Monterey Harbor. More perhaps than any important contemporary American writer, except William Faulkner, his writing has grown out of a special region. It is a region, however, that contains such polar extremes as the hard materialism of Salinas and the bohemianism of the Peninsula. Both have obviously been important in Steinbeck's writing but Salinas came first and is most apparent.

The cultural climate of the Salinas Valley is typical of California agriculture. A tradition of personal individualism goes along with a strongly collectivized economy. As Carey McWilliams has pointed out, the great California valleys show few resemblances to traditional American rural life. The "school-house on the hilltop, the comfortable homes, the compact and easy indolence of the countryside" are noticeably absent. Instead there are the vast orchards, vineyards, and ranches, meticulously tended, irrigated, and smudged but showing little close functional connection with human life. They are (most of them) really farm factories, and their financing and cultivation, and the marketing of their output, have become highly collectivized activities, managed by and for the great owners and packers, the banks, and the utilities. As in most big business, ownership and management are usually sharply separated. The exploitation of labor has exceeded anything known in Western civilization since the early mill towns of England. The operators of this paradise have usually been able to use or usurp the sovereign powers of local or state government whenever necessary to wipe out a threat to their absolutism.

Economically, socially, and culturally it has been an ugly state of affairs. In its extremes of wealth and destitution, in the absence or impotence of any middle group representing the public interest, and in the domination of the organs of civil life by irresponsible private greed, it has been one of the few areas of American life that has closely approximated the Marxian predictions about capitalist society. The proletariat was kept homeless, voteless, and close to or below the starvation point, with the gulf between it and the dominant group widened by racial differences. Civil liberties were nonexistent whenever they remotely threatened the *status quo.* The whole system was impersonal and relentless and individual men of good will on either side were helpless to do much about it. There was no liberal, middle-of-the-road answer that had much reality to it. It is not surprising that Steinbeck's reaction to this aspect of his environment was to explore communist answers in *In Dubious Battle*.

The book is the story of two communists and the strike they organized and directed in the apple country. It is a very "dubious battle" indeed. They don't expect to win the strike—in fact they prefer it that way. Their job is to give the strikers an experience of working together and a feeling of their united strength, and to convince them of the implacable nature of their enemy by a bath of blood that will turn as many of them as possible into all-out revolutionaries. All available tricks and deceits are thrown into the game and friends and sympathizers are sacrificed ruthlessly. (The forces "law and order," to be sure, play their hand as dirtily as they can and leave little to be done in the way of creating grievances and incidents.) One of the communists is killed as the strike begins to disintegrate and the book ends with his faceless corpse propped up on the platform to help his comrade stir up the men to a final burst of violence. It is a study of tactics that make sense only for the long-term end of bloody revolution.

Characteristically, however, Steinbeck's interest in the communists has always been more a matter of what makes them tick as people than of abstract ideology. Why should they go out to face certain beating and possible death from the enemy and betrayal and hatred from the people they are trying to organize? It is this question of motivation that runs through *In Dubious Battle*, is singled out in the story, "The Raid" in *The Long Valley*, and echoes in Casy in *The Grapes of Wrath*. As near as Steinbeck comes to an answer is Casy's quoting of the "fella in the jail house":

> You didn't do it for fun no way. Doin' it 'cause you have to. 'Cause it's you. . . . Anyways you do what you can . . . the on'y thing you got to look at is that ever' time they's a little step fo'ward, she may slip back a little, but she never slips clear back. You can prove that, an' that makes the whole thing right. An' that means they wasn't no waste even if it seemed like they was.

But there is also the note of doubt, of conflict between faith and skepticism. The doctor of *In Dubious Battle*, who will give everything he's got to help the strikers but who has no real faith in the cause, is one side of the conflict in Steinbeck himself. Interestingly enough, Steinbeck never seems to question the adequacy of the Marxian analysis—he accepts class war and inevitable revolution as the way things are and will be. His doubts go deeper, really; they are doubts as to the nature of mankind itself. The first party for "Doc" in *Cannery Row* is a symbolic dramatization of a feeling that runs all through Steinbeck's writing. Mack and the boys give a surprise party for Doc to show him how much they like him. But Doc doesn't get home when they think he will and the party "she got out of hand." Doc finally gets back to his devasted laboratory and Mack tells him:

It don't do no good to say I'm sorry. I been sorry all my life. This ain't no new thing. It's always like this. . . . I had a wife. Same thing. Ever'thing I done turned sour. . . . If I done a good thing it got poisoned up some way. If I give her a present they was something wrong with it. She only got hurt from me.

There are many variations of this "every man kills the thing he loves" theme in Steinbeck. *Of Mice and Men* is little else. The doctor of *In Dubious Battle* says:

There aren't any beginnings. Nor any ends. It seems to me that man has engaged in a blind and fearful struggle out of a past he can't remember, into a future he can't foresee nor understand. And man has met and defeated every obstacle, every enemy except one. He cannot win over himself. How mankind hates itself. . . . We fight ourselves and we can only win by killing every man.

I would suggest that both Steinbeck's acceptance of Marxian dogma as accurate prophecy and his distrust of humanity are outcomes of his California background, and that a broader perspective on American life offers evidence of another sort.

The historical analysis of Marxism calls for a steady intensification of class warfare, in which the lines are drawn more and more sharply, compromise and gradualism become less and less possible, until the stand-up-and-slug-it-out day of revolution comes. After which all things will be different. A lot of our most able writers have accepted this prognosis for America at one time or another. Often, perhaps, they have done so because its drive-to-a-showdown jibes so neatly with their own personality unbalance. The mixture of social revolt, idealism, spiritual homelessness, and unresolved tension that has been so characteristic of serious American writing since the first World War demands an explosive crisis to bring itself to a tolerable, if only temporary, equilibrium. But it has been an outstanding quality of American evolution since the Civil War that the march of events has by-passed every crisis and that the great showdown never comes. Time and again things have built up to the boiling point, only to subside as new developments broke up rigidities and diverted energies. The revolutionary effects of mass production and technology, and the tremendous reshuffling caused by two world wars seem to have been the factors most responsible.

This by-passing of crises has not been so characteristic of California history as of the country as a whole but I think it can be shown that it has happened there as well—and in one of the worst crisis-spots. When *The Grapes of Wrath* and *Factories in the Field* appeared it looked as if nothing could avert an all-out battle between revolution and fascism in California's great valleys. Conditions were intolerable, tensions were incandescent, and both sides seemed ready and eager to fight it out. But the war raised food prices, created a labor shortage, and brought badly needed industrial ballast to the California economy. The situation may, of course, come to a new boiling point in the future. But the larger picture has changed and goes on changing and there is no show-down.

This blind dynamic of American growth—this refusal to harden into a static shape—is one of the great and hopeful things about this country. It doesn't make things easier for the writers, however, and may be one reason for the short creative life-expectancy of the best of them.

III

American civilization, with its extraordinary melting pot and its many regional variations, is a risky thing to generalize about. But there is certainly a central core of character, custom, and belief that has been the dominant national strain. Americans, by and large, tend to be optimistic, pragmatic, outgoing, gregarious, energetic, and moral. We believe in the home, in education and self-betterment, in religion and moral responsibility; we take eagerly to the new in technics and district the new in social and political institutions; we rate character above intelligence and horse sense above theory. Wherever we have lived for several generations without too much upheaval, these characteristics have become part of a way of life, or a social tradition, or whatever you care to call it, which has a life and strength of its own and shapes the individuals who grow up in it. In spite of variations and breakdowns, this condition of settled society has, for better or worse, made us what we are. It is what we have to start with and to go on from.

American society, in this sense, is probably strongest in the Middle

West. It is noticeably weaker in the Far West and especially weak in Steinbeck's country. There are obvious reasons for this: it is only a hundred years since California was largely unmapped, undeveloped, and very thinly inhabited. It is still subject to upheaval by a great wave of immigrants every twenty years or so and a steady inflow between waves. In the years when it was absorbing the first great comings of Americans, the rigors of the journey, the isolation of the section from the country back East, and the strangeness of the life and the countryside all tended to dilute and efface the habits and culture that the immigrants brought with them. For the most part, the existence of a settled and mature society is exceptional and the typical state of affairs is a condition of formless flux or of unbalanced extremes.

Furthermore, this condition isn't merely a matter of a time lag. The settled American society that we talk about is itself in process of change —so abrupt a series of changes that we can almost say that it is breaking up around our ears. It has lost much of its relevance to the conditions of modern life and it is by no means certain that it will be adaptable enough to make a transition of any smoothness to meet new needs. Since the Far West experienced this pattern of social integration only partially when it was in its prime in the East, now that it is falling apart we can hardly expect to see much more growth of it. Most of the country's intellectuals—which includes the writers—have been cheering on this social breakup for the last twenty-five years. They have carried on a running battle against the restrictions and compulsions of settled society, usually in the name of individual freedom. One of the major differences between the East and the West is that in the East this antisociety drive has about run its course, while in the West it seems to be just getting under way.

The intellectuals of the East have learned that freedom is more complicated than getting away from family and neighbors, or from "the system." The "freedom from" battle has become a rout and such questions as "freedom for what?" and "How do we escape this freedom that we cannot handle?" are the order of the day. It is being discovered— the hard way—that a settled society offers securities and supports without which few individuals can remain integrated.

The Far West, however, is kicking up its heels in an individualistic binge very much like the bohemianism of Greenwich Village of the 20's. The little magazines are feeling their cultural oats in what would look like a real renaissance if we hadn't seen the same thing and its aftermath in the East. In Steinbeck's home country, there are more than a few devotees of what a recent *Harper's* article calls "The New Cult of Sex and Anarchism."

Steinbeck has always had a keen awareness of the importance of the social cement of common purpose as far as small groups are concerned. That he has never extended it to society as a whole is probably because there has been little visible reason in California life for considering such a projection anything but fanciful. And the Marxist slant on things, of course, has its poetic summation in Dos Passos' "All right we are two nations." As Mac puts it in *In Dubious Battle:*

> Men always like to work together. There's a hunger in men to work to-gether. Do you know that ten men can lift nearly twelve times as big a load as one can? It only takes a little spark to get them going. Most of the time they're suspicious, because every time someone gets 'em work-ing in a group the profit of their work is taken away from them; but wait till they get working for themselves.

Lord knows we have come close enough to being two nations often enough (or three, or four, or no nation at all). But always the change and the reshuffling have gone on and when the chips were down we have been one nation. On the other hand, most parts of California have never been places to get any such feeling, and if we don't find it in Steinbeck there's no reason we should expect to. Steinbeck's Cali-fornia contains little fragments of the American character, detached from the whole and dragged over the mountains and the desert with the other immigrant baggage and overdeveloped by the golden sun and the ache of homesickness. The big shots and vigilantes of Salinas show one sort of overdeveloped fragmentation; the fierce Christers of Pacific Grove another. Most of the distribution curves between the mountains and the sea are violently skewed.

Which brings us to another one of Steinbeck's favorite black and white oversimplifications; as he puts it in *Sea of Cortez:*

> the so-called and considered good qualities are invariably concomitants of failure, while the bad ones are the cornerstones of success.

The same idea is somewhat better expressed by Doc in *Cannery Row:*

> The things we admire in men, kindness and generosity, openness, hon-esty, understanding and feeling are the concomitants of failure in our system. And those traits we detest, sharpness, greed, acquisitiveness, meanness, egotism and self-interest are the traits of success.

The duplication shows how fond Steinbeck is of this idea. It may be a reasonable reaction to the Salinas growers and their flunkies, but as an unqualified statement about American life it is absurd. It probably had considerable truth in it in the "Robber Baron" period after the Civil War, when the relatively simple and self-sufficient village economies of agriculture, handcraft and trade were disappearing before the thrust of big business combinations. There were huge rewards then in financial piracy and mercantile buccaneering. But the very process that has changed the typical American career from individual enterprise to wage- or salary-earning for one bureaucracy or another has brought about a lessening of acquisitive pressures. It is still true enough that a man who puts money-getting at the top of his agenda will usually accumulate more of it than a man who doesn't. But unless it is "failure" not to be a millionaire, there are plenty of fields of activity in which the generous virtues are no handicap. In fact, one of the most characteristic "types" in modern life is the go-getter who never quite makes the grade, is always busily outfoxing himself, and affords endless amusement to his more relaxed colleagues.

This key idea of Steinbeck's is, I submit, a California aberration. That it is a key idea is pretty obvious. It crops out in the way he hates his middle-class characters. (There are no capitalist giants in Steinbeck's writing—except for occasional beautifully scatological references to Hearst.) His middle-class men are mean, pudgy creatures, blinking pinkly through spectacles, the slaves of their small anxieties and their neurotic and sexually frigid wives. The lunch-wagon woman in *The Grapes of Wrath* dismisses them collectively as "shitheels." (It should be remembered too that California is perpetually full of tourists, and that to the gawked-at native the American Tourist is not a sympathetic type.)

This hatred of the genteel, the solvent, and the fancypants is, of course, the other side of the sentimentalizing of the paisanos of *Tortilla Flat* and the bums of *Cannery Row*. Which is one of the things Steinbeck is famous for. It doesn't require too complicated an explanation. Everything Steinbeck has written shows the urgency of his need to "bite deeply into living." His environment, however, showed him only a mean, life-denying greed and respectability firmly in the saddle. He tried for a while to find answers and a spiritual home for himself in the dream of social revolution. But the Revolution has its own austerities and narrow righteousness and there was always his deep distrust of humanity's capacity for surpassing itself. But when he had

rejected Man as Success and Man as Citizen, and couldn't quite accept
Man as Reformer or Revolutionary, what was left? Well, there was
Man as Animal, and to be satisfactory he had to be without any other
pretensions. Hence Danny and Pilon and Mack and the boys. It is no-
ticeable, however, that even Steinbeck cannot sustain the celebration
of Man as Animal for long without slipping into a semi-lyrical sort of
fantasy-prose in which the complexities and consequences of real life
are lost in the happy fog of a literary mood. It is undeniable that an
important section of the traditional American character got itself badly
warped by trying to ignore Man as Animal. Writers of our generation
have supplied a corrective reaction which was certainly needed but has
just as certainly been a little more than adequate.

There is one of Steinbeck's books, however, in which his tensions
and conflicts seem to have reached an affirmative equilibrium. The
people in *The Grapes of Wrath* are whole (Man as Man, for a change);
they live with the natural balance of biological, social, and spiritual
needs and assertions that makes the human being. There is no anxiety
over leftist means and ends, no agonizing about the self-hate in man.
For all its sprawling asides and extravagances, *The Grapes of Wrath*
is a big book, a great book, and one of maybe two or three American
novels in a class with *Huckleberry Finn*.

I think it is significant that *The Grapes of Wrath* is about folks who
have the cement of settled society in them. For all their exile and destitution, they are a *people,* and they act as a people to an extent that is
unique in Steinbeck's writing and in the California life which he
knows best. I suggest that it is this social integration—which Steinbeck
has felt and reproduced amazingly well—which is the greatness of this
book. Further, this social integration provides the answers to the di-
chotomies and oversimplifications which torture so much of Steinbeck's
other writing. Against it as a frame of reference, being a responsible
citizen and a jobholder becomes merely playing an honest and digni-
fied part in the common life—rather than the mean abdication of freedom and vitality that is implied by the glorification of Mack and the
boys. The tortured obsession about men killing the thing they love
shows up as the self-pitying indulgence of a romantic individualism
gone sour. The answer to it is in Ma Joad's advice to Uncle John about
his sins:

> Tell 'em to God. Don' go burdenin' other people with your sins. That
> ain't decent. . . . Go down the river an' stick your head under an' whis-
> per 'em in the stream.

The pattern of life that Steinbeck found in the Joads—their strength as a people—has been undergoing the attrition of the city and the machine for several generations. Much of it is gone for good and much that remains is moribund. No amount of nostalgic yearning is going to regenerate it. But the lesson we are painfully learning today is that some sort of settled society—with habits, folkways, common aspirations, sanctions and taboos—is an essential part of human life. The rampant individualism of the frontier days is not only too irresponsibly anarchic for modern economic society but it fails to provide the social fabric that supports individual sanity. A kind of dynamic balance between society and the individual is what we need and the danger of too much individualism is that it can create a reaction to the other extreme. It should go without saying that the social integration we need will have to be relevant to today's conditions of living. But that is a long way from saying (as so much of our literature has said for the last twenty-five years) that all society, or all "capitalist" society, is rotten to the core and must be swept into the ashcan of history before things can be better.

IV

There is a coldness about *The Wayward Bus* that reviewers have variously found unpleasant and a welcome change from previous emotional lushness. The book has few "sympathetic" characters and these are chiefly distinguished by a sort of hard, despairing honesty. One of the best reviews that have appeared [1] points out that the key to Steinbeck's approach in this book is explicitly stated in *Sea of Cortez.*

In a rough way, *Sea of Cortez* occupies about the same place in Steinbeck's work that *Death in the Afternoon* does in Hemingway's. Both are relaxed musings about life and art, written as breathers between novels. There is also something of a parallel in Hemingway tying *Death in the Afternoon* to the lore of the bull ring while Steinbeck uses a cruise to the Gulf of California—to collect tide-pool invertebrates—as his framework. The ritual violence of bull-fighting was Hemingway's peacetime laboratory for the study of death and pure emotion. Marine biology has had a similar fascination for Steinbeck.

---

[1] By Toni Jackson Ricketts in *What's Doing On the Monterey Peninsula,* a small California magazine which began as tourist bait and has matured in a little over a year into a first-rate regional publication. She knows Steinbeck well and her statements about his intent can be accepted as sound.

The part of *Sea of Cortez* that concerns us here is Steinbeck's speculation about what he calls "nonteleological thinking." This seems to be a mixture of philosophical relativism, the rigorous refusal of the scientist to be dogmatic about hypotheses, and a sort of moral fatalism. To quote:

What we personally conceive by the term "teleological thinking" . . . is most frequently associated with the evaluation of causes and effects, the purposiveness of events. This kind of thinking considers changes and cures—what "should be" in the terms of an end pattern (which is often a subjective or an anthropomorphic projection); it presumes the bettering of conditions, often, unfortunately, without achieving more than a most superficial understanding of those conditions. In their sometimes intolerant refusal to face facts as they are, teleological notions may substitute a fierce but ineffectual attempt to change conditions which are assumed to be undesirable, in place of the understanding-acceptance which would pave the way for a more sensible attempt at any change which may still be indicated.

Nonteleological ideas derive through "is" thinking, associated with natural selection as Darwin seems to have understood it. They imply depth, fundamentalism, and clarity—seeing beyond traditional or personal projection. They consider events as outgrowths and expressions rather than as results; conscious acceptance as a desideratum, and certainly as an all-important prerequisite. Nonteleological thinking concerns itself primarily not with what should be, or could be, or might be, but rather with what actually "is"—attempting at most to answer the already sufficiently difficult questions *what* or *how,* instead of *why.*

This is fairly heavy going but it is clear enough that Steinbeck is objecting to wishfulness obscuring facts, and understanding being limited by preconceived notions of what should be the case. No one can quarrel with this. There is a strong implication, however, that to think in terms of "why" and "what might be" is not only risky but downright sinful. This implication is even stronger in the following:

It is amazing how the strictures of the old teleologies infect our observation, causal thinking warped by hope. It was said earlier that hope is a diagnostic human trait, and this simple cortex symptom seems to be a prime factor in our inspection of our universe. For hope implies a change from a present bad condition to a future better one. The slave hopes for freedom, the weary man for rest, the hungry for food. And the feeders of hope, economic and religious, have from these simple strivings of dissatisfaction managed to create a world picture which is very hard to escape. Man grows toward perfection; animals grow toward man; bad grows toward good; and down toward up, until our little mechanism, hope, achieved in ourselves probably to cushion the shock of thought, manages to warp our whole world. . . . To most men the most hateful statement possible is, *"A thing is because it is."* Even those who have managed to drop the leading-strings of a Sunday-school deity are still led by the unconscious teleology of their developed trick.

It should be apparent from these quotations why I said that Steinbeck's "is-thinking" has a large content of moral fatalism. If the height of wisdom is "things are because they are" and thinking in terms of cause and effect and of changes for the better are Sunday-school fatuities, we come to an attitude towards life remarkably oriental and passive. It is not the attitude with which we normally contemplate our house catching fire—nor our world catching fire. For that matter, it is not an attitude which would lead anyone to build a house in the first place—or to do any other creative job based on "what might be." Nor will observation which shuns the "why" of things see very much in the long run. Its only logical end is pure mysticism—a search for objectivity winding up in the absolute subjective.

This line of thought is not new in Steinbeck's writing. The doctor of *In Dubious Battle* is something of a nonteleological thinker. But previously it had been a sort of intriguing sideline. In *Sea of Cortez* it becomes the main channel and in both *Cannery Row* and *The Wayward Bus* Steinbeck is obviously trying to see what he can do with nonteleological literature. I can only speculate as to why his slant on things took this particular turn at this particular time. But the *Sea of Cortez* cruise took place in the spring and early summer of 1940, when the Nazis were overrunning France and the Low Countries. Steinbeck's attitude to the war then was that it was:

> a war . . . which no one wants to fight, in which no one can see a gain —a zombie war of sleep-walkers which nevertheless goes on out of all control of intelligence.

So he collected his invertebrates and watched the teeming tide-pool struggle of eat-and-be-eaten and wondered whether a school of fish mightn't properly be considered an organism in its own right (like "group-man"), and he thought further about war and men:

> When it seems that men may be kinder to men, that wars may not come again, we completely ignore the nature of our species. If we used the same smug observation on ourselves that we do on hermit crabs we would be forced to say, with the information at hand, "It is one diagnostic trait

of *Homo Sapiens* that groups of individuals are periodically infected with a feverish nervousness which causes the individual to turn on and destroy, not only his own kind, but the works of his own kind. It is not known whether this be caused by a virus, some airborne spore, or whether it be a species reaction to some meteorological stimulus as yet undetermined." Hope, which is another species diagnostic trait—the hope that this may not always be—does not in the least change the observable past and present. When two crayfish meet, they usually fiight. One would say that perhaps they might not at a future time, but without some mutation it is not likely that they will lose this trait. And perhaps our species is not likely to forgo war without some psychic mutation which at present, at least, does not seem imminent. And if one places the blame for killing and destroying on economic insecurity, on inequality, on injustice, he is simply stating the proposition in another way. We have what we are. . . . So far the murder trait of our species is as regular and observable as our various sexual habits.

It seems likely that the war was, for Steinbeck, overwhelming evidence of the irrational, self-destructive drive of the human race; that it killed—or at least submerged—the faith and buoyancy that filled *The Grapes of Wrath*; and that it drove him back on the toughminded nihilism of "is-thinking." As noted above, the "golden mean" and the "middle way" are no part of Steinbeck's temperament. When he abandons Man as Man for Man as Biological Freak he goes all the way. He jettisons not only hope and progress but cause and effect as well. Which leaves the vertebrates of *The Wayward Bus*, animated by the simpler forms of protoplasmic irritability, and deprived of even a biological dignity by their silly pretensions that they are up to something noble.

Steinbeck's current "is-thinking" has a lot in common with the search for verbal simplicity and for the hard, clean reality of the physically tangible that characterized Hemingway's writing after the previous war. Both are spiritually weary, sick of abstractions and ideologies, and both find comfort in the evocation of what can be seen, felt, heard, smelled, and tasted. In Steinbeck, this retreat to physical reality takes the form of descriptions of the countryside and its wild life and a meticulous reporting of physical action—especially skilled action. In *The Wayward Bus* some of his reporting is a repetition of what he has done better elsewhere. The repairs to the bus that open the book are of a piece with the burnt-out connecting rod bearing in *The Grapes of Wrath* (including the same superstition about skinned knuckles). The Chicoy lunchroom also has a prototype in the previous book and Mrs. Pritchard had a preview in the story called "The White Quail." But much of the book is fresh and new and if Steinbeck's faith in mankind is at a low ebb, his skill as a writer is becoming keener. There is more precision and control in the prose and the structure than in his other books and it ends with little of the melodrama that has wound up most of his previous novels.

The Wayward Bus is, if less *intensely* regional than some of his other books, the most broadly descriptive of California's countryside and the queer assortments of people encountered there. The accidental grouping of a collection of "characters" in a situation which "brings them out" is more than a novelist's trick. It is itself fairly typical of California life. It symbolizes the endless coming and going, the fragmentary social integration, and the human diversity of the region. In fact, it would be quite plausible to say that Steinbeck's "is-thinking" can be explained without reference to any background of disillusionment in revolution and mankind—that it is simply the way life looks to a thoughtful Californian who has outgrown his youth.

V

In many ways the American West might be a good place in which to see our future cultural pattern shape up. The lack of settled society which we dwelt on above may facilitate new cultural fusions and social forms. Just as America itself diverged widely from its European sources because it encountered the first impact of the industrial revolution with less of a cushioning of habit and institutional inertia than the old country, so the West may adapt to the continuing thrust of change more directly and flexibly than the more static East. There are many rigid extremes in the West, of course, and California in particular has many people who come out only to die, or to postpone dying. But the general configuration is one of flux and change and it is a region to which many come in the hope of some sort of vaguely splendid fulfillment. There is still something of the selective process which colonized and settled America at work and California is a setting in which an inchoate mass of aspiration and restless hope will have to either find new patterns of living or drown itself in the Pacific.

One important area where the West seems to show a hopeful flexibility is in the relation between the intellectual and the common man. In most of the country the cleavages between these two classes is one of the sharpest and most disastrous gulfs in American life. The intellectual is a specialist in abstract thought. He typically works from the general to the particular (and sometimes never arrives at the particular at all) and is articulate to a point where he is often unable to perceive any reality for which he lacks a word. The nonintellectual, on the other hand, deals with particulars almost exclusively. He ordinarily uses abstractions and generalizations only in an uncritical, proverbial way that he has picked up from someone else. For the most part, he is incapable of abstract thinking—being unable to use words precisely or to perceive the niceties of logic. But the intellectual so overvalues words and logic, and generalizes from such a narrow base of experience that his conclusions are often irrelevant and sometimes absurd. More serious, he is usually cut off by his overspecialized work and personality from any broad, functional give-and-take with society as a whole. Consequently, his shortcomings of understanding tend to be self-reinforcing and he becomes more and more isolated culturally from everyone but other intellectuals. Society, meanwhile, is deprived of effective intellectual leadership from its most talented (in this direction) members and becomes ripe for totalitarian manipulation.

This vicious circle is of special importance to writers because they are, in the nature of things, intellectuals, and their job is to give meaning and relationship to the raw stuff of life. And since most readers, critics, and publishers of serious literature are also intellectuals, and since a successful writer usually moves completely out of his social and cultural origins into the rarefied air of the literary world, the unhappy social and individual effects of intellectual isolationism are all too characteristic of contemporary literature.

All of this has to do with Steinbeck because—almost alone among important contemporaries—he seems to have no hankering for the literary life or the isolationism of a typical intellectual. The people he writes about are primarily nonintellectuals and his acquaintance with such people and his intuitive feeling for what makes them tick are probably his greatest strength as a writer. He presumably classifies the typical professional intellectual along with the other middle-class "shitheels" as inferior and inadequate human beings. His best field is the subrational and the inarticulate and many of the reviews of *The Wayward Bus* show that this anti-intellectualism produces confusion among the critics who are called upon to classify and evaluate his writing.

The brilliant Mr. Barzun, for instance, discussed the book in a recent issue of *Harpers'* with a mixture of disdain and incomprehension. The characters of *The Wayward Bus* meet no vital counterparts in Mr. Barzun's frame of reference—exceptionally qualified though he is in the worlds of learning and abstractions—and he could only blather about Steinbeck's using the naturalist tradition without bothering to understand it. On the other hand, there have been some reviews of the book which overpraised it with the maudlin hysteria of someone's maiden aunt trying to live dangerously.

It is typical of Steinbeck—and it is typical of California—that he can study biology and speculate about teleology without losing his interest in, or fellowship with, Mack and the boys. His biggest contribution as a writer may turn out to have been the exploration and colonization of the no-man's-land between intellectual and nonintellectual, rational and subrational. Similarly, the ferment of California may come to play a similar part in the future of America.

As we have suggested above, Steinbeck's *Sea of Cortez* musings suggest that he has grown weary of trying to make responsible sense of life and is experimenting with "nonteleological" reporting. But even the most arid stretches of *The Wayward Bus* pretty well demonstrate the impossibility of writing in a state of abstract omniscience from which cause and effect and good and bad have been filtered. Even among the dip-net heterogeneity of this novel's catch, he obviously likes some and dislikes others, and he finds it necessary to explain how they got the way they are. Both Steinbeck and California are relatively young. I suggest that both may have their most creative days ahead of them. And that it would be intelligent to study them in relation to each other.

The Arthurian Cycle in *Tortilla Flat*

by Arthur F. Kinney

I

The work which first made John Steinbeck famous is one he considered a failure. *Tortilla Flat* (1933) failed, said Steinbeck, because critics and readers never understood what he was trying to do. When Louis Kronenberger rejected the book for Alfred A. Knopf, Steinbeck wrote to his agents in a telling mixture of bitterness and despair:

> The book has a very definite theme. I thought it was clear enough. I had expected that the plan of the Arthurian cycle would be recognized, that my Gawaine and Launcelot, that my Arthur and Galahad would be recognized. Even the incident of the Sangreal in the search of the forest is not clear enough I guess. The form is that of the Malory version, the coming of Arthur and the mystic quality of owning a house, the forming of the round table, the adventures of the knights and finally, the mystic adventures of Danny. However, I seem not to have made any of this clear. The main issue was to present a little known and, to me delightful people. Is not this cycle story or theme enough? [1]

Admitting that apparently it was not, Steinbeck wrote a Preface for his novel in which he pointed out that

> . . . Danny's house was not unlike the Round Table, and Danny's friends were not unlike the knights of it. And this is the story of how that group came into being, of how it flourished and grew to be an organization beautiful and wise. This story deals with the adventuring of Danny's friends, with the good they did, with their thoughts and their

"The Arthurian Cycle in *Tortilla Flat*" by Arthur F. Kinney. From *Modern Fiction Studies*, XI, no. 1 (Spring 1965), 11–20. *Modern Fiction Studies*, © 1965, by Purdue Research Foundation, Lafayette, Indiana. Reprinted by permission of Purdue Research Foundation.

[1] The letter is in Peter Lisca, *The Wide World of John Steinbeck* (New Brunswick, N.J.: Rutgers University Press, 1958), p. 76.

endeavors. In the end, this story tells how the talisman was lost and how the group disintegrated.[2]

The novel is framed by the Arthurian legend. Steinbeck used Malory directly, and perhaps Layamon; he apparently neglected Wace. In *Tortilla Flat,* Danny often functions as Arthur; he begins the book as a young soldier discharged from service and comes home to Monterey. Like Arthur, he comes to his homeland about to found a kingdom; like Arthur, he is young and has just survived some major battles. Arthur's talisman was the precious sword Excalibur, handed to him by the Lady of the Lake. This is an inherited greatness, a legacy predicted by Merlin which makes Arthur leader and king. Danny is presented his legacy —two houses—which were the property of his grandfather, although Steinbeck has no Merlin figure. As Excalibur gave Arthur status, so the ownership of houses and property gives Danny status. Danny and his followers, who feel a deep kinship to him, a bond of brotherhood as strong as the Anglo-Saxon *comitatus,* are the subjects of several episodic adventures, as loosely strung together as Malory's knightly tales. As Malory ends with the death of Arthur, and the final breaking up of his followers, so Steinbeck ends with the death of Danny and the dissolution of his band of *paisanos.* In plot outline, *Tortilla Flat* follows Malory.

Steinbeck also uses a type of chapter heading suggestive of medieval romances: for example, Chapter VI is headed, "How three sinful men, through contrition, attained peace. How Danny's Friends swore comradeship"; and Chapter XVI, "Of the sadness of Danny. How through sacrifice Danny's Friends gave a party. How Danny was Translated." If "translated" is an obsolete term, not common and not *paisano,* Steinbeck did find, happily enough, that the real *paisanos* of Monterey do use a familiar "you" resembling medieval practice. In one of the book's first conversations, after Danny meets Pilon carrying a suspicious bundle on the streets, he approaches with the familiar "thou," saying, "Pilon, my little friend! Where goest thou so fast?" and Pilon replies sadly, "Danny, . . . how knewest thou I had a bottle of brandy under my coat?" (pp. 21–22).

Other similarities between Malory and Steinbeck are far more central. In a discussion of Malory, Muriel Bradbrook has distinguished

[2] John Steinbeck, *Tortilla Flat* (New York: Modern Library, 1937), pp. 9–10. All references are to this edition.

three factors of the medieval romance.[3] First, the heroes must be
knights. Arthur knighted the men of his Round Table. Danny, in
turn, welcomes and initiates all the men who gather at his house. They
are, he tells them, to work closely with one another. They are not to
preempt his bed. It is as simple as that.

Such a bond is the *comitatus,* Miss Bradbrook's second point—the
binding loyalty of men in Arthur's time which superseded even the
bond between a man and a woman. This is a predominant Steinbeck
concern. In the first chapter, Danny tells Pilon, "Pilon, I swear, what
I have is thine. While I have a house, thou hast a house" (p. 26). A
short time later, Pilon is given some money by a hotel guest to purchase some ginger-ale; he takes it and buys wine and then lures two
women into the second house, which he rents from Danny. Danny
arrives and immediately "Pilon fell into his arms and placed everything at Danny's disposal" (p. 36). They share the wine and the women.

This *comitatus* gains its force from mutual respect and understanding, as well as from the traditional code. The men that Danny collects
about him—Big Joe, the Pirate, Jesus Maria, Pilon, Pablo—respect one
another. The men take in the Pirate as a member and accept his five
dogs with him. They let Pilon reason out their activities because he is
fond of his ability at logic. Big Joe's bluntness is accepted, and Jesus
Maria's humanitarian instincts are honored; when he brings home a
sick baby with the corporal, Danny and his friends do everything they
can to save the baby's life. Finally, when they take the Pirate into their
group, they do not insist that he give up his daily occupation of gathering firewood and selling it; they simply accept it.

The most brutal action of *Tortilla Flat* occurs when this *comitatus* is
threatened. When Big Joe steals one of Danny's two blankets, the others gather to demand its reurn. When Big Joe's pants are stolen, they
are brought back at night. The *comitatus* is symbolized for Danny and
his friends not only by the talisman of a house of their own, but by the
collection of quarters the Pirate heaps up to purchase a golden candlestick for Saint Francis; with a threat to this money (Big Joe's theft of
it), comes the most fearful of punishments:

> Pablo threw a bucket of water in Big Joe's face. He turned his head and
> stretched his neck like a chicken, and then he opened his eyes and looked
> dazedly at his friends. They did not speak to him at all. Danny measured

[3] *Sir Thomas Malory,* Bibliographical Series of Supplements to British Book News
on Writers and Their Works, No. 95 (London: Longmans, Green & Co., 1958), pp.
13–14.

his distance carefully, like a golfer addressing the ball. His stick smashed on Big Joe's shoulder; then the friends went about the business in a cold and methodical manner. Jesus Maria took the legs, Danny the shoulders and chest. Big Joe howled and rolled on the floor. They covered his body from the neck down. Each blow found a new space and welted it. The shrieks were deafening. The Pirate stood helplessly by, holding his ax. . . . Then Pilon tore off the blue shirt and exposed the pulpy raw back. With the can-opener he cross-hatched the skin so deftly that a little blood ran from each line. Pablo brought the salt to him and helped him to rub it in all over the torn back. (pp. 202–203)

And the *comitatus* is stronger even than the love of a woman. When Delores Engracia Ramirez leans over her fence to lure Danny, and he courts her by paying two dollars for a vacuum cleaner as a gift, the band rebels: "Wherefore the friends, in despair, organized a group, formed for and dedicated to her destruction" (p. 163).

Besides the knightly character of the heroes and the *comitatus*, Miss Bradbrook found that the Malorian romance limited its subject matter chiefly to men, and only men in youth—her third distinguishing characteristic. There are no children and no old people (save fairies and wizards) in Malory. There are no children (save the corporal's dying baby) and no old people (save the jailer) in Steinbeck.

But Steinbeck's use of the Arthurian legend goes beyond structure and convention; particular incidents are transposed. For example, much of Malory is concerned with the amorous adventures of the knights. Launcelot has affairs with two Elaines, as well as Guinevere. Danny courts Señora Ramirez and, when one of his houses burns to the ground, he continues an affair with Mrs. Morales without winking an eye: "Well," said Danny, "if the fire department can't do anything about it, what does Pilon expect me to do?" (p. 79). Big Joe Portagee is seduced by Tia Ignacia.

In Steinbeck, the adventures with women are not all single love affairs. The entire group gets together to aid Señora Teresina Cortez, whose children starve when the bean crop fails. They decide at once to act in the chivalric manner, and "Theirs was no idle boast. Fish they collected. The vegetable patch of the Hotel Del Monte they raided. It was a glorious game. Theft robbed of the stigma of theft, crime altruistically committed—What is more gratifying?" (p. 232).

The group also works together for the benefit of the Pirate. When he has saved enough quarters from his wood sales, he purchases a golden candlestick and goes to have it blessed. The scenes that follow are the most sentimentalized in the book, yet they are successful. The Pirate is grateful to St. Francis (the patron saint of animals) because he saved a dying dog that trailed the Pirate. But the Pirate has no clothes to wear to church during the service of dedication. Danny and his friends each contribute clothing, and then, left with nothing suitable to wear themselves, stay at home during a service and Mass which is almost as important to them.

The Pirate is Steinbeck's Perceval figure. On the way home from church, the Pirate is so happy with the dedication that he repeats the priest's sermon verbatim to his dogs, gathered in a semicircle in a forest at the edge of the Flat. Like Perceval, who was present at a vision of the Holy Grail, the Pirate's dogs see a vision of St. Francis at the conclusion of the Pirate's service, and, while drinking one night, the Pirate admits he himself saw the patron saint when his dying dog was restored to him.

The Grail imagery, admittedly important to Steinbeck, is the basis for Chapter VIII, which is titled "How Danny's Friends sought mystic treasure on St. Andrew's Eve. How Pilon found it and later how a pair of serge pants changed ownership twice." St. Andrew's Eve in Monterey is "the night when all buried treasure sent up a faint phosphorescent glow through the ground" (p. 125). There is believed to be much treasure in Monterey, and Pilon discovers a blue glow in the middle of the night. It has an eerie reflection for the *paisanos,* much as the Grail has for Perceval an air of eerie mysteriousness about it. But where the Grail is seen in the end by Perceval on his pilgrimage, Steinbeck has the treasure hunt in parody: the treasure, watched all night and dug up in the morning, is a landmarker for a 1915 geodetic survey.

The final scene in Malory before the disintegration of Arthur's knightly band is the madness of Launcelot. He is tricked by Elaine into making love to her, believing in the dark that she is Guinevere. When he learns his mistake, and Guinevere discovers his treachery, he leaps from the window of the bedroom and races into the night raving. For months, he fails to return. Danny's madness imitates Launcelot's. He inherits two houses, and one burns. The one that remains bothers him because it involves responsibility. He is happy as long as the talismanic bond of the Pirate's plan to buy a candlestick holds the group of friends together. But when the Pirate's money is stolen by Big Joe and returned, it is counted: there is enough and the candlestick is bought. There is no more talisman for Danny then; only the house remains with its fearful weight pressing upon Danny's shoulders. One night, he runs off. The friends think he is having an affair, and they rest comfortably. But when Danny fails to return, they become worried. They scout the woods and call for him, but they cannot find him. They then hear reports about Danny: he is inviting young girls into the woods, he has stolen grappa, he has knocked down an old man with a fence picket. At a wharf they learn he has fought and broken windows; finally he has been arrested. Their concern increases. When he steals Pilon's shoes one night, the *comitatus* is broken, and they act. They lay traps, and await his return. He sells his final house to ⸃orelli, the local wine merchant, ridding himself of responsibility and luxuriating in newly acquired wine. When he drains his last supply, he returns broken and weary to his friends. He is sad, and the friends find they can cheer him up only with a party, a party where Danny gets so drunk that he topples in stupor over a cliff to his death. True to their simple but profound understanding of the medieval bond, Danny's friends wait until he is buried and then burn the house. "And after a while they turned and walked slowly away, and no two walked together" (p. 317).

II

Steinbeck also followed Malory thematically. With Danny and his friends, ritual is as strong in contemporary Monterey as it was in medieval England. *Tortilla Flat* opens with ritual. Danny has returned from the war, and, overjoyed to be back, he gets drunk. He is put in jail, but the friendly jailer, Tito Ralph, frees him. Danny spends the night in the woods, and then, true to ritual, he acts the next day as if he were an escaped convict rather than a surreptitiously freed one: "When the brilliant sun awakened Danny about noon, he determined to hide all day to escape pursuit. He ran and dodged behind bushes. He peered out of the undergrowth like a hunted fox. And, at evening, the rules having been satisfied, he came out and went about his business" (p. 20).

Later, when Pilon and Pablo and Jesus Maria are to blame for the burning of Danny's first house, they go about thieving and return to Danny penitent, their arms filled with . . . "oranges and apples and bananas, bottles of olives and pickles, sandwiches of pressed ham, egg sandwiches, bottles of soda pop, a paper carton of potato salad and a copy of the *Saturday Evening Post*" (p. 86). Danny knows he is freed of part of his awful responsibility, and he is happy, but he, too, must act out a role; he calls his friends "dogs of dogs" and "thieves of decent folks' other house" and "spawn of cuttlefish" (p. 86).

Like Malory, Steinbeck makes friendship the highest virtue. It is more than this: it is an unspoken demand and acknowledgment. Arthurs' knights helped one another and others; Danny's friends do likewise. Arthur's knights did not preach religion, but they accepted it. Some, like Perceval, devoted their lives to it. Jesus Maria is a true Christian humanitarian; the Pirate, with his visions, borders on the mystic. With his rosary and his love for the gold candlestick, he is reminiscent of the Cortez sisters kneeling nightly to the Virgin in Steinbeck's *Pastures of Heaven,* his earlier treatment of *paisanos.*

Living is largely a simple affair in both Malory and Steinbeck. There is the elaborate method in courtship, ritual, and story-telling feasts, but aside from this, neither Arthur's knights nor Danny's friends demand much: shelter and a full belly is all they want. The lodging need not be luxurious; modern conveniences are unnecessary. For Arthur's knights, such conveniences were unmanly. For Danny's friends, they represent the burden of property. Pilon takes away even such small items as a wash bowl and pitcher and two red glass vases when he and Danny first move into one of the inherited houses (p. 34).

Finally, Malory was a moralist. Despite his joy in Launcelot's amours and Gawain's adventures, a major concern is the quest of the chalice of the Christ. From the Perceval story on, Malory is more and more centering on the degenerate morals of the court of Arthur; the court is for Malory riddled with vice, begun with infidelity, though no longer limited to it, as Arthur's death approaches. Steinbeck's book, comic as it may be, is also a study in degeneration. But for Steinbeck, the immorality is not so much in Danny and his friends, who seem to be good by being natural, but described implicitly in their comments on the artificial, hypocritical society with which their natural good contrasts.

Danny goes to jail as soon as he returns to Monterey, and Steinbeck's first scathing social comment is seen in Danny's killing dozens of bedbugs in his cell and plastering them on the wall. The corporal whose baby is dying is chastised by the police rather than helped. The welfare league, the pride of an organized society, almost kills Señora Cortez's children: they have arbitrarily decided that her healthy children are not healthy because they have been reared solely on beans. Even the destruction of property is a comment on society's overevaluation of material things.

Because he treats contemporary morality by contrasting it with natural good, Steinbeck writes as moral a treatise of today as Malory did of a romantic past. Moreover, Steinbeck's people are real, and they are of his own time. Malory's remain legendary, even if the concern for morality strengthened his legend.

III

Yet it is the founding of a legend, or an emblem of England and a symbol of her greatness, that is important to Malory. A thief in his later years, a scoundrel of the worst sort, Malory wrote his *Morte d'Arthur* in prison. During the process, his moralistic bent grew. As he Anglicized some romantic tales from his "Fressh bookes," the condemnation of the degenerate grew stronger, and his approval of the Perceval quest grew more fervent.

Steinbeck's morality in *Tortilla Flat* is never fervent; it is relaxed and comic. And if there are imitated incidents, there are also discrepancies.

Some of these have been mentioned. Danny, in founding the group of friends and in donating the house as a talisman, is the modern Arthur. But in pursuing Mrs. Morales and Señora Ramirez, he is antithetical to Arthur; in his flight of madness, he becomes not Arthur, but Launcelot.

The confusion begins here, but it pervades Steinbeck's novel. The Pirate resembles Perceval in his humble and rustic background, but in seeking treasure, he is likened to Galahad. If Steinbeck desires the geodetic landmarker to represent the Grail (and such seems to be the case), then it is Pilon and Big Joe who discover the treaure. Neither one elsewhere in the book can be identified as a Galahad or Perceval figure. Elaine, a simple but greedy young girl who causes Launcelot's madness through involvement with Guinevere, has no counterpart in Steinbeck. There is no Merlin in *Tortilla Flat*. Finally, Danny dies an heroic death (parodied), yet there is no suggestion of incarnation as there is in Malory, and no suggestion of Arthur's (Danny's) return as there is in Layamon.

There are other central distinctions. Malory centered his work around the *comitatus,* the French system of courtly love, and the reverence of morality. Steinbeck upholds the English *comitatus.* But the complex code of behavior in courtly love, except for the few dealings with Señora Ramirez, is snuffed out in Steinbeck. The detailed courtship, which results in both lust and adoration of the mistress, is reduced in Steinbeck to lust alone.

This simplification of courtship is indicative. The vices of promiscuity and adultery in courtly love were partly compensated for by the virtues of obedience, devotion, and service. Nothing compensates Steinbeck's vice of lust; it becomes itself virtuous. The double standard so elaborate and meaningful in medieval England is negated for the single standard of desire in Steinbeck. This impinges on Malory's third concern: morality. Arthur became, for Malory, a moral norm, just as Perceval and Galahad were spiritual norms. There is no moral norm in Steinbeck. All the *paisanos* follow the same code, and it is riddled with vice. They oppose the order of Torelli, but he becomes too much the fool character, the buffoon, the victim, to be given the exalted role of moral norm. The moral norm of Monterey, in its keeping of jails, arresting drunks, and sending out dietitians and fire engines, is parodied and satirized. The contrast of Monterey's laws and the *paisanos'* code works against Monterey: only where the *paisanos* show the weakness of organized society is there a contrast, and there the friends of Danny turn their vices into the virtues of a moral norm. Thus the double standard is crushed, no standard is maintained in place of it, and *Tortilla Flat* fails as a wholly moral comment. The moral norm is blurred early in Malory, but by the time Perceval enters, the edges have become increasingly sharper; the moral norm never does exist in Steinbeck.

Just as the moral seriousness of Malory underlay serious acceptance of the adventures he recounted, so Steinbeck's negation of morality underlies the more comic adventures of his heroes. For Launcelot did great deeds; Danny, in courting Señora Ramirez, gives her a vacuum cleaner with no motor. Malory's heroes were, evil or good, somehow taller than men. They were of the stature of greatness. Steinbeck's are merely lovable; worse, they can also be laughable or foolish. As such, Malory and Steinbeck are at opposite poles.

IV

Yet it is the comic that is Steinbeck's salvation. For he has faced as squarely as any contemporary writer the problem of adapting an old myth or legend to modern times. It is a project at once promising and treacherous. If the legend fits the facts, as Steinbeck early suggested, then the facts take on a new richness and the new work takes on an immediate universality. But the price to pay for this is heavy. For if one follows a legend, as Steinbeck also saw, then the previous knowledge of the legend eliminates a necessary ingredient of any creative work—that of suspense. There is less interest in a story if one knows how it will end, and the interest changes to an intellectual comparison of processes. Moreover, to rework an old form is to presuppose both authors have the same concerns, the same philosophic viewpoints, the same ethical standards. It is to deny the years or even centuries of intervening history and intellectual attainment. This is a difficult and improbable position.

Steinbeck solves this dilemma by using both horns to his advantage. He takes the general outline of the Malory epic to guide his major development. It is, for Steinbeck, suggestive but not determinative. To create a new work, Steinbeck changes the character relationship, changes the ending, and then, perhaps in an intuitive way, takes the sharp edge off the old heroic conventions by making them comic.

Hence the chapter headings juxtapose the grand style with the unimportant subject (vacuum cleaners, pants). The *comitatus* is undermined: the earlier quotation in this study—"Pilon, I swear, what I have is thine. While I have a house, thou hast a house"—is followed by "Give me a drink" (p. 26). The grand status of Danny is likened to the new status of Señora Ramirez, but this comes with a vacuum cleaner without a motor owned by a woman in a district with no electricity! Pilon's thoughts of heaven are undercut by Steinbeck's aside ("Hear this, recording angel!") (p. 39) and immediately after his flight of mysticism, Pilon thinks only of obtaining some wine (p. 42).

In Malory, the Grail was sought by the religious; in Steinbeck, the treasure in the forest is sought by all who want money. The tales in Steinbeck are recalled not at feasts in the great hall, but at all-night parties, where Danny's friends drink dollar wine from old fruit jars until they are in a stupor. Even the saint, who appears in a vision to the mystic Pirate, speaks very much unlike a saint; according to the Pirate, St. Francis tells him, "Be good to little doggies, you dirty man" (p. 209). Perhaps the best-known comic revision comes in Danny's death, for, as Steinbeck tells it, "Even now, when the people speak of Danny's Opponent [wine], they lower their voices and look furtively about. They heard Danny charge to the fray [the imaginary bout a drunkard fights]. They heard his last shrill cry of defiance, and then a thump. And the silence" (p. 301). This is enough to turn the modern rendition of Malory into a very well-executed mock-epic.

Indeed, Steinbeck doubly assured his mock-epic treatment by appending to his explanation in the preface the broad hint that this was a parody. He writes: "It is well that this cycle be put down on paper so that in a future time scholars, hearing the legends, may not say as they say of Arthur and of Roland and of Robin Hood—'There was no Danny nor any group of Danny's friends, nor any house. Danny is a nature god and his friends primitive symbols of the wind, the sky, the sun.' This history is designed now and ever to keep the sneers from the lips of sour scholars" (p. 10).

Malory created in his most manly and courageous knight, Launcelot, the most immoral and decadent, a paradox of morality. Launcelot was the lover of Guinevere as well as other women, and therefore the greatest traitor, in one sense, to Arthur. At the same time, Malory introduced more orthodox morality through the Grail quest. He attempted to solve the dilemma by having Launcelot father the man who would find the Grail, thus redeeming his family line.

If Steinbeck denies vice and virtue for a single standard of natural action neither moral nor immoral, then he erases the problem that is still only apparently solved in Malory. Steinbeck, at least, gains consistency. And in developing a comic tone, a mock-epic development, Steinbeck at once keeps close to his reader the Arthurian cycle, while he himself remains a good step in aesthetic distance from it. The result is that what is apparently naiveté in Steinbeck is in actuality perceptive control.

The result, therefore, is a successful transposition of the legend. Steinbeck avoided the dangers of too close a parallel. At the same time, he used the advantages inherent in choosing legend for modern treatment. In forging such a middle road between the danger and the advantage, he turned a possibility into profit, treacherous going into triumph: *Tortilla Flat* is quite possibly the best Arthurian story for which a modern society can serve as basis.

In Dubious Battle[1]

by André Gide

27 September [1940]

In Dubious Battle by John Steinbeck. Impeccable translation of a most remarkable book. If I were less tired, I should enjoy praising it. But I could do so only at too great length. It is the best (psychological) portrayal that I know of Communism, and perfectly lighted. If it leaves the capitalist and bourgeois counterpart in the shadow, at least it very cleverly gives one a glimpse of this in the dialogues, and that is enough. The main character is the crowd; but from that amorphous and vague mass there stand out various individuals in whom the variegated aspects of the problem are set forth without the discussion's ever cluttering and interrupting the action. And likewise there stand out against the vast general movement, in harmony or opposition with the great wave of common interests, the passions or individual interests of the leaders or minor characters; and all this presented so fairly that one cannot take sides for or against the flood of demands any more than the author has done. The legitimacy of those demands, like the outcome of the struggle itself, remains "dubious." Especially dubious the legitimacy of using treacherous means to bring about the triumph of even the most legitimate cause. But Steinbeck reveals admirably (yet without *demonstrating* anything) how those who are refused all other means of fighting are led and forced to treachery, injustice, deliberate cruelty; and how the noblest and most generous characters are distorted thereby. Whence the great distress inherent throughout this beautiful and painful book.

From *The Journals of André Gide*, Volume IV, 1939–1949, trans. Justin M. O'Brien (New York: Alfred A. Knopf, 1951), p. 48. Copyright © 1951 by Alfred A. Knopf, Inc. Reprinted by permission of the publisher.

[1] [Title supplied by Editor.]

When a certain stage of history is reached, everything appears in the guise of a problem. And man's responsibility increases as that of the gods decreases.

It devolves upon man alone, in the final reckoning, to solve all these problems which he alone has presumably raised.

The Unity of *In Dubious Battle*: Violence and Dehumanization

by Howard Levant

In Dubious Battle comprises a specific and general narrative. Jim Nolan's specific education in violence fuses with the general narrative of a strike of apple pickers in the Torgas Valley in the early 1930s. Explicitly the novel raises a number of immediate and suspenseful questions: Will the strike be won? What will happen to Jim, Mac, Doc, London, Lisa? Implicitly these questions involve a judgment of whether idealistic aims can be squared with power tactics. The ideological basis permits considerable depth of motivation in the central figures. This is especially true of Jim Nolan.

Steinbeck's initial problem is to outline Jim's history to the time that he enters the novel. At once Steinbeck accomplishes two things. *In Dubious Battle* begins with an individual, Jim, not with an abstract event. Also the objective, dramatic quality of the novel appears when Jim talks about himself as part of the process of joining the Communist Party, for this disguises necessary background material. A controlled series of images sets the tone and sharpens the meaning of Jim's awareness that he had been "dead" and now is partly "alive." Thus, the first lines of the novel: "At last it was evening. The lights in the street outside came on, and the neon restaurant sign on the corner jerked on and off, exploding its hard red light in the air." [1] The sign conveys the ugly, mechanical "illumination" which Jim has experienced. And, of his family, Jim begins: "My mother had light blue eyes. I remember they looked like white stones" (p. 21). Eyes like stones

"The Unity of *In Dubious Battle*: Violence and Dehumanization" by Howard Levant. From *Modern Fiction Studies* XI, no. 1 (Spring 1965), 21–33. *Modern Fiction Studies*, © 1965, by Purdue Research Foundation, Lafayette, Indiana. Reprinted by permission of Purdue Research Foundation.

[1] John Steinbeck, *In Dubious Battle* (New York: Covici-Friede, 1936), p. 9. Subsequent references to this edition are incorporated in the text.

connote a living-death; this suggestion reappears in an image uniting
eye and death references in a machine image: "mother was quieter
even than before. She moved kind of like a machine, and she hardly
ever said anything. Her eyes got a kind of dead look, too" (p. 22). This
sequence illuminates the inner sense of Jim's background—his father
is a drunken, fighting man, his sister runs away to a life of sin, his
mother suffers and dies silently—and deepens the implications of Jim's
introduction to Joy, an old Party man, whose life suggests the useless
violence of Jim's father: " 'This is Joy,' said Mac. 'Joy is a veteran,
aren't you, Joy?' 'Damn right,' said Joy. His eyes flared up, then almost
instantly the light went out of them again" (p. 24). This sequence indicates Jim's own passage from death to life, from "dead" eyes to "his
eyes flared up." Jim is aware of his symbolic passage, for he describes
his "conversion" to the Party as a coming alive. The effect of this connected imagery is to strip Jim of his dead past and to establish him as
a *tabula rasa.*

Mac is the mature Party man who is responsible for Jim's education:
"I'll train you, and then you can train new men. Kind of like teaching
hunting dogs by running them with the old boys, see?" (p. 36). Here
the imagery suggests a friendly concern that connotes life; its reverse
is the deadness of Jim's previous life.[2]

Once such values are presented within the framework of a symbolic
passage from death to life, Steinbeck provides relevant, supporting
events in the objective world. On their way to organize a strike, riding
the rails, Mac and Jim meet men like themselves who attempt to treat
them cruelly. Jim's education begins, then, when the evil he observes
in these men suggests to him that all men are capable of evil, and,
therefore, need to be manipulated to achieve the goal of the good life.
So, through the practical example, Jim deduces the conflict between
ends and means and accepts the validity of the paradox that good may
come out of evil. Steinbeck avoids any abstract statement of these
propositions; everything is realized drama.

The fruit pickers are a collection of people who "travel with" their
"natural leaders," London and Dakin (pp. 58–59, p. 66, p. 88). To have
a strike at all, Mac has to destroy the almost pure democracy of the
fruit pickers and substitute a rigid organization with himself at its
head. Mac does this by gaining the confidence of the men and by forc-
ing them to recognize their genuine unity. A chance situation provides

---

[2] Later, as the strike develops into ambiguous violence, the imagery of the hunt
takes on a more ominous aspect.

Mac an opportunity and prefigures the development of the novel. London's daughter, Lisa, is in labor. Mac offers himself as an experienced midwife—a lie—and proceeds to direct events. He puts all of the men to boiling water and collecting white rags. After Mac delivers the child successfully, the chances of the strike being "born" appear excellent. As the birth is an organic figure of the strike, so the strike's moral ambiguity is prefigured in the birth. Mac's aim in helping Lisa is tactical, a kind of humanitarian expediency. Mac explains to Jim: "We've got to use whatever material comes to us. That was a lucky break. We simply had to take it. 'Course it was nice to help the girl, but hell, even if it killed her, we've got to use everything" (p. 66). Jim accepts this rule of ends and means. It works and it corresponds to what he has learned on the rails and in the camp. And the weak point in Mac's reasoning is concealed, or, not figured in events this early in the novel. The evident facts are that Mac does manipulate the men on the train, does help Lisa, and knows the men feel a joyful unity as they work in common for a good cause. Yet Mac has to work within a large margin of chance. He understands enough psychology to play on groups and individuals and enough medicine to know that antiseptics are useful, but he does not know if he can sway London, safely deliver Lisa's baby, or form the men into a group. He must pretend to be in total control when he knows he is not; he must use magic, science, or whatever lies at hand to bridge the gap between his knowledge and his ignorance. So the implications of the birth operate together as an analogue of the larger tension between ends and means. The enormous chances that Mac has to take and the thin logic which justifies those chances suggest that Mac will fail to connect ends and means at some point. The immediate fact is that, having the men in his power, Mac can promote a strike. On a deeper level, it is certain the strike cannot produce good.

Jim remains the lyrical voice, the innocent. Jim tends to be corrupted by Mac's knowing use of tactics because he does not realize they may absorb principle. Mac can distinguish between what is right and what has to be done; Jim admires Mac too much and is too green to make that distinction.

The novel's general organization supports these particulars. The first nine chapters set up the economic conditions which are the solidly realized background of Jim's education. The indictment of buccaneering capitalism is credible in its specification, which is assumed to be the entire context of individual experience. On the other hand, the ambiguous quality of the strike is evident by the end of Chapter Eight, when Mac tells Jim that the strikers cannot win, and, in any case, the Party's real aim is to train the men through bitter experience to become willing spearheads of the ultimate revolution. This unscrupulous long-term purpose negates the ostensibly humanitarian short-term purpose to raise wages and improve working conditions. Still, the direct and indirect force which the owners use against the strikers tends to justify ambiguous strike tactics, and this complicates what could become a simple moral choice.

Steinbeck's conception of group-man is an important aspect of this grim development of the novel. Group-man is a collection of individuals, created in periods of great tension to function with enormous strength as a single organism. Group-man is defined by analogy with a group of animal cells. The qualifying fact is that group-man is a creature of violence; it is formed by and produces violence. Limited as a weapon, it is the only effective weapon the strikers have. Obviously, being so qualified, group-man is involved in the ambiguities of the strike and contributes to them.

This concept is developed as a metaphor. The fruit pickers are the raw materials of the cell. The Party men are the "senses," leading group-man into significant action to the extent that personified violence can be led. Jim is one of these "senses." His education and the history of the strike tend to be subsumed in the need to force the creation of group-man and to maintain its period of existence. As the strike continues and the force circling the strike increases, Jim comes to accept the notion of violence as an end in itself. This is Jim's ultimate corruption, as we shall see, and, in this, his personal development corresponds to the development of the strike.

However, following the birth of Lisa's baby, the immediate fact is that Mac has to convince London and Dakin that a strike is necessary. Jim is kept in events when he finds the clinching argument: " 'Where you going when we get the apples picked, Mr. Dakin?' 'Cotton,' said Dakin. 'Well, the ranches over there are bigger, even. If we take a cut here, the cotton people will cut deeper.' Mac smiled encouragement and praise. 'You know damn well they will,' he seconded" (p. 88). Jim's argument reflects Mac's knowledge of tactics and marks Jim's change from pupil to practitioner. This is made specific in Mac's later praise: " 'That was a smart thing, Jim. She was beginning to drag when you brought in that thing about that cotton. That was a smart thing.' 'I want to help,' Jim cried. 'God, Mac, this thing is singing all over me. I don't want to sleep. I want to go right on helping' " (p. 90). Furthermore, Mac suggests that Jim's insights are superior to his; that as he, Mac, is a workhorse, Jim is a revolutionist genius. The distinction strengthens the dramatic quality of the novel in that the two men are given explicitly different personalities. These distinctions keep the history of the strike from collapsing into a set of abstract ideas. Men rather than ideas govern the history of the strike. Thus Jim's personality determines the use of group-man, not the "objective" force of Marxian "laws." Now "coming alive" means to Jim becoming an expert in power tactics, and while this is lyrical as an ideal ("this thing is singing all over me") the process demands inhuman responses ("I don't want to sleep"). Therefore, from this point on, so far as it is Jim's history, the novel is concentrated on two parallel developments in Jim's education: his loss of humanity, and, correspondingly, his growing self-confidence in his ability to lead group-man. The parallel history of the strike consists of increasingly frantic and violent efforts by the leaders—increasingly, that means Jim—to form group-man, to keep it alive, and to lead it. Jim does this but he fails to see that group-man is a force that uses and destroys his sense of his own humanity. Here the technical problem is to permit the reader to see what group-man is and does while keeping that insight from the leading characters.

Steinbeck manages with extraordinary skill by using a controlled allegorical figure, Dan, to spell out the nature of group-man (for the reader) very early in the novel.[3] Jim works with Dan in the orchard while he and Mac are attempting to create the strike, and Dan's fall through a rotten ladder is the specific event that forces the strike into being.[4] So Dan has an organic reason to be in the novel, apart from his more artificial role which is to personify History. Steinbeck makes even this artifice as plausible and organic as he can. Dan is an old, old man who has experienced many strikes, all of them unsuccessful. His experience lends distance and historic content to the extended struggle between worker and owner, for Dan is essentially a pre-Marxian worker in view of his innocent memories and a humility or lack of faith which has experienced group-man as "that big guy" who springs into life but is too unstable for any prolonged fight (p. 73). Yet Mac is ironically

[3] Much later, Doc Burton invents the term "group-man" in an argument with Mac about its true nature. But its nature is suggested explicitly by Dan at this early point.
[4] Steinbeck plays on "birth" and "born" in connecting the birth of Lisa's baby and the initial possibility of a strike. It does not strain Freudian imagery to observe that Dan's "fall" is equated with the "birth" of the strike; but Steinbeck does well, I am sure, to suggest this rather mechanical parallel very lightly.

mistaken in fearing that Jim may be "converted to hopelessness" by History (p. 79). Jim can only learn from History that group-man must be led by a strong hand. So arrogant a presumption of strength of will is an index to the extent of Jim's corruption. That is, Dan's penultimate function is to play off Jim's Promethean certainty.

Dan's view of group-man is not contradicted or supported at once, but Jim's certainty seems increasingly ambiguous as we learn more of group-man. The details of Joy's death and its consequences indicate the strength and weakness of group-man. Joy arrives on a train with a group of unknowing strikebreakers recruited in the city. When he attempts to exhort the strikebreakers, Joy is shot to death by some unknown townsman. The train engine is a symbol of the mechanical force which is capable of destroying the unstable force that is group-man. The charged writing in these passages invites the reading which I propose: "The engine panted rhythmically, like a great, tired animal. London cupped his hands around his mouth . . . His voice was cut off by a shriek of steam. A jet of white leaped from the side of the engine, drowning London's voice, blotting out every sound but its own swishing scream" (p. 167). The violence of Joy's death at this moment causes the first "birth" of group-man, and for the time its power is greater than mechanical power: "Suddenly the steam stopped . . . A strange, heavy movement started among the men . . . The guards aimed with their guns, but the line [of striking men] moved on, unheeding, unseeing . . . the boxcar doors were belching silent men who moved slowly in. The ends of the long line curled and circled slowly around the center of the dead man, like sheep around a nucleus . . . The guards were frightened; riots they could stop; but this slow, silent movement of men with the wide eyes of sleepwalkers terrified them" (pp. 168–169). These passages indicate the strength and weakness of group-man. Its strength is in the surprise and force of its biological formation in contrast with the artifices (engines, guns) of mechanical power, and in the consequent terror which it inspires. Its limitations are involved in its strength. Men need the stress of violent emotion ("blood") to become group-man; the "organism" is sheeplike; its power depends on surprise, mass, and a kind of moral recognition by those opposing it. Group-man is limited also by its physical needs. After Joy's funeral, news arrives that food has been obtained; group-man dissolves into a collection of hungry men. Since the "organism" uses up huge amounts of energy, its lifetime is limited and it is dependent on its biological needs. Even worse, as Mac and London confess to

Jim, group-man is too unpredictable, too morally ambiguous to be directed effectively by anyone; and this echoes Dan's experienced pessimism.

In spite of the evidence against the chance of a deliberate *use* of group-man, Jim remains confident that he can create and use group-man. This conviction is a measure of Jim's will to power by way of violence.

Dramatic contrast is evident in different points of view. Jim's conviction is balanced against Doc Burton's fear that group-man is a non-human beast with no normal dimension, and can be used, therefore, as an indiscriminate means to any end. Doc's fear is based on moral values; thus it is superior to Dan's blind pessimism. But Doc's point of view is qualified by a flaw in his nature and by the developing conditions of the strike. Thus Doc suffers bitterly from his scientific detachment. He is unable to join with men or to have any deeply human contacts. His emotional deadness is indicated by the identifying tag, "his sad eyes," which qualifies the impact of his nay-saying by suggesting the death-life imagery at the opening of the novel (pp. 129, 130, 141, 147, 199, 258). The implication is that Doc may be condemning what he cannot share. Finally, Doc's ambiguous attitude toward group-man lies in his characteristically distrusting hope that group-man may be some kind of a new, living God (pp. 260–261).

Mac's point of view is also contrasted with Doc's, and implicitly with Jim's, on an equally ambiguous basis. Mac's love of individuals conflicts with a willingness to use people for the ideal aim of gaining the good life through a revolution. Mac is a humanitarian under Party discipline. He can say to Jim: "Don't you go liking people, Jim. We can't waste time liking people" (p. 121). Mac can idealize men with equal force and validity.

Jim, Mac, and Doc suggest a balanced series of responses to group-man and to the necessities of the strike. Because Doc is permitted the most eloquent language, the dialectical victory may seem to be his. But to think so is to substitute correct doctrine for Steinbeck's interest in dramatic conflict, and to ignore the qualification of Doc's point of view along with his very presence in the strike camp. In fact the dialectical quarrel between Mac and Doc parallels their differing roles. Mac is a good man whose opportunistic tactics are justified in large part by the detailed tactics of the owners. Doc's good intentions are paralyzed by his analytical mind, and paradox is the result. Doc accepts the Calvinistic position that social change is pointless because evil is inherent in men, but he does what he can to help men and to ensure social change. Doc is the objective scientist, but he finds his distance from men painful. Doc stays distant, but his benevolence is evident to everyone and he is loved by the men he cares for. These complexities or contradictions encourage dramatic conflict rather than doctrinal certainties. Jim's certainty strengthens this pattern, since it does not imply a synthesis. Jim is another sort of creature, a man who comes to love violence and power. This contributes to the depth and intensity of the dramatic conflict.

I do not imply that Steinbeck fails to resolve the novel. The interfused final stages of the strike and of Jim's education provide a resolution of great force, and derives in large part from the context which we have been examining.

Mac's idea that everything has its "use" in view of the needs of the strike—or the revolution—is qualified when Mac refuses to "use" Jim, first, out of love for him, and, later, out of respect for Jim's special talents as a leader. But a change occurs halfway through the novel when Mac confesses to Jim that he is "so scared the strike'll crack," and adds, "I feel like it's mine" (pp. 192–193). Mac's humanly credible feelings contrast with Jim's certainty. Jim suggests a historic parallel from Herodotus for the use of violence. That is, Jim not only takes over leadership, but directs the strike toward violence.

The change is clarified by Jim's visit to Dan. Their conversation defines the function of leadership in the context of group-man:

> [Dan's] eyes grew soft and childlike. "I'll lead 'em," he said gently. "All the hundreds o' years that's what the workin' stiffs needed, a leader. I'll lead 'em through to the light. All they got to do is just what I say. I'll say, 'You lazy bastards get over there!' an' by Christ, they'll git, 'cause I won't have no lazy bastards. When I speak, they got to jump, right now." And then he smiled with affection. "The poor damn rats," he said. "They never had nobody to tell 'em what to do. They never had no real leader." "That's right," Jim agreed. "Well, you'll see some changes now," Dan exclaimed. "You tell 'em I said so. Tell 'em I'm workin' out a plan. I'll be up and around in a couple of days. Tell 'em just to have patience till I get out an' lead 'em." "Sure I'll tell 'em," said Jim. (p. 282)

The technical function of this passage is similar to the Elizabethan device of the play within the play. A single scene or episode seems to be detached from the main action, but in fact clarifies or foreshadows the main action indirectly and in an exaggerated fashion. So, indirectly, and prior to the event, Steinbeck provides an evaluation of the strike's development into pure violence under Jim's leadership. Dan's feverishly exaggerated projection of the private will is less dangerous than Jim's actual authoritarian rule which operates silently, behind the scenes, and therefore appears to be selfless.

Still, in this extraordinary novel, Dan becomes more than the semi-allegorical voice of History. He is drawn into an organic relationship with Jim's education and the progress of the strike through the suggestion that both he and Jim are sick with gangrene. The implication is that Dan's imaginary rule and Jim's actual direction of the strike into violence are not separated into dream and fact but are similarly consequences of fever. Significantly, Jim absorbs much of Mac's function as a leader after he has been put out of direct action by a bullet wound, and Jim's faith in violence increases proportionately as the wound infects. Neither Mac, London, nor Jim can be aware that Jim has gangrene because Jim could not influence events or even remain on the scene if his illness were recognized. Credibility is dealt with by the suggestion of a relationship between Jim and Dan. Dan's physical decline is observed in a detail that could not be justified on its own merits. And, by this point, Doc has been removed.

Jim's attitude toward violence conflicts now with Mac's. Mac will do anything for the cause, but he reacts against violence while Jim welcomes it. This distinction is repeated throughout the second half of the novel, but it is put most forcefully at first appearance when Mac has to smash the face of a boy found planning to snipe at the strikers' camp: " 'I hope they don't catch anybody else; I couldn't do it again.' 'You'd have to do it again,' said Jim. Mac looked at him with something of fear in his eyes. 'You're getting beyond me, Jim. I'm getting scared of you. I've seen men like you before . . . I know you're right. Cold thought to fight madness. I know all that. God Almighty, Jim, it's not human. I'm scared of you' " (p. 280). The novel is able to develop in terms of Jim's inhuman logic because in theory Mac accepts Jim's faith in violence. The distinction is that Mac remains human in practice, since more removed from a worship of violence than Jim.

The dramatic question at this point is to what extent "cold thought" is valid in practice. The answer is supplied by an action—by Jim's control of group-man in its final appearance in the novel. The discouraged strikers are jolted into group-man by the "blood" of a violent fight between London and a potential leader and possible spy named Burke. London does not know what to do with group-man until Jim gestures toward a roadblock which the strikers had refused to attack earlier. Now the roadblock is smashed easily. "Cold thought" is evident in the fact that Jim works out of sight, through the apparent leadership of London, for Jim wants the reality rather than the appearance of power. But "cold thought" is an illusory control. Jim and Mac are nearly attacked when the men come back from the roadblock, and only the speedy disintegration of group-man saves them. Jim is permitted a recognition of the horror of what he has directed when he reports to Mac: "It was like all of them disappeared, and it was just one big—animal, going down the road" (p. 322).

However, even when it is clear that the battle is lost as well as dubious, Jim and Mac are caught too deeply to wish to escape from the consequences which they perceive. And the initial, humanitarian purpose is lost in the violence which subsumes the strike. The final stage of Jim's education corresponds to the final stage of the strike, for in each instance means determine ends and tactics swallow up principle.

The ambiguity of "use" is explicitly the literary tool which Steinbeck depends on to suggest these points in dramatic terms. The strike is increasingly a struggle to gain power; thus it demands the use of many persons. But only Mac, Doc, and Jim choose to be used. The rest is manipulation. Even knowing choices are not free of ambiguity. Doc is in the camp for multiple reasons; his humanitarianism and his scientific wish to observe group-man in action are too divergent to be resolved. Mac is realist enough to admit the truth of power: "Everybody hates us; our own side and the enemy. And if we won, Jim, if we put it over, our own side would kill us" (p. 161). Jim chooses becaues he wishes to come alive at first, but his inhuman desire to "use" power reaches a peak just before his death when he offers to pull off his bandage "and get a flow of blood" to provide the shock that group-man needs to get itself "born" (p. 348). Jim leaves the novel in this ultimate impersonalization, his face "transfigured" so that "a furious light of energy seemed to shine from it" (p. 348). He manages to lose himself so completely, to be "used," that very little of the human is left; perhaps it is not bearing down too hard on the metaphor to suggest that Jim's "transfigured" face is godlike because it is not human.

Steinbeck does not depend only on this climax of ambiguity. Jim's final education is clarified from several points of view. Doc and Lisa state ambiguous and qualified opinions that refer to Jim's education and to the development of the strike.

Doc's ultimate reality is original sin: " '. . . man has met and defeated every obstacle, every enemy except one. He cannot win over himself. How mankind hates itself!' Jim said, 'We don't hate ourselves, we hate the invested capital that keeps us down.' 'The other side is made up of men, Jim, men like you. Man hates himself . . .' " (p. 259). Nevertheless, Doc's loneliness invalidates this certainty, and he ends by asking Jim for the secret of happiness.

A similar ambiguity governs Lisa's view of the good life. Her recall of a simpler, agrarian world is concrete in its detail; its weakness is its utter nostalgia, its lack of reference. Still, Lisa's pragmatism forces her to accept violence only if it is clearly a means to a good end: "I wisht we lived in a house with a floor, an' a toilet close by. I don't like this fightin' " (p. 271). And her point of view is fully relevant when it implies the chance of love. It is no accident that Lisa is paired nearly always with Jim. Her indifference to the strike and her concentration on her baby are counterparts to Jim's inhuman avowal of violence. Her admission that she "likes" Jim, near the end of the novel, balances Jim's accusation of Mac: ". . . sometimes I get the feeling that you're not protecting me for the Party but for yourself" (p. 343). So "use" appears.

This dialectic between Mac, Doc, and Lisa involves then a rather complete range of human affection, from male friendship or its lack to female love, and suggests that Jim's avowal of violence denies his humanity.

Within this very human context, it is significant that Mac's response to Jim's murder is sorrow for the death of a man, not regret for the loss of a superior Party man. Mac has, of course, a duty to the Party. Hence, he tries to stir the strikers by showing them Jim's faceless body, and in speaking to them he repeats essentially an earlier speech over Joy's body. All of this would seem to lend credence to the opinion of several critics that *In Dubious Battle* is too impersonal to have very much ultimate meaning.[5] Such critics fail to observe that Mac's addition of a single word, "Comrades," to his basic speech

[5] Harry Thornton Moore, *The Novels of John Steinbeck* (Chicago: Normandie House, 1939), pp. 41–42, provides a good summary of the matter. For a consideration and rejection of the general matter, see Peter Lisca, *The Wide World of John Steinbeck* (New Brunswick, New Jersey: Rutgers University Press, 1958), pp. 126–127.

is an expression of personal loss, stated in the only way possible for a field organizer, and all the more affecting because of its context of official duty: "Mac shivered. He moved his jaws to speak, and seemed to break the frozen jaws loose. His voice was high and monotonous. 'This guy didn't want nothing for himself—' he began. 'Comrades! He didn't want nothing for himself—' " (p. 349). The initial adjectives and verbs indicate great emotional turmoil in themselves; they are a context for the use of "Comrades!" The term cannot be taken wholly as an invitation to join the Party, for London joins in a calmer atmosphere; nor simply as a stab at creating group-man, since "blood," Jim's faceless, propped-up body, is mainly what is required. Instead, the term is universal: brothers. It contains the best of Jim. His most human aspect is his wish to help "the poor bastards." So Mac delivers a dirge for Jim that is in excess of the strict needs of the occasion. Nor is irony missing. Mac balances the inhumanity of capitalism, not Jim's own inhumanity, against the idealized portrait of the dead man. Sentimentality is avoided through irony, not by coldness. Jim's desire to "use" himself fully had tended to separate him from humanity; Mac's "use" of Jim's corpse tends to return Jim to humanity. Therefore, a seeming impersonality is in fact an aspect of Steinbeck's control of structure and materials.

Mac's dirge ends the novel at a high point, but the ending is not an inconclusive suggestion that what we have witnessed will go on. Personalities do not exactly repeat. Nor does Steinbeck squeeze a stupidly optimistic wedge into the ending; there is no implication that all will be fine or that a return to the happy pre-industrial past is in view. The one encouraged hope is that human feelings may survive—at a price. Jim has to die before he can return to humanity. The paradox is Christian rather than Marxian, and tough-minded rather than optimistic. It brings to mind Steinbeck's own vision of "a terrible kind of order" in the novel, before it was published, and his post-publication comment that "he was trying to write this story without looking through 'the narrow glass of political or economic preconception.' " [6] Such objectivity precludes mere optimism as well as a merely brutal or cynical interpretation that would strip the novel of any moral content, reduce Mac to a simply opportunistic revolutionary, and so forth. André Gide is correct, I think, in his estimation of the novel's dialogue: "The variegated aspects of the problem are set forth without the discussion's ever cluttering and interrupting

[6] Moore, p. 41; Lisca, p. 127.

the action." [7] For the dialogue has a sustained dramatic quality which is in keeping with the functional unity of the novel.

A dramatic quality is characteristic of this novel in other respects. It governs the arrangement of large forces into opposing pairs: city and country, orchard and bank, Party and capitalism, even life and death. The flaw in this arrangement is that representatives of the propertied class are handled rather abstractly and are dimly characterized *vis-à-vis* more realized and complex figures such as Jim, Mac, or Doc. But Steinbeck does maintain a number of points of view regarding the strike and the power situation in general. The resulting sense of complexity and specification does much to keep the novel from any collapse into an unsuitable simplicity. The pairing of characters is equally a contribution to the novel's dramatic quality. Mac and Jim are leaders in the field, but they are sharply distinguished in spite of their common function. London and Dakin are both "natural" leaders, but they are quite different from each other. Dakin is like Anderson, who lets the men camp on his small holding, and both men break up when their loved possessions are destroyed in the course of the strike. London is like Al, Anderson's son, and both men join the Party as a result of their experience in the strike. Even the men of violence are distinguished from each other. They include such different types as Jim's father, Sam, Joy, and Burke. Group-man is a particularly complex entity. It is "good" so far as it is the strikers' main weapon, and "evil" so far as its basis in violent emotion leads to a repulsive and dangerous lack of moral direction as the strike develops. Consequently, group-man becomes the main symbol of the "dubious battle."

All phases of the use of language are governed by the novel's dramatic quality. The fruit pickers speak an uncensored, idiomatic language that is their own in expression and in rhythm. Mac is an unconsciously expert mimic. Jim begins with lyrical outbursts of speech that do not disappear altogether, although in time Jim tends to use more frequently a flat but forceful diction that becomes the progress of his education. Doc speaks the somewhat abstract language of ideas. The languages of "the other side," of the owners and of business, are represented by the orchard superintendent and by the new president of the Fruit Growers' Association. Their brusque or unctuous diction is tonally patriotic, hearty, and threatening by turns. What-

---

[7] André Gide, *The Journals of André Gide,* trans. by Justin O'Brien (New York: Alfred A. Knopf, Inc., 1951), 27 September 1940. [Reprinted here, pp. 47-48.]

ever the range of the spoken language, Steinbeck takes care to use the
exact word, tone, and rhythm. The people are *made* to talk, to reveal themselves through their speech.[8] The defect of this objectivity
is evident in the remote quality of the language whenever there is
observation from the author's point of view, as in descriptive passages.
Steinbeck was aware that a dramatic structure could not include an
explicit control: "In one of his first letters about the work in progress, he wrote, 'I guess it is a brutal book, more brutal because there
is no author's moral point of view.' "[9] The question is whether the
novel suffers greatly from the lack of warmth in description and from
the concentration on suspense in the events. An answer involves two
points. First, motivation and characterization are sufficiently complex,
and there is adequate specification in the detailed narratives of the
strike and of Jim's education, as well as in the language which the
various characters use. Second, the brutal objective tone is an organic
part of the whole tissue of the "dubious battle." But the concentration on suspense is a genuine limitation of the objective dramatic
quality. It prevents the novel from attaining a thoroughly philosophical level of absolute insight, and provides some justification for
Freeman Champney's suggestion that Steinbeck's materials are peculiar to California—are local rather than universal.[10] But, as we have
seen, the novel's permanence is a matter of reference to its artistic
value.

Thus, by aiming for and by largely achieving a harmony between
structure and materials, by selecting and arranging events in terms
of a design, and by subordinating characterization, thematic motifs,
symbols, and style to those considerations, Steinbeck was able to create
particular kinds of people in the context of a certain historical situation, and this, in the paradox of art, lies outside of history although
the environment which permits the artistic construct to assume its
necessary shape is history.

[8] Consult Lisca, pp. 110–112, for a letter in which Steinbeck discusses "the speech
of working men." In fact language accounts for much of the "adequacy of specification" in Steinbeck's best efforts.

[9] Lisca, p. 114.

[10] Freeman Champney, "John Steinbeck, Californian," *Antioch Review*, VII (Fall
1947), pp. 345–362. [Reprinted here, pp. 18–35.]

End of a Dream

by Warren French

Of Mice and Men marks the end of the first period in Steinbeck's literary career in several ways. First, this was the work that brought him at last really impressive national recognition and substantial reward and thus brought him face to face with the problems of a man in the limelight. Like Danny in *Tortilla Flat,* Steinbeck had achieved a position from which there was no turning back. Secondly, *Of Mice and Men* is the book in which Steinbeck found at last the form he had been struggling for—the method of objective storytelling which is really a fictionalized play. All of Steinbeck's novels had contained extraneous material (like the "Caporal" episode in *Tortilla Flat,* in which the *paisanos* expressed out-of-character views). The short stories to be collected into *The Red Pony* perfectly blended form and content, but it was not until *Of Mice and Men* that Steinbeck achieved the same structural soundness in a complex narrative.

Thirdly, in this novel Steinbeck at last discovered how to present the point underlying *Cup of Gold* in a convincing, contemporary setting. Behind the piratical trappings of the first novel stalked the ironic perception that maturity means the destruction of dreams. Other dreamers had learned this lesson in Steinbeck's novels; but Henry Morgan had been the only Steinbeck hero to survive his disillusionment. George in *Of Mice and Men* is the first contemporary figure in a Steinbeck novel to "split" before the onslaught of civilization rather than go under. Steinbeck had at last found the figure that could disentangle the grail quest from the mists of legend and make its futility explicit in down-to-earth terms.

Of Mice and Men is Steinbeck's last novel to be directly influenced by Arthurian legend. In *The Grapes of Wrath,* the writer turns to Biblical traditions for his analogues. This change makes his allegories more generally comprehensible because of the wide familiarity with Biblical imagery. There is an "ivory tower" quality about even Steinbeck's most realistic novels before *The Grapes of Wrath*; and it was probably his months of living among the migrants that enabled him to shake off the lingering effects of the—to American eyes—somewhat remote myths that had long provided the framework for his novels.

Although other critics have not noted to what extent *Of Mice and Men* is an Arthurian story, the fundamental parallels—the knightly loyalty, the pursuit of the vision, the creation of a bond (shared briefly by Candy and Brooks), and its destruction by an at least potentially adulterous relationship—are there. They are, however, so concealed by the surface realism of the work that one unfamiliar with Steinbeck's previous Arthurian experiments would be hardly likely to notice them. The one obvious Arthurian hangover is George, who is not only remarkably loyal to his charge—the feeble-minded Lennie—but also remarkably pure.

George not only warns Lennie against the blandishments of Curley's wife, but is himself obviously impervious to her charms. While the other ranch hands are excited by her presence, George says only, "Jesus, what a tramp!" When invited to join the boys in a Saturday night trip to a neighboring town's "nice" whorehouse, George says that he "might go in an' set and have a shot," but "ain't puttin' out no two and a half." He excuses himself on the ground that he is saving money to buy a farm, but not even Galahad might have found it politic to profess chastity in a bunkhouse. George seems to have stepped, in fact, not out of Malory's Arthurian stories but Tennyson's. When he is told that Curley boasts of having his glove full of Vaseline in order to keep his hand soft for his wife, George says, "That's a dirty thing to tell around."

George is noticeably more critical of Curley's wife than Steinbeck is. *Of Mice and Men* is not so completely objective as *In Dubious Battle*; Steinbeck editorializes occasionally, for example, after the girl has been killed:

> . . . the meanness and the plannings and the discontent and the ache for attention were all gone from her face. She was very pretty and simple, and her face was sweet and young.

George shows no such sympathy, and it is important to notice that the author is more flexible than his character, because it is a sign that he is not being carried away by his vision as are the characters sometimes assumed to represent his viewpoint. The Arthurian flavor here is faint, but unmistakable. Like Jim Nolan, George is a last Galahad, dismounted, armed only with a fading dream, a long way from Camelot. Steinbeck is his historian, not his alter ego.

One does not need to justify a search for an allegory in *Of Mice and Men* since the author has spoken of the book as symbolic and microcosmic. Just what the universal drama enacted against a Salinas Valley backdrop may be is not, however, so obvious as first appears. Unquestionably it concerns a knight of low estate and a protégé who share a dream, a dream that cannot come true because the protégé lacks the mental capacity to be conscious enough to know his own strength or to protect himself from temptation.

At first glance, it appears that nature is the culprit and that this is an ironic, deterministic fable like Stephen Crane's "The Open Boat." It is an indifferent nature that makes men physically strong but mentally deficient; dreaming is man's only defense against a world he never made. "The best-laid schemes o' mice an' men [gang] aft agley," Burns said, providing Steinbeck with a title, because man is at the mercy of forces he cannot control which ruthlessly but indifferently destroy the illusions he has manufactured. The book may be read in this naturalistic manner, and those who speak of it as sentimental must think of it as an expression of Steinbeck's outraged compassion for the victims of chaotic forces.

Such a reading, however, does not do the story justice. If George stood helplessly by and saw Lennie destroyed, the novel might be called deterministic; but he doesn't. George has a will, and he exercises it to make two critical decisions at the end of the novel—to kill Lennie and to lie about it.

George could, of course, have killed Lennie simply to protect the giant brute from the mob; but, since Lennie doesn't know what is going on anyway, it is easy to oversentimentalize George's motives. Actually he has reasons of his own for pulling the trigger. Steinbeck makes it clear that George had tremendous difficulty bringing himself to destroy Lennie, although Lennie will not even know what has happened. What George is actually trying to kill is not Lennie, who is only a shell and a doomed one at that, but something in himself.

Peter Lisca points out that Lennie's need for George is obvious, but that George's need for Lennie, though less obvious, is as great. In his most candid appraisal of himself, George says, "I ain't so bright neither, or I wouldn't be buckin' barley for my fifty and found. If I was even a

little bit smart, I'd have my own little place. . . ." He needs him, however, as more than just a rationalization for his own failure, for George
not only protects but *directs* Lennie. Lennie doesn't speak unless
George permits him to; and, in the fight in which Curley's hand is
broken, Lennie refuses even to defend himself until George tells him
to. George, of course, directs Lennie partly to protect him from com-
mitting acts he could not mentally be responsible for, but George is
not a wholly altruistic shepherd. Another aspect of the relationship
becomes apparent when George tells Slim that Lennie, "Can't think of
nothing to do himself, but he sure can take orders." Since George gives
the orders, Lennie gives him a sense of power.

One aspect of the dream that George repeatedly describes to Lennie
also needs scrutiny. The ritual ("George's voice became deeper. He
repeated his words rhythmically.") begins "Guys like us, that work on
ranches, are the loneliest guys in the world. . . . They ain't got nothing to look ahead to" and continues "with us it ain't like that . . .
because [here Lennie takes over from George] I got you to look after
me, and you got me to look after you, and that's why." The dream not
only gives a direction to their lives, but also makes them feel different
from other people. Since this sense of difference can mean little to
Lennie, it is part of the consolation George receives from the dream.
George wants to be superior. With Lennie gone, his claim to distinction
will be gone. Thus when George shoots Lennie, he is not destroying
only the shared dream. He is also destroying the thing that makes him
different and reducing himself to the status of an ordinary guy. He is
obliged to acknowledge what Willy Loman in Arthur Miller's *Death
of a Salesman*, for example, could never acknowledge but what Henry
Morgan accepted when he turned respectable in *Cup of Gold*—his own
mediocrity. George is much like Willy Loman; for he is forced to recognize the same self-deflating realization Biff Loman vainly tries to impress upon his father: he is a "dime a dozen." Because of their relationship, George has actually been able to remain as much a "kid" as
Lennie; shooting him matures George in more than one way.

It is equally important that George lies to the posse after the shooting. If the experience had not matured him, he had here his opportunity for a grand gesture. He could either destroy himself along with
Lennie and the dream or, by an impassioned confession, force his enemies to destroy him. George, who by Romantic standards has little left
to live for, chooses to go on living and to say that he had to shoot Lennie in self-defense. Actually the maturing effect of the experience upon

George has been apparent from the moment when, in reply to Candy's offer to help him carry out the dream, he says: "—I think I knowed from the very first. I think I know'd we'd never do her. He usta like to hear about it so much I got to thinking maybe we would." With Lennie gone, George will not try to keep the dream alive. When Slim leads George up toward the highway at the end of the novel, the wonder is not that George is badly shaken by his experience, but that he is alive at all.

Despite the grim events it chronicles *Of Mice and Men* is not a tragedy, but a comedy—which, if it were Shakespearean, we would call a "dark comedy"—about the triumph of the indomitable will to survive. This is a story not of man's defeat at the hands of an implacable nature, but of man's painful conquest of this nature and of his difficult, conscious rejection of his dreams of greatness and acceptance of his own mediocrity. Unfortunately, the allegory is less clear in the play version than in the novel, since Steinbeck, probably to provide a more effective curtain, eliminates George's last conversation with Slim and ends with the shooting of Lennie. The original ending would also probably have been too involved for playgoers to follow after experiencing the emotions engendered by the climactic episodes.

Lennie has been viewed sometimes as an example of Steinbeck's preoccupation with subhuman types; actually Lennie is not a character in the story at all, but rather a device like a golden coin in *Moby Dick* to which the other characters may react in a way that allows the reader to perceive their attitudes. So intensely focused upon the relationship between George and Lennie is the novel that the other characters are likely to be overlooked; yet each makes an important contribution to the narrative and provides a clue to Steinbeck's conception of the human condition.

The protest against racial discrimination and the treatment of the aged through the characters of Brooks and Candy needs no elaboration. The symbolism of Curley and his ill-fated bride is perhaps summed up in her statement that they married after she "met him out to Riverside Dance Palace that same night." There is a sordid echo of Fitzgerald and the "lost generation" here; for, like the Buchanans in *The Great Gatsby*, these are "careless people" who smash up things and "let other people clean up the mess." It is true that the girl is smashed up herself, but, unlike Curley, she did have dreams and disappointments. He simply, like the Buchanans, retreats into his "vast carelessness." The wife, not George, is the one in the novel who is destroyed when, instead of controlling her dreams, she allows them to control her; and Curley, not Lennie, is actually the willfully animalistic type.

The most interesting characters—except for George and Lennie—are Carlson and Slim, two other ranch hands, who have the last words in the novel. They are complements, symbolizing, on one hand, the insensitive and brutal; on the other, the kindly and perceptive. "Now what the hell ya suppose is eatin' them two guys?" are Carlson's words —the last in the book—as Slim and George sadly walk off for a drink. Undoubtedly this sums up Steinbeck's concept of an unperceptive world's reaction to the drama just enacted. The uncomprehending responses to his books had given Steinbeck sufficient grounds for being aware of this "practical" attitude and through Carlson he strikes back at the men to whom Doctor Burton in *In Dubious Battle* attributes the world's "wild-eyed confusion." But Steinbeck also suggests that such men have the last word.

This bitterly ironic view is expressed through the major incident involving Carlson: the shooting of Candy's old dog. All Carlson can see about the dog is that "he don't have no fun . . . and he stinks to beat hell." He has no feelings about the animal, and, because his reactions are entirely physical, no concept that anyone else might have feelings about it. He is the same kind of man as the agitators Steinbeck condemned in *In Dubious Battle*—insensitive, violent, fanatical. This "practical" man's only contributions to the group are destructive.

To balance this destructive force, Steinbeck introduces and awards the next-to-last word to the jerkline skinner, Slim, the man who alone understands and tries to comfort George at the end of the novel. Steinbeck breaks his editorial silence, as he does in speaking of Curley's wife, to make it absolutely clear to the reader how Slim is to be regarded. "His ear heard more than was said to him," the author writes, "and his slow speech had overtones not of thought, but of understanding beyond thought." "His authority," the reader is told, "was so great that his word was taken on any subject, be it politics or love." What matters most, however, is the professional standing of this paragon:

> He moved with a majesty only achieved by royalty and master craftsmen. He was a jerkline skinner, capable of driving ten, sixteen, even twenty mules with a single line to the leaders. He was capable of killing a fly on the wheeler's butt with a bull whip without touching the mule.

The important thing about this passage is the emphasis placed upon skill and craftsmanship; here is the really "practical" man—not the callous boor, but the man who is able to do his job exceedingly well. We are to meet him again in *Cannery Row* and *The Wayward Bus*. It is notable that he is not a dreamer, but a doer. In another editorial aside that sets the tone for the whole book, Steinbeck points out that among other things with which the shelves where the ranch hands kept their personal belongings were loaded were "those Western magazines ranch men love to read and scoff at and secretly believe." Underneath the surface most men are not only dreamers, but unsuccessful dreamers; the real heroes are not these dreamers, but the doers. The heroic "doers," however, are not those who act only for personal aggrandizement, but those who try to do their best out of an affection for their craft and who feel compassionate rather than scornful toward the dreamers. With *Of Mice and Men*, Steinbeck himself unmistakably joins this class of craftsmen, for he not only shows compassion for the plight of the dreamer, but he accomplishes in the manner of a master craftsman his intention to sort out and evaluate the categories of men. Having mastered his craft, he was ready to execute his masterpiece.

Thematic Rhythm in *The Red Pony*

by Arnold L. Goldsmith

Underlying Steinbeck's four short stories which make up *The Red Pony* are thematic rhythms, structural balance, and a seasonal symbolism which skillfully integrate the whole work and relate it to his Emersonian mysticism found in later books such as *The Grapes of Wrath* (1939) and *Sea of Cortez* (1941). "The Leader of the People," added by Steinbeck in 1938 to the three stories first published as *The Red Pony* in 1937, is an integral part of the whole work, but readers of college anthologies usually find one of the stories published separately or the first three as a unit, and thus miss a good opportunity to study Steinbeck's subtle extension of the themes expressed in "The Gift," "The Great Mountains," and "The Promise."

The central figure unifying all four stories is Jody Tiflin. Like Hemingway's early hero Nick Adams, Jody is being initiated into a violent world where danger lurks everywhere, pain and death are imminent, and the best laid plans of mice and boys often go astray. In the first story Jody is ten, in the next apparently a year older, and in the third and fourth, probably twelve. The adventures of both youths are intended to teach them the need for stoic endurance in order to survive in an imperfect and cruel world. In this sense, Hemingway's stories and *The Red Pony* can be considered *bildungsromans,* but there are some significant differences. Because of Jody's age, sex plays much less a part of his initiation than it does in Nick's, whose experiences are not just vicarious. And violence, which explodes all around Nick and finally wounds him in the war, destroys only the things Jody loves, not harming him physically. Where Nick's wounds are both physical and psychic, Jody's are only psychic, and we do not know whether they have a permanent effect on him. The third story

"Thematic Rhythm in *The Red Pony*" by Arnold Goldsmith. From *College English* XXVI, no. 5 (February 1965), 391–94. Copyright © 1965 by the National Council of Teachers of English. Reprinted by permission of the publisher and the author.

ends with Jody's thrill at the birth of his new colt, but even this thrill is dampened by pain: "He ached from his throat to his stomach. His legs were stiff and heavy. He tried to be glad because of the colt, but the bloody face, and the haunted, tired eyes of Billy Buck hung in the air ahead of him." [1] The last story substitutes the tired face of Jody's grandfather for that of Billy Buck, but the optimism implied in the title as well as Jody's kindness to the old man are adequate evidence of the kind of adjustments Jody will make in life.

More important than the above contrasts is the fact that Steinbeck composed *The Red Pony* as an integrated whole, while Hemingway wrote the Nick Adams stories sporadically at different times during his literary career. All four stories in *The Red Pony* take place in the Salinas Valley, where Steinbeck himself grew up as a boy. The stories are filled with realistic and lyric descriptions of the Valley's flora and fauna (*e.g.*, horned toads, newts, blue snakes, lizards, buzzards, rabbits, hoot-owls, turkeys, coyotes, muskmelons, oakwoods, and black cypresses) which Steinbeck knew as intimately as Thoreau knew the woods, ponds, and fields around Concord.

The time sequence of the stories can be worked out as follows. "The Gift" begins in late summer and ends around Thanksgiving, the beginning of the winter with its rainy season in California. The reader of Hemingway's *A Farewell to Arms* is certainly familiar with the association of rain with disease, violence, and death, and such seasonal symbolism is most appropriate in the story about the death of Jody's pony suffering from pneumonia. "The Great Mountains" begins in the "heat of a midsummer afternoon" (p. 53), probably a year after the first story began. It spans less than twenty-four hours, ending the next morning. "The Promise" begins that spring and ends eleven months later, in a January rain, once again an appropriate setting for the death of the mare Nellie and the birth of her colt. "The Leader of the People" takes place a couple of months later, in March, probably the same year that the mare died. The same unity of time and place found in the second story is evident here also. As in "The Great Mountains," the story begins on an afternoon and ends the next morning.

This analysis of the time sequence helps illuminate the structural symmetry of the stories. Just as Hemingway in *A Farewell to Arms* alternates a book of war with a romantic interlude for dramatic con-

---

[1] John Steinbeck, *The Red Pony* (New York, The Viking Press, 1945), p. 104. Hereafter, all references to *The Red Pony* will be to this edition and page numbers will be enclosed in parentheses.

trast, Steinbeck follows the violence of the first story with the tragic quiet of the second, with this same pattern repeated in the third and fourth sections. Where the first and third stories are about the violent deaths of horses, the second and fourth are about the twilight years of two old men.

The basic thematic rhythm unifying the four stories in *The Red Pony* is the life-death cycle. This organic theory of life ending in death which in turn produces new life is the major theme of Hemingway's "Indian Camp," where Nick Adams witnesses the Caesarean delivery of an Indian baby and the violent death of the father. It is the same cycle of life and death implicit in Whitman's image of the "cradle endlessly rocking."

In *The Red Pony* we see this rhythm in the cycle of the seasons, the buzzards flying overhead, the life and death of Jody's pony Galiban, the death of the buzzard Jody kills with his bare hands, the approaching death of the paisano Gitano and the old horse Easter (his very name suggesting life in death), and the two opposing sets of mountains: Galiban (jolly, populated, suggesting life) and the Great Ones (ominous, mysterious, suggesting death, a place where we must all go eventually), the little bird Jody kills with his slingshot and then beheads and dissects, the death of Nellie and the birth of her colt, and the approaching death of Jody's old grandfather, the old leader of the people, with the implication that Jody is to be the new one. All of these objects and incidents represent the never-ending rhythm of life and death to which Jody is continually exposed. The subtle expression of this theme can even be found at the beginning of "The Leader of the People," when Billy Buck rakes the last of the old year's haystack, an action which implies the end of one season and the beginning of the next. In terms of the story, life is ending for the grandfather, but it is just beginning for Jody.

The most obvious example of Steinbeck's conscious effort to present this theme in *The Red Pony* is the sharp contrast he develops in "The Promise" between the black cypress tree by the bunkhouse and the water tub. Where the cypress is associated with death, the never-ending spring water piped into the old green tub is the symbol of the continuity of life. The two paragraphs where Steinbeck explains the effect these things have on Jody should be given in full:

> Jody traveled often to the brush line behind the house. A rusty iron pipe
> ran a thin stream of water into an old green tub. Where the water spilled

over and sank into the ground there was a patch of perpetually green grass. Even when the hills were brown and baked in the summer that little patch was green. The water whined softly into the trough all the year round. This place had grown to be a center-point for Jody. When he had been punished the cool green grass and the singing water soothed him. When he had been mean the biting acid of meanness left him at the brush line. When he sat in the grass and listened to the purling stream, the barriers set up in his mind by the stern day went down to ruin.

On the other hand, the black cypress tree by the bunkhouse was as repulsive as the water-tub was dear; for to this tree all the pigs came, sooner or later, to be slaughtered. Pig killing was fascinating, with the screaming and the blood, but it made Jody's heart beat so fast that it hurt him. After the pigs were scalded in the big iron tripod kettle and their skins were scraped and white, Jody had to go to the water-tub to sit in the grass until his heart grew quiet. The water-tub and the black cypress were opposites and enemies. (pp. 91–92)

As Jody daydreams about his colt, he finds himself under the black cypress and superstitiously moves over to the green grass near the trilling water. "As usual the water place eliminated time and distance" (p. 93).

Jody's communion with nature, a semi-mystical experience in which time and place are eliminated, is not very different from the withdrawal into the wilderness of Jim Casy in *The Grapes of Wrath*. Casy adds a religious dimension to the experience when he says, "There was the hills, an' there was me, an' we wasn't separate no more. We was one thing. An' that ore thing was holy." [2] The most explicit statement Steinbeck has made on this mystical feeling of oneness of the animate and inanimate is in *Sea of Cortez*, where he wrote:

groups melt into ecological groups until the time when what we know as life meets and enters what we think of as non-life: barnacle and rock, rock and earth, earth and tree, tree and rain and air. And the units nestle into the whole and are inseparable from it . . . And it is a strange thing that most of the feeling we call religious, most of the mystical outcrying which is one of the most prized and used and desired reactions of our species, is really the understanding and the attempt to say that man is related to the whole thing, related inextricably to all reality, known and unknowable. This is a simple thing to say, but the profound feeling of it made a Jesus, a St. Augustine, a St. Francis, a Roger Bacon, a Charles

---

[2] John Steinbeck, *The Grapes of Wrath* (New York, Random House, 1939), p. 110.

Darwin, and an Einstein. Each of them in his own tempo and with his own voice discovered and reaffirmed with astonishment the knowledge that all things are one thing and that one thing is all things.[8]

Throughout his literary career John Steinbeck has attempted to render dramatically his passionate belief in the oneness of all life, and *The Red Pony* is no exception, as the life-death cycle and Jody's romantic communion with nature will attest. But there is one final example which should be mentioned because of its effective fusion of character, theme, and setting. It occurs in "The Great Mountains." To Jody, these mountains represent the mystery of the unknown, unlived life, but to the old man they stand for the mystery of death. Beyond them lies the sea—eternity. As Gitano rides off into the mountains, he carries a long rapier with a golden basket hilt, a family heirloom passed down to him by his father. This rapier adds just the right touch of myth and folklore to the ancient legend of an old man returning to his birthplace to die. It echoes the classic tradition of such weapons as the magical sword of King Arthur and Beowulf, the shield of Achilles, even the long rifle of Natty Bumppo. To Jody, Gitano is "mysterious like the mountains. There were ranges back as far as you could see, but behind the last range piled up against the sky there was a great unknown country. And Gitano was an old man, until you got to the dull dark eyes. And in behind them was some unknown thing" (p. 68). Thus the mountains are an extension of Gitano, and Gitano is an extension of the old horse with its ribs and hip-bones jutting out under its skin. All three objects blend into one as Jody watches them disappear in the distance, lying in the green grass near the water-tub, the symbol of timelessness:

> For a moment he thought he could see a black speck crawling up the farthest ridge. Jody thought of the rapier and Gitano. And he thought of the great mountains. A longing caressed him, and it was so sharp that he wanted to cry to get it out of his breast. He lay down in the green grass near the round tub at the brush line. He covered his eyes with his crossed arms and lay there a long time, and he was full of a nameless sorrow. (p. 72)

[8] John Steinbeck, *The Log from the Sea of Cortez* (New York, The Viking Press, 1951), pp. 216–217.

The Grapes of Wrath

by Peter Lisca

Steinbeck's trek from Oklahoma to the cotton fields of California in the fall of 1937 was not the first of such forays made to observe his materials at first hand. He had made several trips into the agricultural areas of California in preparation for his strike novel, and immediately after completing *Of Mice and Men* in September of 1936 he had gone to observe the squatters' camps near Salinas and Bakersfield. There he gathered materials for "Dubious Battle in California" (*Nation*, Sept. 12, 1936) and a series of seven other articles called "The Harvest Gypsies," which appeared in the *San Francisco News*, October 5–12, 1936.[1] On his return from this trip he wrote to Ben Abramson, "California is not very far from civil war. I hope it can be averted." (JS-BA, 10/?/36) He expressed the same concern to his agents: "I just returned yesterday from the strike area of Salinas and from my migrants in Bakersfield. This thing is dangerous. Maybe it will be patched up for a while, but I look for the lid to blow off in a few weeks. Issues are very sharp here now. . . . My material drawer is chock full." (Steinbeck to McIntosh and Otis [hereafter MO], 10/?/36)

During one period that autumn Steinbeck lived in one of the federal migrant camps in central California and wrote to Lawrence Clark Powell, "I have to write this sitting in a ditch. I'm out working—may go south to pick a little cotton. Migrants are going south now and I'll probably go along."[2] After the publication of *The Grapes of Wrath* these migrants sent Steinbeck a patchwork dog sewn from pieces of

"The Grapes of Wrath." From *The Wide World of John Steinbeck* by Peter Lisca (New Brunswick, N.J.: Rutgers University Press, 1958), pp. 144–77. Copyright © 1958 by Rutgers, The State University. Reprinted by permission of the publisher.

[1] This series of articles is more widely known as "Their Blood Is Strong," the title given them when, with an epilogue, they were reprinted in pamphlet form under the auspices of the Simon J. Lubin Society of California in the spring of 1938.

[2] Lawrence Clark Powell, "Toward a Bibliography of John Steinbeck," *Colophon*, 3 (Autumn, 1938), pp. 562–563.

shirttails and dresses and bearing around its neck a tag with the inscription "Migrant John."

The *San Francisco News* articles are straight-forward reports of living conditions among migrant workers, along with suggestions and appeals for a more enlightened treatment of these people. Although they contain several details which were later incorporated in *The Grapes of Wrath,* these articles are significant primarily as a record of Steinbeck's attitude toward the people and conditions which he was to use as the materials of his great novel. Actually, the extremes of poverty, injustice, and suffering depicted in these articles are nowhere equaled in *The Grapes of Wrath.*

Steinbeck was still trying to understand the total situation. He did not go into the field to substantiate a ready-made theory. When the editors of *Occident* asked him for an article of a political nature, he refused, saying, "Generalities seem to solidify so quickly into stupidities. A writer can only honestly say—'This is the way it seems to me at this moment.' " He didn't think he knew enough about the situation and didn't wish to retire into some "terminology." Steinbeck did, however, allow the editors to print his letter of refusal, part of which follows:

> The changes go on so rapidly and it is so hard to see! Sad that it will be so easy in fifty years. Of course there is a larger picture one can feel. I suppose the appellations communist and fascist are adequate. I don't really think they are. I'm probably making a mistake in simply listening to men talk and watching them act, hoping that the projection of the microcosm will define the outlines of the macrocosm. There will come a time and that soon, I suppose, when such a position will be untenable, when we'll all put on blinders and put our heads down, and yelling some meaningless rallying cry, we'll do what men of every other time have done—tear the guts out of our own race.[3]

Unlike Doc in *In Dubious Battle,* however, Steinbeck's attempt to understand did not make him a dispassionate observer. In the autumn of that same year he was planning to accept a Hollywood contract of a thousand dollars a week for six weeks' work on *Of Mice and Men* so that he could give two dollars apiece to three thousand migrants. Pascal Covici flew out to the coast to talk him out of it. Early in 1938, in the midst of work on the new novel, he wrote his agents, "I must go over into the interior valleys. There are five thousand families starving to death over there, not just hungry, but actually starving. . . .

[3] *Occident* (Fall, 1936), p. 5.

In one tent there are twenty people quarantined for smallpox and two of the women are to have babies in that tent this week. . . . Talk about Spanish children. The death of children by starvation in our valleys is simply staggering. . . . I'll do what I can. . . . Funny how mean and how little books become in the face of such tragedies." [4] When *Life* offered to send him into the field with a photographer to write about the migrants, he informed his agents that he would accept no money other than expenses—"I'm sorry but I simply can't make money on these people. . . . The suffering is too great for me to cash in on it." (JS-MO, 3/?/38) It is this great compassion which accounts for the difference in tone between *In Dubious Battle* and *The Grapes of Wrath*.

But this compassion, this honest indignation, did not carry Steinbeck into propagandism or blind him to his responsibilities as a novelist. "The subject is so large that it scares me," he wrote. "And I am not going to rush it. It must be worked out with care." (JS-MO, 1/?/37) By June of 1938 he finished a sixty-thousand-word novel called *L'Affaire Lettuceberg*. To his agents and publishers, who were expecting the book and had announced it variously as *Oklahoma* and *Lettuceberg*, he sent the following joint letter:

This is going to be a hard letter to write. I feel badly about it. You see this book is finished and it is a bad book and I must get rid of it. It can't be printed. It is bad because it isn't honest. Oh! the incidents all happened but—I'm not telling as much of the truth about them as I know. In satire you have to restrict the picture and I just can't do satire. . . . I know that a great many people would think they liked this book. I, myself, have built up a hole-proof argument on how and why I liked it. I can't beat the argument, but I don't like the book. And I would be doing Pat a greater injury in letting him print it than I would by destroying it. Not once in the writing of it have I felt the curious warm pleasure that comes when work is going well. My whole work drive has been aimed at making people understand each other and then I deliberately write this book, the aim of which is to cause hatred through partial understanding. My father would have called it a smart-alec book. It was full of tricks to make people ridiculous. If I can't do better I have slipped badly. And that I won't admit—yet. . . . (JS-MO, 6/?/38)

Such a letter makes ridiculous any insinuation that Steinbeck's "social protest" was literary opportunism. It is Steinbeck's corollary to Hem-

[4] Lewis Gannett, "Introduction," *The Portable Steinbeck* (New York, 1946), pp. xx–xxi.

ingway's ideal of writing "truly," without "tricks," and without "cheating."

Steinbeck continued to work on his big novel all that summer, and by autumn it was in its final stages. "I am desperately tired," he wrote, "but I want to finish. And mean. I feel as though shrapnel were bursting about my head. I only hope the book is some good. Can't tell yet at all. And I can't tell whether it is balanced. It is a slow plodding book but I don't think that it is dull." [5] On September 16, 1938, he sent Pascal Covici the book's title—*The Grapes of Wrath*—saying, "I like the soft with the hard and the marching content and the American revolutionary content." Three months later he suggested to Covici that the "Battle Hymn of the Republic" be printed somewhere in the book, possibly as end pages. (Steinbeck to Pascal Covici [hereafter PC], 12/22/38)

The completion of *The Grapes of Wrath* late in 1938 left Steinbeck exhausted. He was confined to bed for some weeks and forbidden on doctor's orders to read or write. But he conscientiously saw the book through the press. As in the publication of *In Dubious Battle,* there arose the problem of printable language. Steinbeck's stand was again firm. He warned the publishers that no words must be changed; even "shit-heels" must remain. (JS-PC, 1/15/39) Also, he refused to have included in the book a page reproduced in his own handwriting. He insisted on keeping his personality out of it. The book was to stand on its own merits, even if it meant a loss in sales. He didn't want "that kind" of reader anyway. (JS-PC, 2/23/39) In April, 1939, The Viking Press brought out *The Grapes of Wrath.*

The Grapes of Wrath did not have a chance of being accepted and evaluated as a piece of fiction. From the very beginning it was taken as substantial fact and its merits debated as a document rather than as a novel. This was to be expected in a decade which had produced such motion pictures as Pare Lorentz' *The River* and *The Plow That Broke the Plains;* such books as Dorothea Lange's and Paul S. Taylor's *An American Exodus: A Record of Human Erosion,* Archibald MacLeish's *Land of the Free,* Erskine Caldwell's and Margaret Bourke-White's *You Have Seen Their Faces,* and the WPA collection of case histories called *These Are Our Lives,* to cite only a few. The line between social documentation and fiction has never been so hazy, and this lack of a definite line resulted in works like *Land of the Free,* which is neither

[5] *Ibid.,* p. xxiv.

an illustrated text nor a book of pictures with captions, but a form in itself. Often what was intended as social documentation and reportage had a literary value achieved only rarely in proletarian fiction—Ruth McKenney's *Industrial Valley* being an example.

Even aside from the fact that *The Grapes of Wrath* came in such a period, Steinbeck's novel had the vulnerability of all social fiction—it was subject to attack on its facts. It is not within the scope of this study to present an exhaustive analysis either of the attack made on his facts and their defense or of the sociological and political consequences of the book, but a small sampling of the relevant literature may indicate the nature of that social-political-economic controversy which eclipsed *The Grapes of Wrath* as a novel.

Within two months after the publication of *The Grapes of Wrath*, there appeared a slim volume called *Grapes of Gladness: California's Refreshing and Inspiring Answer to John Steinbeck's "Grapes of Wrath."* This title, a remnant from the age of pamphleteering, was affixed to the story of a family of migrants who came to California poverty-stricken and found that everyone, including the banks and growers, welcomed them with open arms. They were given free land, loaned money, and lionized. In an "Addenda" to this soap opera, the author tries to break down some of Steinbeck's "facts." [6]

Another book, *The Truth About John Steinbeck and the Migrants*, tells of its author's own experiences on a trip which he made, disguised as a migrant, just to see what conditions really were. This "migrant" found that he was able to average four dollars a day on wages and that almost all the growers begged him to stay with them and live in the ranch house all year round. In an essay which prefaces this sojourn in the land of Canaan, the author calls *The Grapes of Wrath* "a novel wherein naturalism has gone berserk, where truth has run amuck drunken upon prejudice and exaggeration, where matters economic have been hurled beyond the pale of rational and realistic thinking." [7]

Defenses of the book's accuracy were no less vehement. Professors of sociology, ministers, and government officials put themselves on record that Steinbeck's information was accurate.[8] The subject was debated on radio programs such as "Town Meeting," and the book was publicly

[6] Marshal V. Hartranft, *Grapes of Gladness: California's Refreshing and Inspiring Answer to John Steinbeck's "The Grapes of Wrath"* (Los Angeles, 1939).

[7] George Thomas Miron, *The Truth About John Steinbeck and the Migrants* (Los Angeles, 1939), p. 5.

[8] For details, see Martin Staples Shockley, "The Reception of *The Grapes of Wrath* in Oklahoma," *American Literature*, 15 (January, 1954), 351–361.

reviewed before mass audiences. Before making the motion picture,
Zanuck sent private detectives to ascertain the accuracy of the novel
and found conditions even worse than described by Steinbeck.[9] The
author himself, accompanied by a photographer, visited hundreds of
migrant camps, took notes and made a pictorial record which was
later printed in *Life* as evidence that the motion picture had not
exaggerated. The book itself was both banned and burned on both
political and pornographic grounds from Buffalo, New York, to California, and Archbishop Spellman's denunciation of it appeared in all
the Hearst papers. Not the least antagonism was fomented in Oklahoma, whose native sons found themselves degraded and abused and
whose bookstores found that the novel's circulation exceeded even
that of *Gone With the Wind*. Oklahoma Congressman Lyle Boren
denounced the book in Congress, maintaining that "the heart and brain
and character of the average tenant farmer of Oklahoma cannot be
surpassed and probably not equaled by any other group. . . ." He
called the book itself "a black, infernal creation of a twisted, distorted
mind." The Oklahoma Chamber of Commerce tried to stop the filming
of the picture.[10] No American novel since *Uncle Tom's Cabin* has created such an immediate reaction on so many levels.

While the exploration of these frenzied reactions to the factual details of *The Grapes of Wrath* is more pertinent to sociology and perhaps even psychology than it is to either the history or criticism of
literature, critical reactions to the novel's social philosophy do come
within the scope of this study.

One extreme position is best stated by the author of *The Truth
About John Steinbeck and the Migrants*, who "can think of no other
novel which advances the idea of class war and promotes hatred of

[9] Margaret Marshall, "Writers in the Wilderness," *The Nation*, 149 (November
25, 1939), p. 579.

[10] Shockley, "The Reception of *The Grapes of Wrath* in Oklahoma," p. 357. The
reader interested in pursuing this topic further may find useful, in addition to
items already cited, the following: Carey McWilliams, "California Pastoral," *Antioch
Review*, 2 (March, 1942), 103–121; *The La Follette Committee Transcript*, vol. 51;
Wilson Library Bulletin, 14 (October, 1939), pp. 102, 165, and vol. 13 (May, 1939),
p. 640; Carey McWilliams, "What's Being Done About the Joads?" *The New Republic*, 100 (September 20, 1939), pp. 178–180; Frank J. Taylor, "California's 'Grapes
of Wrath,'" *Forum and Century*, 102 (November, 1939), pp. 232–238; *Look* (January
16, 1940); Leon Whipple, "Novels on Social Themes," *Survey Graphic*, 28 (June,
1939), p. 401; Richard Neuberger, "Who Are the Associated Farmers?" *Survey
Graphic*, 28 (September, 1939), 517–521, 555–557; the Nazi Bund's *Deutscher Weckruf
und Beobachter*, edited by Fritz Kuhn; Carey McWilliams, *Factories in the Field*
(Boston, 1939). Others are listed by Shockley.

class against class . . . more than does *The Grapes of Wrath*." [11] It is
directly opposed by Stanley Edgar Hyman: "Actually, as a careful
reading makes clear, the central message of *The Grapes of Wrath* is an
appeal to the owning class to behave, to become enlightened, rather
than to the working class to change its own conditions." [12]

That it could not have been Steinbeck's intention to urge organized
revolt is indicated not only in his letter retracting *L'Affaire Lettuceberg*, but also in the series of articles which he wrote for the *San Francisco News* in October of 1936. The first of these articles ends with the
warning that "California . . . is gradually building up a human structure which will certainly change the State, and may, if handled with
the inhumanity and stupidity that have characterized the past, destroy
the present system of agricultural economics." [13] Steinbeck makes a
similar point at the end of his article in *The Nation*: "It is fervently
to be hoped that the great group of migrant workers so necessary to
the harvesting of California's crops may be given the right to live
decently, that they may not be so badgered, tormented, and hurt that
in the end they become avengers of the hundreds of thousands who
have been tormented and starved before them." [14] In his third article
of the *News* series appears another warning that "a continuation of
this approach [intimidation and repression] constitutes a criminal en-
dangering of the peace of the State." [15] In the final article of this series,
Steinbeck offers three suggestions: first, that migrant laborers be al-
lotted small "subsistence" farms on which they can live and work when
there is no call for migrant labor; second, that a Migratory Labor
Board be created to help allot labor where needed and to determine fair
wages; third, that vigilante-ism and terrorism be punished. Steinbeck's
proposed alternative to this solution has a keen logic: "If, on the other
hand, as has been stated by a large grower, our agriculture requires
the creation and maintenance of a peon class, then it is submitted that
California agriculture is economically unsound under a democracy." [16]
There is certainly no Marxian class war or Bolshevik revolutionary

[11] Miron, *The Truth About John Steinbeck and the Migrants*, p. 7. See also Elizabeth N. Monroe, *The Novel and Society* (Chapel Hill, 1941), p. 272, and Earle
Birney, review of *The Grapes of Wrath* in *The Canadian Forum*, 19 (June, 1939),
p. 94.
[12] "Some Notes on John Steinbeck," *Antioch Review*, 2 (Summer, 1942), p. 195.
[13] "The Harvest Gypsies," *San Francisco News*, October 5, 1936, p. 3.
[14] "Dubious Battle in California," *The Nation*, 143 (September 12, 1936), p. 304.
[15] "The Harvest Gypsies," *San Francisco News*, October 7, 1936, p. 6.
[16] "The Harvest Gypsies," *San Francisco News*, October 12, 1936, p. 8.

ardor here. Steinbeck's statement about an American "peon" class is milder even than that of Walt Whitman in "Notes Left Over." "If the United States," said Whitman, "like the countries of the Old World, are also to grow vast crops of poor, desperate, dissatisfied, nomadic, miserably-waged populations . . . then our republican experiment, notwithstanding all its surface-success, is at heart an unhealthy failure."

Actually, as Frederick I. Carpenter has observed, Steinbeck's social philosophy had three roots: "For the first time in history, *The Grapes of Wrath* brings together and makes real three skeins of American thought. It begins with the transcendental oversoul, Emerson's faith in the common man, and his Protestant self-reliance. To this it joins Whitman's religion of the love of all man and his mass democracy. And it combines these mystical and poetic ideas with the realistic philosophy of pragmatism and its emphasis on effective action." Jim Casy "translates American philosophy into words of one syllable, and the Joads translate it into action." [17]

Another critic, Chester E. Eisinger, taking note of Carpenter's observations, suggests that there must be added a fourth skein of American thought—the agrarianism of Jefferson: "Because he had faith in the common man and thus gave his thinking a broad popular basis, Steinbeck was closer to Jeffersonianism than were the Southern Agrarians, who sought to resurrect not only an agricultural way of life but also the traditional cultural values of Europe. Steinbeck was concerned with democracy, and looked upon agrarianism as a way of life that would enable us to realize the full potentialities of the creed. Jefferson, of course, held the same." [18]

Steinbeck had dealt with this theme of man's relationship to the land earlier—in *To a God Unknown* and *Of Mice and Men*. In these works the relationship is mystical, symbolic, and mythical. While these values persist in *The Grapes of Wrath*, man's identification with the growth cycle is also seen as pragmatic, socially practical in Jeffersonian terms. The human erosion pictured in the book is as much the result of a separation from the land as it is of poverty. And because for the absentee growers their land has become a column of figures in a book,

---

[17] "The Philosophical Joads," *College English*, 2 (January, 1941), pp. 324–325. The resemblance of Casy to Emerson is also noted by Floyd Stovall in his *American Idealism* (Norman, Oklahoma, 1943), p. 164.

[18] "Jeffersonian Agrarianism in *The Grapes of Wrath*," *University of Kansas City Review*, 14 (Winter, 1947), p. 150.

they too are suffering an erosion—a moral one. Jefferson would have had no difficulty understanding what Steinbeck was getting at in one of his *San Francisco News* articles—that the loss of land led to a loss of dignity, which he defined not as a sense of self-importance, but as "a register of man's responsibility to the community": "We regard this destruction of dignity, then, as one of the most regrettable results of the migrant's life since it does reduce his responsibility and does make him a sullen outcast who will strike at our government in any way that occurs to him." [19]

Although *The Grapes of Wrath* brings together these four important skeins of American thought, it can be considered one of our great American novels only to the extent that it succeeds in realizing these ideas in the concrete forms of art. As Alex Comfort has put it, "The critical importance of a writer's ideas is this: if their scope is insufficient to cover the material he deals with, and to cover it in a coherent manner, irrespective of their immediate truth, they may render him unable to write at that level which, by common agreement, we call major literature." [20]

The ideas and materials of *The Grapes of Wrath* presented Steinbeck with the most difficult problem of structure he had faced so far. Neither the variations on a single line of action and development that he had used in *Cup of Gold, To a God Unknown, In Dubious Battle,* and *Of Mice and Men* nor the episodic structure of *The Pastures of Heaven* and *Tortilla Flat* could handle the scope and diversity of *The Grapes of Wrath.* His position was not unlike that of Tolstoy in writing *War and Peace.* Tolstoy's materials were, roughly, the adventures of the Bezukhov, Rostov, and Bolkonski families on the one hand, and the Napoleonic wars on the other. And while these two blocks of material were brought together in the plot development, there was enough material about the Napoleonic wars left over so that the author had to incorporate it in separate, philosophic interchapters. Steinbeck's materials were similar. There were the adventures of the Joad family and there was also the Great Depression. And, like Tolstoy, he had enough material left over to write separate, philosophic interchapters.

In the light of this basic analogy, Percy Lubbock's comments on the structural role of these two elements in *War and Peace* become signif-

[19] "The Harvest Gypsies," *San Francisco News,* October 8, 1936, p. 16.
[20] *The Novel and Our Time* (Letchworth, Hertfordshire, England, 1948), p. 8.

icant for an analysis of structure in *The Grapes of Wrath*: "I can discover no angle at which the two stories will appear to unite and merge
in a single impression. Neither is subordinated to the other, and there
is nothing above them . . . to which they are both related. Nor are
they placed together to illustrate a contrast; nothing *results* from their
juxtaposition. Only from time to time, upon no apparent principle
and without a word of warning, one of them is dropped and the other
resumed." [21]

In these few phrases Lubbock has defined the aesthetic conditions
not only for *War and Peace*, but for any other piece of fiction whose
strategies include an intercalary construction—*The Grapes of Wrath*,
for example. The test is whether anything *"results"* from this kind of
structure.

Counting the opening description of the drought and the penultimate chapter on the rains, pieces of straightforward description allow-
able even to strictly "scenic" novels (Lubbock's term for materials
presented entirely from the objective point of view), there are in *The
Grapes of Wrath* sixteen interchapters, making up a total of just under
a hundred pages—almost one sixth of the book. In none of these chapters do the Joads, Wilsons, or Wainwrights appear.

These interchapters have two main functions. First, by presenting
the social background they serve to amplify the pattern of action created by the Joad family. To this purpose, thirteen of the sixteen chapters are largely devoted. Chapter 1, for example, describes in panoramic
terms the drought which forces the Joads off their land. Chapter 5 is
mostly a dialogue between two generalized forces, the banks and the
farmers, presenting in archetype the conflict in which the Joads are
caught up. Chapters 7 and 9 depict, respectively, the buying of jalopies
and the selling of household goods. Chapter 11 describes at length a
decaying and deserted house which is the prototype of all the houses
abandoned in the dust bowl. Other chapters explore, through the col-
lage technique of chapters 7 and 9, the nature of that new, nomadic
society which the Joads are helping to form (14, 17, 23). Almost every
aspect of the Joads' adventures is enlarged in the interchapters and
seen as part of the social climate.

The remaining three intercalary chapters (19, 21, and 25) have the
function of providing such historical information as the development
of land ownership in California, the consequent development of migrant labor, and certain economic aspects of the social lag. These three

---

[21] *The Craft of Fiction* (New York, 1945), p. 33.

"informative" chapters make up only nineteen of the novel's six hundred odd pages. Scattered through the sixteen interchapters are occasional paragraphs whose purpose is to present, with choric effect, the philosophy or social message to which the current situation gives rise. For the most part, these paragraphs occur in four chapters—9, 11, 14, and 19.

While all these various materials are obviously ideologically related to the longer, narrative section of the novel (five hundred pages), there remains the problem of their aesthetic integration with the book as a whole. Even a cursory reading will show that there is a general correspondence between the material of each intercalary chapter and that of the current narrative portion. The magnificent opening description of the drought sets forth the condition which gives rise to the novel's action. Chapter 5 deals with the banks' foreclosing of mortgages, which forces the sharecroppers to emigrate. Highway 66 is given a chapter as the Joads begin their trek on that historic route. The chapters dealing with migrant life on the highway appear interspersed with the narrative of the Joads' actual journey. The last intercalary chapter, 29, describes the rain and flood in which the action of the novel ends.

A more careful reading will make it evident that this integration of the interchapters into a total structure goes far beyond a merely complementary juxtaposition. There is in addition an intricate interweaving of specific details. The chapter about the banks, for example, comes immediately after Tom and Casy see the deserted Joad farmhouse and is itself followed by a narrative chapter particularizing many of that chapter's generalities: As with the anonymous house in the intercalary chapter (5), one corner of the Joad house has been knocked off its foundation by a tractor. The man who in the interchapter threatens the tractor driver with his rifle becomes Grampa Joad, except that where the anonymous tenant does not fire, Grampa shoots out both headlights. The tractor driver in the intercalary chapter, Joe Davis, is a family acquaintance of the anonymous tenant, as Willy is an acquaintance of the Joads in the narrative chapter. The general dialogue between banks and tenants in the intercalary chapter is particularized by Muley in the narrative chapter: "Well, the guy that come aroun' talked nice as pie. 'You got to get off. It ain't my fault.' 'Well,' I says, 'Whose fault is it? I'll go an' nut the fella.' 'It's the Shawnee Lan' an' Cattle Company. I jus' got orders.' 'Who's the Shawnee Lan' an' Cattle Company?' 'It ain't nobody. It's a company.' Got a fella crazy. There wasn't nobody you could lay for." The jalopy sitting in the Joads' front yard is the kind of jalopy described in chapter 7. Chapter 8 ends with Al Joad driving off to sell a truckload of household goods. Chapter 9 is an intercalary chapter describing destitute farmers selling such goods, including many items which the Joads themselves are selling—pumps, farming tools, furniture, a team and wagon for ten dollars. In the following chapter the Joads' truck returns empty, the men having sold everything for eighteen dollars—including ten dollars they got for a team and wagon. Every chapter is locked into the book's narrative portion by this kind of specific cross-reference, which amplifies the Joads' typical actions to the dimensions of a communal experience.

Often, this interlocking of details becomes thematic or symbolic. The dust which is mentioned twenty-seven times in three pages of chapter 1 comes to stand not only for the land itself, but also for the basic situation out of which the novel's action develops. Everything which moves on the ground, from insects to trucks, raises a proportionate amount of dust; "a walking man lifted a thin layer as high as his waist." When Tom returns home after four years in prison and gets out of the truck which has given him a lift, he steps off the highway, and performs the symbolic ritual of taking off his new, prison-issue shoes and carefully working his bare feet into the dust. He then moves off across the land, "making a cloud that hung low to the ground behind him."

One of the novel's most important symbols, the turtle, is presented in what is actually the first intercalary chapter (3). And while this chapter is a masterpiece of realistic description (often included as such in Freshman English texts), it is also obvious that the turtle is symbolic and its adventures prophetic allegory. "Nobody can't keep a turtle though," says Jim Casy. "They work at it and work at it, and at last one day they get out and away they go. . . ." (p. 28) The indomitable life force which drives the turtle drives the Joads, and in the same direction—southwest. As the turtle picks up seeds in its shell and drops them on the other side of the road, so the Joads pick up life and take it across the country to California. (As Grandfather in "The Leader of the People" puts it, "We carried life out here and set it down the way those ants carry eggs.") As the turtle survives the truck's attempt to smash it on the highway and as it crushes the red ant which runs into its shell, so the Joads endure the perils of their journey.

This symbolic value is retained and further defined when the turtle specifically enters the narrative. The incident with the red ant is echoed two hundred and seventy pages later when another red ant runs over "the folds of loose skin" on Granma's neck and she reaches up with her "little wrinkled claws"; Ma Joad picks it off and crushes it. In chapter 3 the turtle is seen "dragging his high-domed shell across the grass." In the next chapter, Tom sees "the high-domed back of a land turtle" and, picking up the turtle, carries it with him. It is only when he is convinced that his family has left the land that he releases the turtle, which travels "southwest, as it had been from the first," a direction which is repeated in the next two sentences. The first thing which Tom does after releasing the turtle is to put on his shoes, which he took off when he left the highway. Thus, not only the turtle but also Tom's connection with it is symbolic, as symbolic as Lennie's appearance in *Of Mice and Men,* with a dead mouse in his pocket.

In addition to this constant knitting together of the two kinds of chapters, often the interchapters themselves are further assimilated into the narrative portion by incorporating in themselves the techniques of fiction. There are no more than a half-dozen paragraphs in the book which are aimed directly at the reader or delivered by the author. The general conflict between small farmers and the banks, for example, is presented as an imaginary dialogue, each speaker personifying the sentiments of his group. And although neither speaker is a "real" person, they are dramatically differentiated and their arguments embody details particular to the specific social condition. Each speaker is like the chorus in a Greek tragedy.[22] This kind of dramatization is also evident in those chapters concerned with the buying of used cars, the selling of household goods, the police intimidation of migrants, and others.

These structural techniques for integrating the two parts of *The Grapes of Wrath* are greatly implemented by a masterful command of prose style. In his novels after *To a God Unknown,* Steinbeck had demonstrated the variety of prose styles that he could weld into the very meaning of a novel—prose styles as different as those of *Tortilla Flat* and *In Dubious Battle.* In *The Grapes of Wrath* there is such a number of strategically employed prose styles that the novel almost amounts to a *tour de force.* No Steinbeck novel begins so auspiciously:

To the red country and part of the gray country of Oklahoma, the last rains came gently, and they did not cut the scarred earth. The plows

[22] For an excellent discussion of this point, see Joseph Warren Beach, *American Fiction, 1920–1940* (New York, 1942), pp. 337–338.

crossed and recrossed the rivulet marks. The last rains lifted the corn
quickly and scattered weed colonies and grass along the sides of the roads
so that the gray country and the dark red country began to disappear
under a green cover. In the last part of May the sky grew pale and the
clouds that had hung in high puffs for so long in the spring were dissi-
pated. The sun flared down on the growing corn day after day until a
line of brown spread along the edge of each green bayonet. The clouds
appeared, and went away, and in a while they did not try any more. The
weeds grew darker green to protect themselves, and they did not spread
any more. The surface of the earth crusted, a thin hard crust, and as the
sky became pale, so the earth became pale, pink in the red country and
white in the gray country.

This opening paragraph is as carefully worked out as an overture to
an opera. The themes of *red, gray, green,* and *earth* are announced and
given parallel developments: *red* to pink, *gray* to white, *green* to
brown, and ploughed *earth* to thin hard *crust*. The pervading structural rhythm of each sentence is echoed in the paragraph as a whole,
a paragraph promising a story of epic sweep and dignity.

The extent to which this style is indebted to the Old Testament can
be strikingly demonstrated by arranging a similar passage from the
novel according to phrases, in the manner of the Bates Bible, leaving
the punctuation intact:

> *The tractors had lights shining,*
> *For there is no day and night for a tractor*
> *And the disks turn the earth in the darkness*
> *And they glitter in the daylight.*
>
> *And when a horse stops work and goes into the barn*
> *There is a life and a vitality left,*
> *There is a breathing and a warmth,*
> *And the feet shift on the straw,*
> *And the jaws champ on the hay,*
> *And the ears and the eyes are alive.*
> *There is a warmth of life in the barn,*
> *And the heat and smell of life.*
>
> *But when the motor of a tractor stops,*
> *It is as dead as the ore it came from.*
> *The heat goes out of it*
> *Like the living heat that leaves a corpse.*

The parallel grammatical structure of parallel meanings, the simplicity of diction, the balance, the concrete details, the summary sentences,

the reiterations—all are here. Note also the organization: four phrases for the tractor, eight for the horse, four again for the tractor. Except for the terms of machinery, the passage might be one of the Psalms.

It is this echo—more, this pedal point—evident even in the most obviously "directed" passages of the interchapters, which supports their often simple philosophy, imbuing them with a dignity which their content alone could not sustain. The style gives them their authority:

> Burn coffee for fuel in the ships. Burn corn to keep warm, it makes a hot fire. Dump potatoes in the rivers and place guards along the banks to keep the hungry people from fishing them out. Slaughter the pigs and bury them, and let the putrescence drip down into the earth.
>
> There is a crime here that goes beyond denunciation. There is a sorrow here that weeping cannot symbolize. There is a failure here that topples all our success. The fertile earth, the straight tree rows, the sturdy trunks, and the ripe fruit. And children dying of pellagra must die because a profit cannot be taken from an orange.

These passages are not complex philosophy, but they may well be profound. The Biblical resonance which gives them power is used discreetly, is never employed on the trivial and particular, and its recurrence has a cumulative effect.

There are many other distinct prose styles in the interchapters of *The Grapes of Wrath*, and each is just as functional in its place. There is, for example, the harsh, staccato prose of chapter 7, which is devoted to the sale of used cars:

> Cadillacs, La Salles, Buicks, Plymouths, Packards, Chevvies, Fords, Pontiacs. Row on row, headlights glinting in the afternoon sun. Good Used Cars.
>
> Soften 'em up, Joe. Jesus, I wisht I had a thousand jalopies! Get 'em ready to deal, an' I'll close 'em.
>
> Goin' to California? Here's jus' what you need. Looks shot, but they's thousan's of miles in her.
>
> Lined up side by side. Good Used Cars. Bargains. Clean, runs good.

A good contrast to this hectic prose is offered by chapter 9, which presents the loss and despair of people forced to abandon their household goods. Here the style itself takes on a dazed resignation:

> The women sat among the doomed things, turning them over and looking past them and back. This book. My father had it. He liked a book. *Pilgrim's Progress*. Used to read it. Got his name on it. And his pipe— still smells rank. And this picture—an angel. I looked at that before the

first three come—didn't seem to do much good. Think we could get this
china dog in? Aunt Sadie brought it from the St. Louis Fair. See? Wrote
right on it. No, I guess not. Here's a letter my brother wrote the day before he died. Here's an old-time hat. These feathers—never got to use
them. No, there isn't room.

At times, as in the description of a folk dance in chapter 23, the
prose style becomes a veritable chameleon:

> Look at that Texas boy, long legs loose, taps four times for ever' damn
> step. Never see a boy swing aroun' like that. Look at him swing that
> Cherokee girl, red in her cheeks and her toe points out. Look at her pant,
> look at her heave. Think she's tired? Think she's winded? Well, she ain't.
> Texas boy got his hair in his eyes, mouth's wide open, can't get air, but
> he pats four times for ever' darn step, an' he'll keep a-goin' with the
> Cherokee girl.

No other American novel has succeeded in forging and making in-
strumental so many prose styles.

The number of such passages which could be cited is almost endless.
Those cited thus far suggest a number of influences—the Bible, Dos
Passos' "Newsreel" technique, folk idiom, Walt Whitman, Hemingway,
and perhaps Carl Sandburg's *The People, Yes,* although the latter's
diction is much more strident than that of *The Grapes of Wrath.* Another influence on this prose is certainly the narrative style of Pare
Lorentz in his scripts for the motion pictures *The Plow That Broke
the Plains* and *The River.* Steinbeck had met Lorentz and discussed
this style with him, listening to recordings of Lorentz' radio drama
Ecce Homo! [23] Lorentz too had made use of the Old Testament, but
the influence on him of Whitman and Sandburg was perhaps stronger,
as the following passage from *The River* makes clear:

> *Down the Missouri three thousand miles from the Rockies;*
> *Down the Ohio a thousand miles from the Alleghenies;*
> *Down the Arkansas fifteen hundred miles from the Great Divide;*
> *Down the Red, a thousand miles from Texas;*
> *Down the great Valley, twenty-five hundred miles from Minnesota,*
> *Carrying every rivulet and brook, creek and rill,*
> *Carrying all the rivers that run down two-thirds the continent—*
> *The Mississippi runs to the Gulf.*[24]

[23] Joseph Henry Jackson, "Introduction," Limited Edition of *The Grapes of Wrath*
(New York, 1940), pp. viii–ix.
[24] *The River* (New York, 1938), unpaginated. According to the "Preface," the text
for this book was taken verbatim from the motion picture of the same name.

The debt of Steinbeck's intercalary chapter on Highway 66 to this kind of writing is obvious: "Clarksville and Ozark and Van Buren and Fort Smith on 64, and there's an end of Arkansas. And all the roads into Oklahoma City, 66 down from Tulsa, 270 up from McAlester. 81 from Wichita Falls south, from Enid north. Edmond, McLoud, Purcell. 66 out of Oklahoma City; El Reno and Clinton, going west on 66. Hydro, Elk City. . . ." But Steinbeck demonstrates a much greater range than Lorentz, and was capable of much greater variety; only in this chapter did he resort to the easy device of cataloguing America. And in this chapter the catalogue is functional, representing the more detailed progress the Joads are making.

The great variety of prose style and subject matter found in these interchapters not only has value as Americana, but creates a "realism" far beyond that of literal reporting. In addition, this variety is important because it tends to destroy any impression that these interchapters, as a group, constitute a separate entity. They are a group only in that they are not a direct part of the narrative. They have enough individuality of subject matter, prose style, and technique to keep the novel from falling into two parts, and to keep the reader from feeling that he is now reading "the other part."

Because Steinbeck's subject in *The Grapes of Wrath* is not the adventures of the Joad family so much as the social conditions which occasion them, these interchapters serve a vital purpose. As Percy Lubbock has pointed out, the purely "scenic" or objective technique "is out of the question . . . whenever the story is too big, too comprehensive, too widely ranging to be treated scenically, with no opportunity for general and panoramic survey. . . . These stories . . . call for some narrator, somebody who *knows*, to contemplate the facts and create an impression of them." [25]

Steinbeck's story certainly is "big," "comprehensive," and "wide ranking." As we have seen, however, he took pains to keep the novel from falling into two independent parts. The cross-reference of detail, the interweaving symbols, the dramatization, and the choric effects are techniques designed to make the necessary "panoramic" sections tend toward the "scenic." An examination of the narrative portion of *The Grapes of Wrath* will reveal, conversely, that its techniques make the "scenic" or narrative sections tend toward the "panoramic." Steinbeck worked from both sides to make the two kinds of chapters approach each other and fuse into a single impression.

[25] *The Craft of Fiction*, p. 40.

This tendency of the narrative or dramatic portion of *The Grapes of Wrath* toward the pictorial can be seen readily by comparing the book with another of Steinbeck's group-man novels, *In Dubious Battle,* which has a straightforward plot development and an involving action. Of course, things happen in *The Grapes of Wrath,* and what happens not only grows out of what has gone before but grows into what will happen in the future. But while critics have perceived that plot is not the organizational principle of the novel, they have not attempted to relate this fact to the novel's materials as they are revealed through other techniques, assuming instead that this lack of plot constitutes one of the novel's major flaws.[26]

Actually, this lack of an involving action is effective in at least two ways. It could reasonably be expected that the greatest threat to the novel's unity would come from the interchapters' constant breaking up of the narrative's line of action. However, the very fact that *The Grapes of Wrath* is *not* organized by a unifying plot works for absorbing these intercalary chapters smoothly into its texture. A second way in which this tendency of the "scenic" towards the "panoramic" is germane to the novel's materials becomes evident when it is considered that Steinbeck's subject is not an action so much as a situation. Description, therefore, must often substitute for narration.[27]

This substitution of the static for the dynamic also gives us an insight into the nature and function of the novel's characters, especially the Joads, who have been called "essentially symbolic marionettes" [28] and "puppets with differentiating traits," [29] but seldom real people. While there are scant objective grounds for determining whether a novel's characters are "real," one fruitful approach is to consider fictional characters not only in relation to life, but in relation to the *rest* of the fiction of which they are a part.

In his Preface to *The Forgotten Village,* which immediately followed *The Grapes of Wrath,* Steinbeck comments on just these relationships:

[26] Harry Thornton Moore, for example, refers to Steinbeck's failure to provide *The Grapes of Wrath* with "a proportioned and intensified drama," a "vital conflict," or a "continuity of suspense." *The Novels of John Steinbeck* (Chicago, 1939), pp. 59, 69.

[27] For an excellent discussion of this point, see Claude-Edmonde Magny, *L'âge du roman américain* (Paris, 1948), p. 187.

[28] Alfred Kazin, *On Native Grounds* (New York, 1942), p. 397.

[29] George F. Whicher, "Proletarian Leanings," *The Literature of the American People,* ed. by A. H. Quinn (New York, 1951), p. 960.

A great many documentary films have used the generalized method, that is, the showing of a condition or an event as it affects a group of people. The audience can then have a personalized reaction from imagining one member of that group. I have felt that this is the more difficult observation from the audience's viewpoint. It means very little to know that a million Chinese are starving unless you know one Chinese who is starving. In *The Forgotten Village* we reversed the usual process. Our story centered on one family in one small village. We wished our audience to know this family very well, and incidentally to like it, as we did. Then, from association with this little personalized group, the larger conclusion concerning the racial group could be drawn with something like participation.[30]

This is precisely the strategy in *The Grapes of Wrath*. Whatever value the Joads have as individuals is "incidental" to their primary function as a "personalized group." Kenneth Burke has pointed out that ". . . most of the characters derive their role, which is to say their personality, purely from their relationship to the basic situation."[31] What he takes to be a serious weakness is actually one of the book's greatest accomplishments. The characters are so absorbed into the novel's materials that the reader's response goes beyond sympathy for the individuals to moral indignation at their social condition. This is, of course, precisely Steinbeck's intention. And certainly the Joads are adequate for this purpose. This conception of character is a parallel to the fusing of the "scenic" and "panoramic" techniques in the narrative and interchapters.

Although the diverse materials of *The Grapes of Wrath* made organization by a unifying plot difficult, nevertheless the novel does have structural form. The action progresses through three successive movements, and its significance is revealed by an intricate system of themes and symbols.

The Grapes of Wrath is divided into thirty consecutive chapters with no larger grouping, but even a cursory reading reveals that the novel is made up of three major parts: the drought, the journey, and California. The first section ends with chapter 10. It is separated from the second section, the journey, by *two* interchapters. The first of these chapters presents a picture of the deserted land—"The houses were left

[30] "Preface," *The Forgotten Village* (New York, May, 1941).
[31] *The Philosophy of Literary Form* (Baton Rouge, 1941), p. 91.

vacant on the land, and the land was vacant because of this." The second interchapter is devoted to Highway 66 and is followed by chapter 13, which begins the Joads' journey—"The ancient overloaded Hudson creaked and grunted to the highway at Sallisaw and turned west, and the sun was blinding." The journey section extends past the geographical California border, across the desert to Bakersfield. This section ends with chapter 18, "And the truck rolled down the mountain into the great valley," and the next chapter begins the California section by introducing the reader to labor conditions in that state. Steinbeck had this tripartite division in mind as early as September of 1937, when he told Joseph Henry Jackson that he was working on "the first of three related longer novels." [82]

Like the prose style of the philosophical passages in the interchapters, this structure has its roots in the Old Testament. The novel's three sections correspond to the oppression in Egypt, the exodus, and the sojourn in the land of Canaan, which in both accounts is first viewed from the mountains. This parallel is not worked out in detail, but the grand design is there: the plagues (erosion), the Egyptians (banks), the exodus (journey), and the hostile tribes of Canaan (Californians).

This Biblical structure is supported by a continuum of symbols and symbolic actions. The most pervasive symbolism is that of grapes. The novel's title, taken from "The Battle Hymn of the Republic," ("He is trampling out the vintage where the grapes of wrath are stored") is itself a reference to Revelation: "And the angel thrust in his sickle into the earth, and gathered the vine of the earth, and cast it into the great winepress of the wrath of God." (14:19) Similarly, in Deuteronomy: "Their grapes are grapes of gall, their clusters are bitter. Their wine is the poison of serpents. . . ." (32:32); in Jeremiah: "The fathers have eaten sour grapes, and their children's teeth are set on edge." (31:29) Sometimes this meaning of the symbol is stated in the novel's interchapters: "In the souls of the people the grapes of wrath are filling and growing heavy, heavy for the vintage."

Steinbeck also uses grapes for symbols of plenty, as the one huge cluster of grapes which Joshua and Oshea bring back from their first excusion into the rich land of Canaan is a symbol of plenty, a cluster so huge that "they bare it between two on a staff." (Numbers, 12:23) It is this meaning of grapes that is frequently alluded to by Grampa Joad:

[82] "John Steinbeck, A Portrait," *Saturday Review of Literature*, 16 (September 25, 1937), p. 18.

"Gonna get me a whole big bunch a grapes off a bush, or whatever, an'
I'm gonna squash 'em on my face an' let 'em run offen my chin." Although Grampa dies long before the Joads get to California, he is symbolically present through the anonymous old man in the barn (stable),
who is saved from starvation by Rosasharn's breasts: "This thy stature
is like to a palm tree, and thy breasts to clusters of grapes." [33] (Canticles, 7:7) Rosasharn's giving of new life to the old man is another reference to the orthodox interpretation of Canticles "I [Christ] am the
rose of Sharon, and the lily of the valleys" (2:1); and to the Gospels:
"take, eat; this is my body." Still another important Biblical symbol is
Jim Casy (Jesus Christ), who will be discussed in another connection.

Closely associated with this latter symbolic meaning of grapes and
the land of Canaan is Ma Joad's frequent assertion that "We are the
people." She has not been reading Carl Sandburg; she has been reading
her Bible. As Sairy tells Tom when he is looking for a suitable verse to
bury with Grampa, "Turn to Psalms, over further. You kin always get
somepin outa Psalms." And it is from Psalms that she gets her phrase:
"For he is our God; and we are the people of his pasture, and the
sheep of his hand." (95:7) They are the people who pick up life in
Oklahoma (Egypt) and carry it to California (Canaan) as the turtle
picks up seeds and as the ants pick up their eggs in "The Leader of
the People." These parallels to the Israelites of Exodus are all brought
into focus when, near the end of the novel, Uncle John sets Rose of
Sharon's stillborn child in an old apple crate (like Moses in the basket),
sets the box in a stream "among the willow stems," and floats it toward
the town saying, "Go down an' tell 'em."

As the Israelites received the new Law in their exodus, so the migrants develop new laws: "The families learned what rights must be
observed—the right of privacy in the tent; the right to keep the past
black hidden in the heart; the right to refuse help or accept it, to offer
help or to decline it; the right of a son to court and the daughter to be
courted; the right of the hungry to be fed; the rights of the pregnant
and the sick to transcend all other rights." Chapter 17 can be seen as
the Deuteronomy of *The Grapes of Wrath*. It is this context which

---

[33] I cannot resist quoting Harry Slochower's interpretation of this scene: "The re-
incarnation of Grampa is also suggested by the theme of grapes. Grampa had been
looking forward to squashing the grapes of California on his face, 'a-nibblin' off it
all the time.' The man in the barn is reduced to such baby acts, 'practicing' them
as he drinks Rose of Sharon's milk. The grapes have turned to 'wrath,' indicated
by the fact that the first milk of the mother is said to be bitter." *No Voice Is
Wholly Lost* (New York, 1945), footnote p. 304.

makes of the Joads' journey "out west" an archetype of mass migration.[34]

Through this supporting Biblical structure and context there are interwoven two opposing themes which make up the book's "plot." One of these, the "negative" one, concerns itself with the increasingly straitened circumstances of the Joads. At the beginning of their journey they have $154, their household goods, two barrels of pork, a serviceable truck, and their good health. As the novel progresses they become more and more impoverished, until at the end they are destitute, without food, sick, their truck and goods abandoned in the mud, without shelter, and without hope of work. This economic decline is paralleled by a similar decline in the family's morale. In his *San Francisco News* articles Steinbeck had described the gradual deterioration of family and of human dignity which accompanies impoverished circumstances. This is illustrated by the Joads, who start off as a cheerful group full of hope and will power and by the end of the novel are spiritually bankrupt. As Steinbeck had noted about the migrants around Bakersfield three years earlier, they "feel that paralyzed dullness with which the mind protects itself against too much sorrow and too much pain." [35] When the Joads enter their first Hooverville they catch a glimpse of the deterioration which lies ahead of them. They see filthy tin and rug shacks littered with trash, the children dirty and diseased, the heads of families "bull-simple" from being roughed up too often, all spirit gone and in its place a whining, passive resistance to authority. Although the novel ends before the Joads come to this point, in the last chapter they are well on their way.

And as the family declines morally and economically, so the family unit itself breaks up. Grampa dies before they are out of Oklahoma and lies in a nameless grave; Granma is buried a pauper; Noah deserts the family; Connie deserts Rosasharn; the baby is born dead; Tom becomes a fugitive; Al is planning to leave as soon as possible; Casy is killed; and they have had to abandon the Wilsons.

These two "negative" or downward movements are balanced by two

---

[34] Bernard Bowron persistently ignores this wider frame of reference. He calls *The Grapes of Wrath* "a triumph of literary engineering" because of the great "artfulness—I do not say great art" with which the book utilizes the "romance-formula" of such covered wagon stories as *The Way West*. *The Grapes of Wrath,* says Mr. Bowron, "derives from the 'Westward' novel both the structure and the values that give it its emotional horsepower." See "The Grapes of Wrath: a 'Wagons West' Romance," *Colorado Quarterly,* 3 (Summer, 1954), pp. 84–91.

[35] "The Harvest Gypsies," *San Francisco News,* October 6, 1936, p. 3.

"positive" or upward movements. Although the primitive family unit is breaking up, the fragments are going to make up a larger group. The sense of a communal unit grows steadily through the narrative—the Wilsons, the Wainwrights—and is pointed to again and again in the interchapters: "One man, one family driven from the land; this rusty car creaking along the highway to the west. I lost my land, a single tractor took my land. I am alone and I am bewildered. And in the night one family camps in a ditch and another family pulls in and the tents come out. The two men squat on their hams and the women and children listen. . . . For here 'I lost my land' is changed; a cell is split and from its splitting grows the thing you [owners] hate—'We lost *our* land!' " Oppression and intimidation only serve to strengthen the social group; the relief offered by a federal migrant camp only gives them a vision of the democratic life they can attain by cooperation, which is why the local citizens are opposed to these camps.

Another of the techniques by which Steinbeck develops this theme of unity can be illustrated by the Joads' relationship with the Wilson family of Kansas, which they meet just before crossing the Oklahoma border. This relationship is developed not so much by explicit statements, as in the interchapters, as by symbols. Grampa Joad, for example, dies in the Wilsons' tent and he is buried in one of the Wilson's blankets. Furthermore, the epitaph which is buried with Grampa (in Oklahoma soil) is written on a page torn from the Wilsons' Bible—that page usually reserved for family records of births, marriages, and deaths. In burying this page with Grampa, the Wilsons symbolize not only their adoption of the Joads, but their renouncing of hope for continuing their own family line. Also, note that it is the more destitute Wilson family which embraces the Joads. Steinbeck makes of the two families' relationship a microcosm of the migration's total picture, its human significance.

This growing awareness on the part of the people *en masse* is paralleled by the "education" and "conversion" of Tom and Casy. At the beginning of the book, Tom's attitude is individualistic. He is looking out for himself. As he puts it, "I'm still laying my dogs down one at a time," and "I climb fences when I got fences to climb." His first real lesson comes when Casy strikes out against the trooper to save his friend and then gives himself up in his place. The section immediately following is that of the family's stay at a federal migrant camp, and here Tom's education is advanced still further. By the time Casy is killed, Tom is ready for his conversion, which he seals by revenging his mentor. While Tom is hiding out in the cave, after having struck down the vigilante, he has time to think of Casy and his message, so that in his last meeting with his mother, in which he asserts his spiritual unity with all men, it is evident that he has moved from material and personal resentment to ethical indignation, from particulars to principles.

This last meeting between mother and son takes place under conditions reminiscent of the prenatal state. The entrance to the cave is covered with black vines, and the interior is damp and completely dark, so that the contact of mother and son is actually physical rather than visual; she gives him food. When Tom comes out of the cave after announcing his conversion, it is as though he were reborn. When Tom says, "An' when our folks eat the stuff they raise an' live in the houses they build—why I'll be there," he is paraphrasing Isaiah: "And they shall build houses and inhabit them, they shall not build and another inhabit; they shall not plant and another eat." (65:21–22)

The development of Jim Casy is similar to that of Tom. He moves from Bible-belt evangelism to social prophecy. At the beginning of the book he has already left preaching and has returned from his sojourn "in the hills, thinkin', almost you might say like Jesus went into the wilderness to think His way out of a mess of troubles." But although Casy is already approaching his revelation of the Oversoul, it is only through his experiences with the Joads that he is able to complete his vision. As Tom moves from material resentment to ethical indignation, from action to thought to action again, so Casy moves from the purely speculative to the pragmatic. Both move from stasis to action. Casy's Christ-like development is complete when, pointed out as "that shiny bastard" and struck on the head with a pick handle, he dies saying, "You don't know what you're a-doin'." [36]

Those critics are reading superficially who think that Steinbeck "expects us to admire Casy, an itinerant preacher, who, over-excited from his evangelistic revivals, is in the habit of taking one or another of the girls of his audience to lie in the grass." [37] Actually, Casy himself perceives the incongruity of this behavior, which is why he goes "into the wilderness" and renounces his Bible-belt evangelism for a species of social humanism, and his congregation for the human race. His development, like that of Tom, is symbolic of the changing social condition

---

[36] Further parallels between Casy and Christ have been pointed out recently in Martin Shockley's "Christian Symbolism in *The Grapes of Wrath*," *College English*, 18 (November, 1956), pp. 87–90.

[37] Elizabeth N. Monroe, *The Novel and Society* (Chapel Hill, 1941), p. 18.

which is the novel's essential theme, paralleling the development of the
Joad family as a whole, which is, again, but a "personalized group."
Casy resembles Emerson more than he does Sinclair Lewis' Elmer Gan-
try or Erskine Caldwell's Semon Dye. For like Emerson, Casy discovers
the Oversoul through intuition and rejects his congregation in order to
preach to the world.

Because these themes of "education" and "conversion" are not the
central, involving action of the novel, but grow slowly out of a rich
and solid context, the development of Tom and Casy achieves an authority lacking in most proletarian fiction. The novel's thematic organization also makes it possible for Steinbeck successfully to incorporate the widest variety of materials, and, with the exception of
romantic love, to present the full scale of human emotions. This ac-
complishment is a great one when it is considered that the point of
view in the narrative sections is absolutely objective. At no point are
we told what the characters feel or think, only what they do or say.

The ability of this thematic structure to absorb incidents is illustrated by the early morning "breakfast" scene. One version of this little
scene, a first-person narrative, had appeared as a short sketch in *The
Long Valley*. This earlier version is a well-written piece of description
—the girl and her baby, the three men, the smell of early morning
breakfast, the hospitality extended a stranger. But somehow the emotion apparently felt by the author is not conveyed to the reader. Steinbeck concludes the piece lamely: "That's all. I know, of course, some
of the reasons why it was pleasant. But there was some element of great
beauty there that makes the rush of warmth when I think of it." (LV,
92) Although this incident was completely rewritten for *The Grapes
of Wrath*, what makes it effective there is its context. This bit of normal human activity, warmth, and tenderness is Tom's first experience
in the refuge of the federal migrant camp, immediately following
a night of vigilante horror and cringing flight. It constitutes for him
a renewal of faith in his fellow man. In this connection, it is significant
that whereas both Dos Passos' *U.S.A.* and *Manhattan Transfer* end
with the protagonist hitchhiking *away* from home, the group, Steinbeck's novel begins with Tom coming home, joining the group.[38]

This ability of Steinbeck's thematic organization to absorb incidents
organically into its context is also important for an understanding of

[38] For an excellent contrast of Steinbeck and Dos Passos, see Harry Slochower,
"John Dos Passos and John Steinbeck, Contrasting Notions of the Communal Personality," in *Byrdcliffe Afternoons* (Woodstock, New York, January, 1940), pp. 11–27.

the last scene, of which there has been much criticism. Typical of this criticism is Bernard De Voto's contention that the ending of the novel is "symbolism gone sentimental." [39] The novel's materials do make a climactic ending difficult. Steinbeck had faced the same problem in *In Dubious Battle,* where he had solved it by "stopping on a high point." (JS-MO, 2/4/35) By this same solution in *The Grapes of Wrath,* Steinbeck avoids three pitfalls: a *deus ex machina* ending; a summing-up, moral essay; and a new level of horror. The novel's thematic treatment makes it possible for him to avoid these choices by bringing his novel to a "symbolic" climax without doing violence to credulity, structure, or theme.[40]

This climax is prepared for by the last interchapter, which parallels in terms of rain the opening description of drought. The last paragraphs of these chapters are strikingly similar:

> The women studied the men's faces secretly. . . . After a while the faces of the watching men lost the bemused perplexity and became hard and angry and resistant. Then the women knew that they were safe and that there was no break.

> The women watched the men, watched to see whether the break had come at last. . . . And where a number of men gathered together, the fear went from their faces, and anger took its place. And the women sighed with relief, for they knew it was all right—the break had not come. . . .

With this latter paragraph the novel is brought full circle. The last chapter compactly re-enacts the whole drama of the Joads' journey in one uninterrupted continuity of suspense. The rain continues to fall; the truck and household goods must be abandoned; the little mud levee collapses; Rosasharn's baby is born dead; the boxcar must be abandoned; they take to the highway in search of food and find instead a starving man. Then the miracle happens. As Rose of Sharon offers her breast to the old man (this is my body and my blood), the novel's two counterthemes are brought together in a symbolic paradox. Out

---

[39] "American Novels: 1939," *Atlantic Monthly,* 165 (January, 1940), p. 68.

[40] For parallels to this scene, see Maupassant's "Idylle"; Byron's *Childe Harold,* Canto IV, Stanzas CXLVIII–CLI; Rubens' painting of old Cimon drawing milk from the breast of Pero; and an eighteenth-century play called *The Grecian's Daughter,* which is discussed in Maurice W. Disher's *Blood and Thunder* (London, 1949), p. 23. See also Celeste T. Wright, "Ancient Analogues of an Incident in John Steinbeck," *Western Folklore,* 14 (January, 1955), pp. 50–51.

of her own need she gives life; out of the profoundest depth of despair comes the greatest assertion of faith.

Steinbeck's great achievement in *The Grapes of Wrath* is that while minimizing what seem to be the most essential elements of fiction—plot and character—he was able to create a "well-made" and emotionally compelling novel out of materials which in most other hands have resulted in sentimental propaganda.[41]

[41] George Bluestone, *Novels into Film* (Baltimore, 1957) appeared too late to be included in the present discussion. Mr. Bluestone's chapter on *The Grapes of Wrath* illuminates several aspects of that novel, particularly the function of animal imagery. [Reprinted below, pp. 102–21.]

The Grapes of Wrath

by George Bluestone

In his compact little study of California writers, *The Boys in the Back Room*, Edmund Wilson comments on the problems inherent in the close affiliation between Hollywood and commercial fiction:

> Since the people who control the movies will not go a step of the way to give the script writer a chance to do a serious script, the novelist seems, consciously or unconsciously, to be going part of the way to meet the producers. John Steinbeck, in *The Grapes of Wrath*, has certainly learned from the films—and not only from the documentary pictures of Pare Lorentz, but from the sentimental symbolism of Hollywood. The result was that *The Grapes of Wrath* went on the screen as easily as if it had been written in the studios, and was probably the only serious story on record that seemed equally effective as a film and as a book.[1]

Indeed, not only did Steinbeck learn from Pare Lorentz; he also received, through Lorentz, his first introduction to Nunnally Johnson, the screen writer who did the movie adaptation of his novel.[2] And Bennett Cerf, the publishing head of Random House, must have had none other than Steinbeck in mind when he wrote, "The thing an author wants most from his publisher these days is a letter of introduction to Darryl Zanuck." [3] For if Steinbeck was fortunate in having Pare Lorentz as a teacher and Nunnally Johnson as a screen writer, he was one of the few who earned the coveted letter to Darryl Zanuck, the producer of *The Grapes of Wrath*. Add Gregg Toland's photography, Alfred Newman's music, and John Ford's direction, and one

"The Grapes of Wrath." From *Novels into Film* by George Bluestone (Baltimore: The Johns Hopkins Press, 1957), pp. 147–69. Copyright © 1957 by the Johns Hopkins Press. Reprinted by permission of the publisher.

[1] Edmund Wilson, *The Boys in the Back Room* (San Francisco, 1941), p. 61.

[2] In conversation with Mr. Johnson.

[3] In *Hollywood Reporter* (January 9, 1941), p. 3; quoted in Leo C. Rosten, *Hollywood: The Movie Colony, The Movie Makers* (New York, 1941), p. 366.

sees that Steinbeck had an unusually talented crew, one which could be depended upon to respect the integrity of his best-selling book.

Lester Asheim, in his close charting of the correspondence between twenty-four novels and films, seems to corroborate Edmund Wilson's conclusion about the easy transference of Steinbeck's book to John Ford's film. According to Asheim's analysis, the major sequences in the novel bear more or less the same ratio to the whole as the corresponding sequences do in the film:

	per cent of whole	
sequence	*book*	*film*
Oklahoma episodes	20	28
Cross-country episodes	19	22
General commentary	17	—
Government camp episodes	15	18
Hooverville episodes	10	13
Strike-breaking episodes	9	16
Final episodes	10	3
	100	100

And when Asheim goes on to explain that, if one ignores the major deletions which occur in the transference and considers only those episodes in the novel which appear in the film, the percentage of both book and film devoted to these central events would be virtually identical, his observation seems, at first, to be providing indisputable proof for Wilson's claim.[4]

Yet, to follow through Wilson's primary analysis of Steinbeck's work is to come at once on a contradiction which belies, first, his comment on the ineluctable fitness of the novel for Hollywood consumption and, second, his implication that Steinbeck, like the novelists whom Bennett Cerf has in mind, had written with one eye on the movie market. For it is central to Wilson's critical argument that the "substratum which remains constant" in Steinbeck's work "is his preoccupation with biology."[5] According to Wilson's view, "Mr. Steinbeck almost always in his fiction is dealing either with the lower animals or with human beings so rudimentary that they are almost on the animal level."[6] Tracing the thematic seams that run through Steinbeck's prose, Wilson notes the familiar interchapter on the turtle

[4] Lester Asheim, "From Book to Film" (Ph.D. dissertation, University of Chicago, 1949), pp. 55–56.
[5] Wilson, p. 42.
[6] *Ibid.*, pp. 42–43.

whose slow, tough progress survives the gratuitous cruelty of the truck driver who swerves to hit it. This anticipates the survival of the Joads, who, with the same dorsal hardness, will manage another journey along a road, emerging like the turtle from incredible hardships surrounded by symbols of fertility, much like the turtle's "wild cat head" which spawns three spearhead seeds in the dry ground. And Wilson notes, too, the way in which the forced pilgrimage of the Joads, adumbrated by the turtle's indestructibility, is "accompanied and parodied all the way by animals, insects and birds," as when the abandoned house where Tom finds Muley is invaded by bats, weasels, owls, mice, and pet cats gone wild.

This primary biological analysis seems to contradict Wilson's more casual statement on the film, since the screen version, as evolved by Nunnally Johnson and John Ford, contains little evidence of this sort of preoccupation. And when Asheim concludes, after a detailed comparison, that to one unfamiliar with the novel there are no loose ends or glaring contradictions to indicate that alterations have taken place,[7] we begin to uncover a series of disparities which, rather than demonstrating the ease of adaptation, suggests its peculiar difficulties. We are presented in the film with what Asheim calls "a new logic of events," a logic which deviates from the novel in several important respects. Tracing these mutations in some detail will illuminate the special characteristics of book and film alike. The question immediately arises, how could *The Grapes of Wrath* have gone on the screen so easily when the biological emphasis is nowhere present?

Undeniably, there is, in the novel, a concurrence of animal and human life similar to that which appears in the work of Walter Van Tilburg Clark, another western writer who transcends regional themes. Even from the opening of the chapter which depicts the pedestrian endurance of the turtle, creature and human are linked:

> The concrete highway was edged with a mat of tangled, broken, dry grass, and the grass heads were heavy with oat beards to catch on a dog's coat, and foxtails to tangle in a horse's fetlocks, and clover burrs to fasten in a sheep's wool; sleeping life waiting to be spread and dispersed, every seed armed with an appliance of dispersal, twisting darts and parachutes for the wind, little spears and balls of tiny thorns, and all waiting for animals and for the wind, for a man's trouser cuff or the hem of a woman's skirt, all passive but armed appliances of activity, still, but each possessed of the anlage of movement.

[7] Asheim, p. 161.

Here, the central motifs of the narrative are carefully, but inobtrusively enunciated, a kind of generalized analogue to the coming tribulations of the Joads: a harsh, natural order which is distracting to men and dogs alike; a hostile, dry passivity which, like the dormant blastema, is at the same time laden with regenerative possibilities. From the opening passages ("Gophers and ant lions started small avalanches . . .") to the last scene in which an attempt is made to beatify Rose of Sharon's biological act, the narrative is richly interspersed with literal and figurative zoology. Tom and Casy witness the unsuccessful efforts of a cat to stop the turtle's slow progress. In the deserted house, Muley describes himself as having once been "mean like a wolf," whereas now he is "mean like a weasel." Ma Joad describes the law's pursuit of Pretty Boy Floyd in animal terms: "they run him like a coyote, an' him a-snappin' an' a-snarlin', mean as a lobo." Young Al boasts that his Hudson jalopy will "ride like a bull calf." In the interchapter describing the change, the growing wrath triggered by the wholesale evictions of the tenant farmers, the western states are "nervous as horses before a thunder storm."

Later, Ma Joad savagely protests the break-up of the family: "All we got is the family unbroke. Like a bunch of cows, when the lobos are ranging." Later still, Tom tells Casy that the day he got out of prison, he ran himself down a prostitute "like she was a rabbit." Even the endless caravans of jalopies are described in terms which echo the plodding endurance of the turtle. After a night in which "the owls coasted overhead, and the coyotes gabbled in the distance, and into the camp skunks walked, looking for bits of food . . ." the morning comes, revealing the cars of migrants along the highway crawling out "like bugs." After the relatively peaceful interlude of the Government Camp, Al comments on the practice of periodically burning out the Hoovervilles where the dispossessed farmers are forced to cluster: ". . . they jus' go hide down in the willows an' then they come out an' build 'em another weed shack. Jus' like gophers." And finally, toward the end, Ma expresses her longing to have a settled home for Ruth and Winfield, the youngest children, in order to keep them from becoming wild animals. For by this time, Ruth and Winnie do, indeed, emerge from their beds "like hermit crabs from shells."

The presistence of this imagery reveals at least part of its service. In the first place, even in our random selections, biology supports and comments upon sociology. Sexual activity, the primacy of the family clan, the threat and utility of industrial machinery, the alienation and hostility of the law, the growing anger at economic oppression, the arguments for human dignity, are all accompanied by, or expressed in terms of, zoological images. In the second place, the presence of literal and figurative animals is more frequent when the oppression of the Joads is most severe. The pattern of the novel, as we shall see, is similar to a parabola whose highest point is the sequence at the Government Camp. From Chapter XXII to the middle of Chapter XXVI, which covers this interlude, the animal imagery is almost totally absent. Densely compacted at the beginning, when Tom returns to find his home a shambles, it recurs in the closing sequences of the strike-breaking and the flood.

The point is that none of this appears in the film. Even the highly cinematic passage depicting the slaughtering of the pigs, in preparation for the journey, is nowhere evident in the final editing. If the film adaptation remains at all faithful to its original, it is not in retaining what Edmund Wilson calls the constant substratum in Steinbeck's work. It is true, one may argue, that biological functions survive in the Joads' elementary fight for life, in the animal preoccupation with finding food and shelter, in the scenes of death and procreation, but this is not what Edmund Wilson has in mind. In the film, these functions are interwoven so closely with a number of other themes that in no sense can the biological preoccupation be said to have a primary value. This type of deletion could not have been arbitrary, for, as Vachel Lindsay showed as early as 1915, animal imagery can be used quite effectively as cinema. Reviewing Griffith's *The Avenging Conscience*, Lindsay is describing the meditations of a boy who has just been forced to say goodbye to his beloved, supposedly forever. Watching a spider in his web devour a fly, the boy meditates on the cruelty of nature: "Then he sees the ants in turn destroy the spider. The pictures are shown on so large a scale that the spiderweb fills the end of the theater. Then the ant-tragedy does the same. They can be classed as particularly apt hieroglyphics. . . ." [8] More recently, the killing of the animals by the boy in *Les Jeux Interdits* shows that biology can still effectively support cinematic themes. In the particular case of *The Grapes of Wrath*, however, the suggestions of the book were abandoned. If, then, we are to understand the mutation, to assess the film's special achievement, we must look elsewhere.

Immediately, a number of other motifs strongly assert themselves

[8] Vachel Lindsay, *The Art of the Moving Picture* (New York, 1915), p. 124.

in Steinbeck's novel: the juxtaposition of natural morality and religious hypocrisy; the love of the regenerative land; the primacy of the family; the dignity of human beings; the socio-political implications inherent in the conflict between individual work and industrial oppression. Consider Casy's impulsive rationalizations in the very early section of the book where he tries, like the Ancient Mariner, to convince his listener and himself at the same time, that his rejection of religious preaching in favor of a kind of naturalistic code of ethics is morally acceptable. Tortured by his sexual impulses as a preacher, Casy began to doubt and question the assumptions which he had been articulating from his rough, evangelical pulpit, began to observe the discrepancy between theoretical sin and factual behavior. He repeats his conclusions to Tom, "Maybe it ain't a sin. Maybe it's just the way folks is. Maybe we been whippin' hell out of ourselves for nothin'. . . . To hell with it! There ain't no sin and there ain't no virtue. There's just stuff people do. It's all part of the same thing. And some of the things folks do is nice, and some ain't nice, but that's as far as any man got a right to say."

Casy retains his love for people, but not through his ministry, and later this love will be transmuted into personal sacrifice and the solidarity of union organization. This suspicion of a theology not rooted in ordinary human needs continues to echo throughout the novel. When Casy refuses to pray for the dying Grampa, Granma reminds him, quite offhandedly, how Ruthie prayed when she was a little girl: " 'Now I lay me down to sleep. I pray the Lord my soul to keep. An' when she got there the cupboard was bare, an' so the poor dog got none.' " The moral is clear: in the face of hunger, religious piety seems absurd. After Grampa's death, the inclusion of a line from Scripture in the note that will follow him to his grave is parodied in much the same way, but Casy's last words at the grave echo his earlier statement: "This here ol' man jus' lived a life an' jus' died out of it. I don't know whether he was good or bad, but that don't matter much. He was alive, an' that's what matters. An' now he's dead, an' that don't matter. . . . if I was to pray, it'd be for the folks that don' know which way to turn." Ma Joad expresses the same kind of mystical acceptance of the life cycle when she tries to tell Rose of Sharon about the hurt of childbearing:

They's a time of change, an' when that comes, dyin' is a piece of all dyin', and bearin' is a piece of all bearin', and bearin' an' dyin' is two pieces of the same thing. An' then things ain't lonely any more. An' then a hurt

don't hurt so bad, 'cause it ain't a lonely hurt no more, Rose-asharn. I
wisht I could tell you so you'd know, but I can't.

Because Ma is so firm in her belief in the rightness of natural
processes, she becomes furious at the religious hypocrites who plague
the migrants. At the Hoovervilles and in the government station, the
evangelists whom Ma characterizes as Holy Rollers and Jehovites are
grimly present, like camp followers. Beginning with polite acceptance,
Ma becomes infuriated when one of these zealots works on Rose of
Sharon, scaring her half to death with visions of hellfire and burning.
Ma represents the state of natural grace to which Casy aspires from the
beginning.

Just as the novel reveals a preoccupation with biology, it is also
obsessed with love of the earth. From the opening lines of the book,
"To the red country and part of the gray country of Oklahoma, the
last rains came gently, and they did not cut the scarred earth," to the
last scene of desolation, the land imagery persists. The earth motif
is woven into the texture complexly, but on the whole it serves two
main functions: first, to signify love; and second, to signify endurance.
Tom makes the sexual connection when, listening to Casy's compul-
sive story, he idly, but quite naturally, draws the torso of a woman
in the dirt, "breasts, hips, pelvis." The attachment of the men for
the land is often so intense that it borders on sexual love. Muley's
refusal to leave, even after the caterpillar tractors have wiped him
out, looks ahead to Grampa's similar recalcitrance. At first, Grampa
is enthusiastic about the prospect of moving to a more fertile land,
and he delivers himself of words verging on panegyric: "Jus' let me get
out to California where I can pick me an orange when I want it. Or
grapes. There's a thing I ain't ever had enough of. Gonna get me a
whole big bunch a grapes off a bush, or whatever, an' I'm gonna
squash 'em on my face, an' let 'em run offen my chin." But when
the moment for departures arrives, Grampa refuses to go. His roots
in the ground are too strong; he cannot bear to tear them up. Very
soon after the family leaves its native soil, Grampa dies of a stroke.
And when Casy says to Noah, "Grampa an' the old place, they was jus'
the same thing," we feel that the observation has a precision which
is supported by the texture of the entire novel. When the Joads get
to California, they will, of course, find that the grapes which Grampa
dreamed of are inaccessible, that the grapes of promise inevitably turn
to grapes of wrath. The land, one interchapter tells, has been possessed
by the men with a frantic hunger for land who came before the Joads.

And the defeated promise is bitterly dramatized in the last scene, when a geranium, the last flower of earth to appear in the novel, becomes an issue dividing Ruthie and Winfield, and results in Ruthie's pressing one petal against Winfield's nose, cruelly. Love and endurance have been tried to their utmost. When the land goes, everything else goes, too; and the water is the emblem of its destruction.

Love of family parallels love of the earth. During the threatening instability of the cross-country journey, Ma Joad acts as the cohesive force which keeps her brood intact. Whenever one of the men threatens to leave, Ma protests, and sometimes savagely. When she takes over leadership of the family, by defying Pa Joad with a jack handle, it is over the question of whether or not Tom shall stay behind with the disabled car. Even after Connie, Rose of Sharon's husband, and Noah, one of the brothers, desert the family, the identity of the clan remains Ma Joad's primary fixation. After half a continent of hardship, Ma articulates her deepest feelings. She tells Tom, "They was a time when we was on the lan'. They was a boundary to us then. Ol' folks died off, an' little fellas came, an' we was always one thing —we was the fambly—kinda whole and clear. An' now we ain't clear no more." The deprivation of the native land, and the alienation of the new, become more than economic disasters; they threaten the only social organization upon which Ma Joad can depend. The fertility of the land and the integrity of the clan are no longer distinct entities; both are essential for survival.

Closely bound up with this theme of familial survival is the theme of human dignity. Clearly, the exigencies of eviction and migration force the problem of brute survival upon the Joads. But just as important is the correlative theme of human dignity. The first time the Joads are addressed as "Oakies," by a loud-mouthed deputy who sports a Sam Browne belt and pistol holster, Ma is so shocked that she almost attacks him. Later, Uncle John is so chagrined by Casy's sacrificial act (deflecting from Tom the blame for hitting the deputy, and going to prison in his stead) that he feels positively sinful for not making an equal contribution. At the Government Camp, a woman complains about taking charity from the Salvation Army because "We was hungry—they made us crawl for our dinner. They took our dignity." But it is Tom who makes the most articulate defense of dignity against the legal harassment to which the Joads have been subjected: ". . . if it was the law they was workin' with, why, we could take it. But it *ain't* the law. They're a-workin' away at our spirits. . . . They're

workin' on our decency." And the final image of Rose of Sharon offer-
ing her breast to the starving farmer is intended as an apotheosis of
the scared girl, recently deprived of her child, into a kind of natural
madonna.

In short, if the biological interest exists, it is so chastened through
suffering that it achieves a dignity which is anything but animal, in
Edmund Wilson's sense of the word. The conflicts, values, and recogni-
tions of the Joads cannot, therefore, be equated with the preoccupa-
tions of subhuman life. The biological life may be retained in the
search for food and shelter, in the cycle of death and procreation, but
always in terms which emphasize rather than obliterate the distinctions between humans and animals. When Steinbeck reminisces about
his carefree bohemian days in Monterey, he is just as nostalgic about
the freedom of assorted drifters, his "interesting and improbable"
characters, as he is about Ed Ricketts' "commercial biological laboratory." [9] Steinbeck's novel may be read, then, as much as a flight from
biological determinism as a representation of it. The story of the pilgrimage to the new Canaan which is California, the cycle of death and
birth through which the Joads must suffer, becomes a moral, as well
as a physical, trial by fire.

The socio-political implications of the Joad story, more familiar
than these correlative themes, serve to counterpoint and define the
anger and the suffering. Throughout the novel, the Joads are haunted
by deputies in the service of landowners, bankers, and fruit growers;
by the contradiction between endless acres in full harvest and streams
of migratory workers in dire straits; by unscrupulous businessmen
who take advantage of the desperate, westbound caravans; by strike-
breakers, corrupt politicians, and thugs. At first, the Joads must draw
from their meager savings to pay for gas and half-loaves of bread;
but as they draw West they must even pay for water. In California,
they cannot vote, are kept continually on the move, are bullied by
the constabulary, and must even watch helplessly as one of the
Hoovervilles is burned out. The only time they earn enough money
to eat comes when they are hired as strike-breakers. Gradually, there
is the dawning recognition that the only possible response to these
impossible conditions is solidarity through union organization, precisely what the fruit growers and their agents dread most. In order
to overcome the fruit growers' divisive tactics, Casy becomes an active

---

[9] John Steinbeck, "Dreams Piped from Cannery Row," *New York Times Theater
Section* (Sunday, November 27, 1955), p. 1.

union organizer and gets killed in the process by a bunch of maraud-
ing deputies. At the end, Tom, in his familiar farewell to Ma Joad,
is trembling on the verge of Casy's solution. "That the end will be
revolution," one reviewer writes, "is implicit from the title on-
wards." [10] Steinbeck ultimately withdraws from such a didactic conclusion, as we shall see in a moment, but that the didactic conclusion
is implicit in the narrative can hardly be denied:

> . . . the companies, the banks worked at their own doom and they did
> not know it. The fields were fruitful, and starving men moved on the
> roads. The granaries were full and the children of the poor grew up
> rachitic, and the pustules of pellagra swelled on their sides. The great
> companies did not know that the line between hunger and anger is a
> thin line. And money that might have gone to wages went for gas, for
> guns, for agents and spies, for blacklists, for drilling. On the highways
> the people moved like ants and searched for work, for food. And the
> anger began to ferment.

Hence the symbolism of the title. Clearly woven through the novel,
and therefore inseparable from Steinbeck's prose, we find these sharp
political overtones. Besides being a novel, writes one reviewer, *The
Grapes of Wrath* "is a monograph on rural sociology, a manual of
practical wisdom in times of enormous stress, an assault on individualism, an essay in behalf of a rather vague form of pantheism, and a
bitter, ironical attack on that emotional evangelistic religion which
seems to thrive in the more impoverished rural districts of this vast
country. . . ." [11]

Along the highways, a new social order is improvised, a fluid but
permanent council in which the family is the basic unit, an order
reaching its almost utopian operation at the Government Camp. According to this scheme, the governing laws remain constant, while
the specific counters are continually replaced, one family succeeding
another, a sort of permanent republic which can accommodate a
populace in constant motion:

> The families learned what rights must be observed—the right of privacy
> in the tent; the right to keep the past black hidden in the heart; the
> right to talk and to listen; the right to refuse help or to decline it; the
> right of son to court and daughter to be courted; the right of the hungry

[10] Earle Birney, "The Grapes of Wrath," *Canadian Forum*, xix (June, 1939), 95.
[11] James N. Vaughan, "The Grapes of Wrath," *Commonweal*, xxx (July 28, 1949),
341-342.

to be fed; the rights of the pregnant and the sick to transcend all other rights. . . .

And with the laws, the punishments—and there were only two—a quick and murderous fight or ostracism; and ostracism was the worst.

Within such a scheme, Ma Joad's fierce maintenance of the family becomes more clear. For without the integrity of the clan, survival is all but impossible. The alternatives are death, which does, in fact, snip the Joad family at both ends, claiming both the grandparents and Rose of Sharon's baby, or, on the other hand, militant struggle through union organization.

If the biological motifs do not appear in the film, these correlative themes are adopted with varying degrees of emphasis. The religious satire, with a single exception, is dropped entirely; the political radicalism is muted and generalized; but the insistence on family cohesion, on affinity for the land, on human dignity is carried over into the movie version.

In the film, the one remnant of tragi-comic religious satire occurs in Tom's first talk with Casy on the way to the Joad house. Casy's probing self-analysis is essentially the same as in the book, and its culmination, "There ain't no sin an' there ain't no virtue. There's just what people do," is a precise copy from the novel. Once the theme is enunciated, however, it is underplayed, recurring almost imperceptibly in the burial scene. Ma's anger at the evangelical camp followers is dropped entirely.

The film-makers must have known that the film was political dynamite. After a difficult decision, Darryl Zanuck began what turned out to be, thematically speaking, one of the boldest films in the history of the movies. The secrecy which surrounded the studios during production has become legend. Even as the film was being shot, Zanuck reportedly received 15,000 letters, 99 per cent of which accused him of cowardice, saying he would never make the film because the industry was too closely associated with big business.[12] And yet, fearful that the Texas and Oklahoma Chambers of Commerce would object to the shooting, on their territory, of the *enfant terrible* of the publishing world, the studio announced that it was really filming another story innocuously entitled, *Highway 66.*[13] It was precisely this fear of criticism, of giving offense to vested interests that was responsible for muting the film's political implications. Lester Asheim has pointed out

[12] Frank Condon, "The Grapes of Raps," *Collier's* (January 27, 1940), p. 67.
[13] *Ibid.*, p. 64.

how the film scrupulously steers clear of the book's specific accusations. Many small episodes showing unfair business practices, for example, were cut from the film version.[14] While the reference to the handbills which flood Oklahoma, luring an excess labor force out West, is carried over into the film, most of the corresponding details are dropped. The complaint about the unfair practices of used-car salesmen; the argument with the camp owner about overcharging; the depiction of the company-store credit racket; the dishonest scales on the fruit ranch; and even the practice, on the part of an otherwise sympathetic luncheon proprietor, of taking the jackpots from his own slot machines—none of these was ever even proposed for the shooting-script. Similarly, all legal authority is carefully exempt from blame. In Tom's angry speech about the indignities foisted upon the family by the local constabulary, everything is retained except his bitter indictment of the deputies, and his line, ". . . they comes a time when the on'y way a fella can keep his decency is by takin' a sock at a cop." [15] In Casy's discourse on the progress of the fruit strike, the line, "An' all the cops in the worl' come down on us" is deleted. Casy's announcement that the cops have threatened to beat up recalcitrant strikers is retained, but the film adds, "Not them reg'lar deputies, but them tin badge fellas they call guards. . . ."

In spite of the revolutionary candor of the interchapters, whenever the film raises questions about whom to see or what to do for recourse or complaint, the novel's evasive answers are used in reply. When Tom asks the proprietor of the Government Camp why there aren't more places like this, the proprietor answers, "You'll have to find that out for yourself." When Muley wants to find out from the City Man who's to blame for his eviction, so that he can take a shotgun to him, the City Man tells him that the Shawnee Land and Cattle Company is so amorphous that it cannot be properly located. The bank in Tulsa is responsible for telling the land company what to do, but the bank's manager is simply an employee trying to keep up with orders from the East. "Then who do we shoot?" Muley asks in exasperation. "Brother, I don't know . . ." the City Man answers helplessly. To add to the mystification, the film supplies a few clouds of its own. In the scene where Farmer Thomas warns Tom and the Wallaces about the impending raid on the Government Camp, the recurring question of "red" agitation comes up again. The "red menace" has

14 Asheim, p. 277.
15 *Ibid.*, p. 256.

become the *raison d'être* for attacks against the squatter camps. Tom, who has heard the argument before, bursts out, "What is these reds anyway?" Originally, according to the script, Wilkie Wallace was to have answered, cribbing his own line from the novel, that according to a fruit grower he knew once, a red is anyone who "wants thirty-cents an hour when I'm payin' twenty-five." In the final print, however, Farmer Thomas answers Tom's question simply but evasively, "I ain't talkin' about that one way 'r another," and goes on to warn the men about the raid.

Even Tom's much-quoted farewell to Ma Joad, retained in the film, is pruned until little remains but its mystical affirmation. And the final words, backing away from Casy's conscious social commitment, are carried over intact:

Ma. I don' un'erstan. . . .
Tom. Me neither, Ma. . . . It's jus' stuff I been thinkin' about. . . .

In the world of the Ford-Johnson film, the politico-economic tendency is merely an urge in search of a name it is never allowed to find. And yet because of the naked suffering, the brute struggle to survive, devoid of solutions in either church or revolution, John Gassner finds that more appropriate than the image of God "trampling out the vintage where the grapes of wrath are stored," from which the title is derived, are the lines, "And here in dust and dirt . . . the lilies of his love appear," [16] which connote neither religion nor politics. According to Gassner, bed-rock is reached in this film, "and it proves to be as hard as granite and as soft as down."

If the religious satire is absent and the politics muted, the love of land, family and human dignity are consistently translated into effective cinematic images. Behind the director's controlling hand is the documentary eye of a Pare Lorentz or a Robert Flaherty, of the vision in those stills produced by the Resettlement Administration in its volume, *Land of the Free* (with commentary by Archibald MacLeish), or in Walker Evans' shots for *Let Us Now Praise Famous Men* (with commentary by James Agee), which, like Lorentz's work, was carried on under the auspices of the Farm Security Administration. Gregg Toland's photography is acutely conscious of the pictorial values of land and sky, finding equivalents for those haunting images of erosion which were popularized for the New Deal's reclamation program and

[16] John Gassner, *Twenty Best Film Plays*, ed. John Gassner and Dudley Nichols (New York, 1943), p. xxvi.

reflected in Steinbeck's prose. The constant use of brooding, dark silhouettes against light, translucent skies, the shots of roads and farms, the fidelity to the speech, manners and dress of Oklahoma farmers—all contribute to the pictorial mood and tone. I am told that some of these exteriors were shot on indoor sound stages at the studios,[17] but even this has worked to the advantage of the film-makers. In the studio, Ford was able to control his composition by precise lighting, so that some of the visuals—Tom moving like an ant against a sky bright with luminous clouds, the caravans of jalopies, the slow rise of the dust storm—combine physical reality with careful composition to create striking pictorial effects. Finally, generous selections of dialogue, culled from the novel, echoing the theme of family affiliation with the land, appear in the final movie version. Grampa's last minute refusal to go, as he clutches at a handful of soil, necessitates Tom's plan to get him drunk and carry him aboard by force. And, as Muley, John Qualen's apostrophe to the land, after the tractor has ploughed into his shack, is one of the most poignant anywhere in films.

In the same fashion, the central episodes depicting Ma Joad's insistence on family cohesion, and Tom's insistence on dignity, are either presented directly or clearly suggested. Ma, to be sure, is made a little less fierce than she is in the novel. Tom still tells Casy the anecdote about Ma's taking after a tin peddler with an ax in one hand and a chicken in the other, but the scene in which she takes a jack handle after Pa, originally scheduled according to the script, is deleted. We never see Ma physically violent.

Tracing through these recurring themes, comparing and contrasting the emphasis given to each, gives us all the advantages of content analysis without explaining, finally, the central difference between Steinbeck's artistic vision and that of the film-makers. This difference does emerge, however, when we compare the two structures.

Some deletions, additions, and alterations, to be sure, reflect in a general way the ordinary process of mutation from a linguistic to a visual medium. On the one hand, the characteristic interchapters in the novel are dropped entirely, those interludes which adopt the author's point of view and which are at once more lyric and less realistic than the rest of the prose. The angry interludes, the explicit indictments, the authorial commentary do not appear, indeed would seem obtrusive, in the film. Translated into observed reality, however, and integrated into the picture within the frame, certain fragments

---

[17] In an interview with Mr. Ford.

find their proper filmic equivalents. For example, the interchapters are mined for significant dialogue, and, in fact, Muley's moving lines, "We were born on it, and we got killed on it, died on it. Even if it's no good, it's still ours. . . ." appear originally in one of these interludes. In the second place, the themes of one or two of these interchapters are translated into a few highly effective montages—the coming of the tractors, the caravans of jalopies, the highway signs along route 66. As Muley begins telling his story, over the candle in the dimly lit cabin, the film flashes back to the actual scene. A series of tractors looming up like mechanical creatures over the horizon, crossing and criss-crossing the furrowed land, cuts to the one tractor driven by the Davis boy, who has been assigned the task of clearing off Muley's farm. Later, as the Joads' jalopy begins its pilgrimage, we see a similar shot of scores and scores of other jalopies, superimposed one upon the other, making the same, slow, desperate cross-country trek. Finally, the central episodes of the trip are bridged by montages of road signs—"Checotah, Oklahoma City, Bethany," and so on to California. These devices have the effect of generalizing the conflicts of the Joads, of making them representative of typical problems in a much wider social context. In every reversal, in every act of oppression, we feel the pressure of thousands.

If the film carries these striking equivalents of Steinbeck's prose, it is partly due to the assistance which Steinbeck offers the film-maker, partly to the visual imagination of the film-maker himself. Except for the freewheeling omniscience of the interchapters, the novel's prose relies wholly on dialogue and physical action to reveal character. Because Steinbeck's style is not marked by meditation, it resembles, in this respect, the classic form of the scenario. Even at moments of highest tension, Steinbeck scrupulously avoids getting inside the minds of his people. Here is Ma right after Tom has left her, and probably forever:

> "Good-by" she said, and she walked quickly away. Her footsteps were loud and careless on the leaves as she went through the brush. And as she went, out of the dim sky the rain began to fall, big drops and few, splashing on the dry leaves heavily. Ma stopped and stood still in the dripping thicket. She turned about—took three steps back toward the mound of vines; and then she turned quickly and went back toward the boxcar camp.

Although this is Steinbeck's characteristic style, it can also serve as precise directions for the actor. There is nothing here which cannot be turned into images of physical reality. Critics who seem surprised at the ease with which Steinbeck's work moves from one medium to another may find their explanation here. Precisely this fidelity to physical detail was responsible, for example, for the success [of] *Of Mice and Men* first as a novel, then as a play, then as a film. And yet, in *The Grapes of Wrath*, the film-makers rethought the material for themselves, and frequently found more exact cinematic keys to the mood and color of particular scenes in the book. Often their additions are most effective in areas where the novel is powerless—in moments of silence. Casy jumping over a fence and tripping, after the boast about his former preaching prowess; Ma Joad burning her keepsakes (the little dog from the St. Louis Exposition, the old letters, the card from Pa); the earrings which she saves, holding them to her ears in the cracked mirror, while the sound track carries the muted theme from "Red River Valley"; the handkerchiefs which Tom and Casy hold to their mouths in the gathering dust; Tom laboriously adding an "s" to "funerl" in the note which will accompany Grampa to his grave; the reflection of Al, Tom, and Pa in the jalopy's windshield at night as the family moves through the hot, eery desert—all these, while they have no precedent in the novel, make for extraordinarily effective cinema. The images are clean and precise, the filmic signature of a consistent collaboration between John Ford and his cameraman.

The deletions, on one level, are sacrifices to the exigencies of time and plot. The dialogue is severely pruned. Most of the anecdotes are dropped, along with the curse words. And the leisurely, discursive pace of the novel gives way to a tightly knit sequence of events. The episodes involving the traveling companionship of the Wilsons; the desertions of Noah and Connie; the repeated warnings about the dismal conditions in California from bitterly disappointed migrants who are traveling home the other way; and countless other small events do not appear in the film story, though a few of them, like Noah's desertion, appeared in the script and were even shot during production. But the moment we go from an enumeration of these deletions to the arrangement of sequences in the final work, we have come to our central structural problem.

As I indicated earlier, the structure of the book resembles a parabola in which the high point is the successful thwarting of the riot at the Government Camp. Beginning with Tom's desolate return to his abandoned home, the narrative proceeds through the journey from

Oklahoma to California; the Hooverville episodes; the Government Camp episodes; the strike-breaking episodes at the Hooper Ranch; Tom's departure; the flooding of the cotton pickers' boxcar camp; the last scene in the abandoned farm. From the privation and dislocation of the earlier episodes, the Joads are continually plagued, threatened with dissolution, until, through the gradual knitting of strength and resistance, the family finds an identity which coincides with its experience at the Government Camp. Here they are startled by the sudden absence of everything from which they have been running— dirty living conditions, external compulsion, grubbing for survival, brutal policemen, unscrupulous merchants. They find, instead, a kind of miniature planned economy, efficiently run, boasting modern sanitation, self-government, co-operative living, and moderate prices. After their departure from the camp, the fortunes of the Joads progressively deteriorate, until that desolate ending which depicts Rose of Sharon's stillborn child floating downstream. The critical response to Steinbeck's shocking ending was almost universally negative. Clifton Fadiman called it the "tawdriest kind of fake symbolism." [18] Anthony West attributed it to the novel's "astonishingly awkward" form.[19] Louis Kronenberger found that the entire second half of the book "lacks form and intensity . . . ceases to grow, to maintain direction," [20] but did not locate the reasons for his dissatisfaction. Malcolm Cowley, in spite of general enthusiasm, found the second half less impressive than the first because Steinbeck "wants to argue as if he weren't quite sure of himself." [21] Charles Angoff was one of a small minority who defended both the ending and the "robust looseness" of the novel as squarely in the narrative tradition of Melville, Cervantes and Thomas Hardy.[22]

Contrast these objections with the general approval of the film's structure. Thomas Burton becomes adulatory over Ford's "incessant physical intimacy and fluency." [23] Otis Ferguson speaks in superla-

[18] Clifton Fadiman, "Highway 66—A Tale of Five Cities," *New Yorker*, xv (April 15, 1939), 81.

[19] Anthony West, "The Grapes of Wrath," *New Statesman and Nations*, xviii (September 16, 1939), 404–405.

[20] Louis Kronenberger, "Hungry Caravan: The Grapes of Wrath," *Nation*, cxlviii (April 15, 1939), 441.

[21] Malcolm Cowley, "American Tragedy," *New Republic*, xcviii (May 3, 1939), 382.

[22] Charles Angoff, "In the Great Tradition," *North American Review*, ccxlvii (Summer, 1939), 387.

[23] Thomas Burton, "Wine from These Grapes," *Saturday Review of Literature*, xxi (February 10, 1940), 16.

tives: "this is a best that has no very near comparison to date. . . . It all moves with the simplicity and perfection of a wheel across silk." [24] Why did the film-makers merit such a sharply contrasting critical reception? Simply because they corrected the objectionable structure of the novel. First, they deleted the final sequence; and second they accomplished one of the most remarkable narrative switches in film history. Instead of ending with the strike-breaking episodes in which Tom is clubbed, Casy killed, and the strikers routed, the film ends with the Government Camp interlude. This reversal, effected with almost surgical simplicity, accomplishes, in its metamorphic power, an entirely new structure which has far-reaching consequences. Combined with the deletion of the last dismal episode, and the pruning, alterations, and selections we have already traced, the new order changes the parabolic structure to a straight line that continually ascends. Beginning with the desolate scene of the dust storm, the weather in the film improves steadily with the fortunes of the Joads, until, at the end, the jalopy leaves the Government Camp in sunlight and exuberant triumph. Even a sign, called for in the original script, which might have darkened the rosy optimism that surrounds the departing buggy, does not appear in the cut version. The sign was to have read, "No Help Wanted." As in the novel, Tom's departure is delayed until the end, but the new sequence of events endows his farewell speech with much more positive overtones. In place of the original ending, we find a line that appears at the end of Chapter XX, exactly two-thirds of the way through the book. It is Ma's strong assurance, "We'll go on forever, Pa. We're the people." On a thematic level, as Asheim points out, the affirmative ending implies that action is not required since the victims of the situation will automatically emerge triumphant. "Thus the book, which is an exhortation to action, becomes a film which offers reassurance that no action is required to insure the desired resolution of the issue." [25] But the film's conclusion has the advantage of seeming structurally more acceptable. Its "new logic" affords a continuous movement which, like a projectile, carries everything before it. The movie solution satisfies expectations which are there in the novel to begin with and which the novel's ending does not satisfactorily fulfill. Hence the critics' conflicting reaction to the two endings. Where the book seems to stop

[24] Otis Ferguson, "Show for the People," *New Republic*, CII (February 12, 1940), 212.
[25] Asheim, p. 157.

and meander in California, the film displays a forward propulsion that carries well on beyond the Colorado River.

Is such an inversion justified? Nunnally Johnson reports that he chose Ma's speech for his curtain line because he considered it the "real" spirit of Steinbeck's book.[26] This might seem at first like brazen tampering. But Johnson further reports that from Steinbeck himself he received *carte blanche* to make any alterations he wished. Steinbeck defended his position on the grounds that a novelist's final statement is in his book. Since the novelist can add nothing more, the film-maker is obliged to remake the work in his own style. If Steinbeck's awareness of the adaptational process is not enough, we may also find internal justification for the film-makers' brilliantly simple reversal. We have seen how the production crew effected alterations which mute the villainy of cops and tradesmen; underplay the religious satire; cloud over the novel's political radicalism. But part of this withdrawal has precedent in the novel itself. The city man's portrayal of the anonymity of the banks; the proprietor's evasive answer to Tom in the Government Camp; Ma and Tom's mystical faith—these are all Steinbeck's. So is the fact that from the beginning Tom is on parole, which he technically breaks by leaving the state. Already he is outside the domain of legal ordinance. Tom is a fugitive who *has* to keep running. If the film's conclusion withdraws from a leftist commitment, it is because the novel does also. If the film vaporizes radical sociology, the novel withdraws from it, too, with Rose of Sharon's final act. The familial optimism of the one and the biological pessimism of the other are two sides of the same coin.

The structural achievement of the cinematic version may account, paradoxically, for the film's troubling reputation. On the one hand, acclamation, box-office success, critical enthusiasm; Jane Darwell winning an Academy Award for her portrayal of Ma Joad; the casting and acting of Henry Fonda, John Carradine, Charlie Grapewin, John Qualen, Frank Darien, Grant Mitchell, and the others, generally considered flawless; Nunnally Johnson sporting a gold plaque on the wall of his studio office in recognition of a fine screenplay; and one reporter poking fun at the grandiose premiere of the film at the Normandie Theater in New York, which was attended by glamorous stars adorned in jewels and furs, and, like a "Blue Book pilgrimage," [27] by the representatives of the very banks and land companies that had

[26] In an interview with the author.
[27] Michael Mok, "Slumming with Zanuck," *Nation*, CL (February 3, 1940), 127–28.

tractored the Joads off their farms. Zanuck and his entourage must have known that the filmic portrait of Steinbeck's book was no serious threat.

On the other hand, the industry's discomfort. *The Grapes of Wrath* came as close as any film in Hollywood's prolific turnout to exposing the contradictions and inequities at the heart of American life. A new thing had been created and its implications were frightening. In spite of its facile conclusion, the film raises questions to which others, outside the fictive world, have had to supply answers. The film's unusual cinematographic accomplishments, its structural unity, its documentary realism, combine to fashion images, embodying those questions, which one may review with profit again and again. If the novel is remembered for its moral anger, the film is remembered for its beauty. And yet the industry has been a little embarrassed by its success. That success and that embarrassment may help explain why Nunnally Johnson has accomplished so little of lasting interest since his work on this film, and why he was last seen completing the scenario for Sloan Wilson's *The Man in the Gray Flannel Suit,* a book of a very different kind! It may explain why John Ford never lists *The Grapes* as one of his favorite films, and why Ford himself offers perhaps the best explanation for the film's unique personality. Tersely, but with just the slightest trace of whimsy and bravado, John Ford remarks, "I never read the book." [28]

[28] In an interview with the author.

Sea of Cortez

by Joseph Fontenrose

Sometime in the late thirties Steinbeck became a partner in Pacific Biological Laboratories, an impressive name for Ed Ricketts' inefficiently managed commercial laboratory, which offered to supply institutions with marine and terrestrial animals of all kinds, alive or preserved, "as strange an operation as ever outraged the corporate laws of California," said Steinbeck after the death of Ricketts in 1948. Ordinarily Ricketts earned enough to maintain himself in the free and solitary life that he relished; he had few wants, few responsibilities, and lived comfortably on an income a shade above subsistence level. But after he became heavily in debt to the bank and was paying out so much in interest that he was faced with bankruptcy, Steinbeck took up the bank loans, "lowered the interest to a vanishing point," and in return received stock in the corporation and a mortgage on the establishment.

Thus, in a sense, Steinbeck became an active biologist. As Ricketts' partner he took a genuine interest in the laboratory's work and, when he had time, participated in it, always, like Ricketts, more interested in the work itself and the knowledge acquired than in prospective profits. Late in 1939, the year in which Ricketts and Calvin published *Between Pacific Tides,* Steinbeck and Ricketts explored marine life on the coast north of San Francisco. Immediately thereafter they planned a scientific trip to the Gulf of California in order "to collect and preserve the marine invertebrates of the littoral . . . to observe the distribution of invertebrates, to see and to record their kinds and numbers, how they lived together, what they ate, and how they reproduced." They engaged a small boat, the "Western Flyer," for a six-week period, got permits from the Mexican government, and sailed

"Sea of Cortez." From *John Steinbeck: An Introduction and Interpretation* by Joseph Fontenrose (New York: Holt, Rinehart and Winston, Inc., 1963), pp. 84–97. Copyright © 1963 by Holt, Rinehart and Winston, Inc. Reprinted by permission of the publisher.

from Monterey on March 11, 1940, returning on April 20. They were in the Gulf, collecting on its shores every day, with two or three exceptions, from March 17 to April 12. Working hard and fast, they collected a great number of marine animals and did not confine themselves strictly to invertebrates. Besides Steinbeck and Ricketts the "Western Flyer" carried its owner, Tony Berry, Tex the engineer, and two seamen, Tiny Colletto and Sparky Enea, Monterey fishermen, who were signed on to steer, cook, fish, and do anything else that needed doing—they even helped collect specimens.

Soon after the "Western Flyer" returned to Monterey on April 20, Steinbeck went back to Mexico, going this time to Mexico City and its vicinity, to help produce the movie *The Forgotten Village*, for which he wrote the script, published in 1941. Then from January to August of 1941 he worked on the manuscript of *Sea of Cortez*, which was published in December. Unless one counts the film script *A Medal for Benny* (published in 1946), this is the only book on which Steinbeck had a collaborator. In fact, Steinbeck wrote the first part, the narrative of the trip—published separately in 1951 as *The Log from the Sea of Cortez*—and Ricketts wrote the second part, a phyletic catalogue. But both men had kept journals during the trip, and Steinbeck drew material for the narrative from Ricketts' journal.

From Cape San Lucas, the southern tip of Lower California, the party moved up the west shore of the Gulf of California to Angeles Bay, and then rounding Angel de la Guardia Island crossed the Gulf to Puerto San Carlos and explored the east shore southwards to Agiabampo Estuary. They stopped at twenty-one collecting stations. The *Log* makes pleasant reading: scientific notes, observations on the animals collected, are mingled with travelogue, philosophy, and *obiter dicta* on all sorts of topics. It is written *con gusto;* it is lively, vivid, and entertaining. We enter into the rhythm of the days, the hard work of collecting, preparing, and storing the specimens, the cruising in Gulf waters, the relaxing on deck after work, the conversations and beer-drinking (beer is almost as important to the *Log* as are the marine invertebrates), the meals and sleep, the visits to Mexican towns. Incidents are given humorous turns. Memorable passages are the accounts of the outboard motor called the Hansen Sea-Cow ("not only a living thing but a mean, irritable, contemptible, vengeful, mischievous, hateful living thing"), the *cantina* at San Lucas, the youth who found the great pearl, the Mexican boys who guided and helped the collecting party. Reminiscent of Norman Douglas' account

(*Siren Land*) of a chicken caught for dinner in a village above Sorrento
is the tale of catching chickens purchased from a woman in La Paz: on
this occasion too the chickens skillfully evaded capture, everybody in
town joined in the chase, and the birds, when finally caught, were
already about plucked.

Although Steinbeck reveals little about himself and Ricketts, aside
from their thoughts, he tells us a good deal about the behavior and
idiosyncrasies of the other four men. We get to know Tony, Tex,
Tiny, and Sparky very well—especially Tiny and Sparky, Italian-
American fishermen and rounders of Monterey, *paesani* rather like
Steinbeck's *paisanos*, men of appetites and humor. And Steinbeck,
who felt at home among the Latin residents of Monterey, Spanish-
Mexican and Italian, was bound to appreciate the people of Mexico,
who have successfully blended Latin and native American cultures.
In *Sea of Cortez* he tells about several encounters with the natives of
Baja California and the opposite coast. Many are illiterate, he says,
and they may be often hungry; they have no physicians and dentists
to relieve their aches and pains; but they have a genuine humanity
that in many more civilized persons has been smothered beneath
blankets of artificial wants, absurd values, and false *personae*. The
Mexican Indians whom they met were outgoing in a wholesome way,
truly interested in their visitors, and always courteous. They con-
firmed Steinbeck's doctrine, preached now for a decade, that money
and possessions poison human relations if they are lifted above human
values.

Nearly every chapter can be divided into two parts, narrative of
events and reflections upon them. The first chapter, about organizing
the expedition, contains a paragraph on man's "atavistic urge toward
danger . . . [whose] satisfaction is called adventure." The second
chapter leaps at once from boats to man's atavistic attraction to boats,
which is so strong that no man can destroy a boat without feeling
guilty of murder; and so Steinbeck turns to reflections on murder as
a "diagnostic trait" of the human species (we may feel guilty afterwards, but we do have a habit of murdering both men and boats).
Chapter 4 tells about leaving Monterey and going out of the bay into
the open Pacific; and again atavism comes into the picture: we are
treated to a discourse on "sea-memory, or sea-thought, which lives
deep in the mind," inherited from the time when all life was in the
sea, and harboring such persistent fantasies as the Old Man of the
Sea and the sea serpent. In Chapter 10 the run from Cape San Lucas to

Pulmo Reef provokes remarks on scientists and their human limitations, and that subject leads to remarks on the time sense, and that to mutations in man. Chapter 14, the longest, begins with collecting on San José Island on Easter Sunday, March 24; a page of narrative is followed by the "Easter sermon" on non-teleological thinking, the philosophical center of the book. So with other chapters.

Obviously *Sea of Cortez* cannot be underestimated as a statement of Steinbeck's point of view, the interpretation of man and society which he expressed in his novels of the thirties and forties. As Lisca has remarked, *Sea of Cortez* stands in the same relation to Steinbeck's fiction as does *Death in the Afternoon* to Hemingway's. In his biological work we see exposed the biological root of his fictional message. His novels had already made plain that his organismic theory of groups owed more to biology than to political theory, in which during the nineteenth century the organismic theory of state or society had considerable vogue. Almost without exception the theorists had the human animal in mind, looking upon state or society as a compound man. This statement is even true of Herbert Spencer, who, being learned in biology, drew arguments and analogies from lower forms of life to support his organismic theory of society. Before Steinbeck, only William McDougall in *The Group Mind* (1920) appears to have extended the conception to every sort of human group—family, mob, corporation, town, as well as state and national society. The young Steinbeck read Spencer and McDougall; but the book which contributed most to his final organismic theory was W. C. Allee's *Animal Aggregations* (1931). Yet we have noticed that Steinbeck's earliest novels show rudiments of the collective animal. Whether Steinbeck found support in Allee's book for his own conclusions or was stimulated by Allee to further study of aggregations, his organismic theory owes more to actual observations—his own and Ricketts'—than to books. In *Sea of Cortez* he points to the kind of organism that he means when he says that a human group is a single organism: it is the colonial animal like the pelagic tunicate:

> There are colonies of pelagic tunicates which have taken a shape like the finger of a glove. Each member of the colony is an individual animal, but the colony is another individual animal, not at all like the sum of its individuals. Some of the colonists, girdling the open end, have developed the ability, one against the other, of making a pulsing movement very like muscular action. Others of the colonists collect the food and distribute it, and the outside of the glove is hardened and protected against

contact. Here are two animals, and yet the same thing . . . So a man of individualistic reason, if he must ask, "Which is the animal, the colony or the individual?" must abandon his particular kind of reason and say, "Why, it's two animals and they aren't alike any more than the cells of my body are like me. I am much more than the sum of my cells and, for all I know, they are much more than the division of me."

The first sentence of the individualistic reasoner's answer to his own question is very like a statement of Doc Burton's in *In Dubious Battle*. So not the human being, but the tunicate or sea whip or sponge serves as model for the human group organism. Steinbeck was later to say in *The Pearl* that "A town is a thing like a colonial animal."

The precise biologist may point out that human groups hardly fit the class of aggregation in which Allee puts tunicates, since the individual animals of the colony are contiguous. But to Steinbeck, as to Herbert Spencer, contiguity of parts matters little: he sees the same phenomenon in schools of fish, where the individuals are not in mutual contact. In speaking of the schools he extends the conception from organized groups to whole species, to ecological communities, to all life:

> The schools swam, marshaled and patrolled. They turned as a unit and dived as a unit. In their millions they followed a pattern minute as to direction and depth and speed. There must be some fallacy in our thinking of these fish as individuals. Their functions in the school are in some as yet unknown way as controlled as though the school were one unit. We cannot conceive of this intricacy until we are able to think of the school as an animal itself, reacting with all its cells to stimuli which perhaps might not influence one fish at all. And this larger animal, the school, seems to have a nature and drive and ends of its own. It is more than and different from the sum of its units. . . . In the little Bay of San Carlos, where they were many schools of a number of species, . . . [we perceived] a larger unit which was the interrelation of species with their interdependence for food, even though that food be each other. A smoothly working larger animal surviving within itself—larval shrimp to little fish to larger fish to giant fish—one operating mechanism. And perhaps *this* unit of survival may key into the larger animal which is the life of all the sea, and this into the larger of the world.

And so the state or national society as a single animal is but an organ of a larger single animal, the human species, and that in turn is an organ of the single animal which is the biosphere. And that is not all; the whole world is a single organism:

. . . species are only commas in a sentence, . . . each species is at once
the point and the base of a pyramid . . . And then not only the meaning but the feeling about species grows misty. One merges into another,
groups melt into ecological groups until the time when what we know as
life meets and enters what we think of as non-life: barnacle and rock,
rock and earth, earth and tree, tree and rain and air. And the units nestle
into the whole and are inseparable from it.

Here is the Oversoul (to which Steinbeck alludes in the "Easter sermon"), and here is the great chain of being. Steinbeck's statement is
near to Leibniz':

> Thus men are linked with the animals, these with the plants and these
> with the fossils, which in turn merge with those bodies which our senses
> and our imagination represent to us as absolutely inanimate. . . . it is
> necessary that all the orders of natural beings form but a single chain, in
> which the various classes, like so many rings, are so closely linked one to
> another that it is impossible for the senses or the imagination to deter-
> mine precisely the point at which one ends and the next begins—all the
> species which, so to say, lie near to or upon the borderlands being equiv-
> ocal, and endowed with characters which might equally well be assigned
> to either of the neighboring species. (Lovejoy's translation.)

Steinbeck is certainly Leibnizian when he says that life "is a unified
field of reality" in which "everything is an index of everything else."
The "feeling we call religious," says Steinbeck, is "the attempt to say
that man is related to the whole thing."

In these higher pantheistic and panpsychic reaches we leave biology
behind. Although his biological studies of animal aggregations shaped
Steinbeck's organismic theory of the human group, biological science
does not really support it; that is, all the evidence that he adduces
can be, and is, explained otherwise. Steinbeck himself designates all
such speculation as "It might be so." Since in *To a God Unknown* he
had already stated through Joseph Wayne the central idea expressed
in the foregoing quotations, it is probable that his belief in the unity
of all being was prior to his formulation of the group-organism theory
as a special application of it. It may be that his reading of Emerson
and Emerson's Romantic predecessors first turned his mind in this
direction. For the organic view of the world is a distinctive and fundamental feature of Romantic thought. The Romantics, revolting against
mechanistic and formistic ideas, turned to the world of living things
for a cosmic pattern. They likened the world to a living animal or
plant, as Morse Peckham has shown: "[The metaphor] is a tree, for

example; and a tree is a good example," being an image that they used often. The interrelation of a tree's component parts is that "of leaves to stem to trunk to root to earth. Entities are an organic part of that which produced them. The existence of each part is made possible only by the existence of every other part."

Steinbeck has much in common with the Romantics. He is usually classed as a realist or naturalist, but these are mere labels, and they hardly suit *To a God Unknown* and *Tortilla Flat*. Moreover, Irving Babbitt the anti-Romantic and Jacques Barzun the pro-Romantic agree on one thing, that realism springs from Romanticism. But in a deeper sense than that, Steinbeck is an heir of the Romantic movement. The organic view of the world renews primitive animism at a more sophisticated level. To the animist, sky and earth, wind and storm, tree and rock are living entities. Out of animism springs myth, and so Steinbeck's biological interpretation and his mythical interpretation of the human condition flow from one and the same source.

In his discourse on the schools Steinbeck recurs to the idea expressed in *In Dubious Battle* that an individual may be a special organ of the group animal:

> . . . we suspect that when the school is studied as an animal . . . , it will be found that certain units are assigned special functions to perform; that weaker or slower units may even take their places as placating food for the predators for the sake of the security of the school as an animal. . . . There would seem to be only one commandment for living things: Survive! And the forms and species and units and groups are armed for survival, fanged for survival, timid for it, fierce for it, clever for it, poisonous for it, intelligent for it. This commandment decrees the death and destruction of myriads of individuals for the survival of the whole.

One function of the individual unit, then, is to die for the good of the whole. Here and elsewhere Steinbeck asserts that the relation of predator to prey is mutually beneficial: in Norway, it seems, the hawks were doing the willow grouse a good turn by preying on them, killing those slow-moving grouse infected with a parasitic disease and thus preventing the spread of the disease to healthy birds. This leads to the conclusion, and Steinbeck does not hesitate to draw it, that no individual's death matters at all, since it is necessary for the survival of the species; the commandment "Survive" is directed to the collective beings. For "to the whole, there is no waste. The great organism, Life, takes it all and uses it all. . . . Nothing is wasted; 'no star is lost.' " Even human sacrifice can be rationalized:

Sometimes one has a feeling of fullness, of warm wholeness, wherein every sight and object and odor and experience seems to key into a gigantic whole. . . . Perhaps among primitive peoples the human sacrifice has the same effect of creating a wholeness of sense and emotion—the good and bad, beautiful, ugly, and cruel all welded into one thing. Perhaps a whole man needs this balance.

Thus natural selection and sacrament have the same meaning, and magic is truly the forerunner of science. The sacrifices of Joseph Wayne, Jim Nolan, and Jim Casy expressed an at-one-ment with the universe.

To the panthesist the world must be exactly as it is, and everything has its place—cruelty, pain, crime, death. To the biological pantheist the universe is one great ecological community: every unit has its niche and is related to every other unit. In such a world blame is out of the question; we cannot even speak of causes, because everything is just what it is, and every fact "[is] so because it's so." This is what Steinbeck means by non-teleological thinking. Was it by design that Steinbeck and Ricketts "discussed intellectual methods and approaches" as they collected on Easter Sunday? At any rate this was one day among others. They rejected what they called teleology, thinking in terms of cause-effect and end patterns, since, they held, this kind of thinking is both superficial and fallacious, prone to the *post hoc, ergo propter hoc* error. The teleologist asks "Why?" and is easily satisfied with an answer that assigns a cause. The non-teleologist asks, not "Why?" but "How?" and "What?" (can he really answer "What?" more easily than "Why?"). He is not satisfied until he has seen the whole picture, which, of course, he never can see completely. Steinbeck calls it " 'is' thinking," a tough-minded, statistical, relational way of dealing with phenomena, which brings a deeper understanding and acceptance. The key word here is "acceptance": action for change may be indicated when all conditions of a problem have been discovered, as when a physician correctly prescribes after making a correct diagnosis; but in general one will be satisfied with things as they are, having understood. To take Steinbeck's preliminary example: what does one do about unemployment (as it still stood in America in 1930–40)? Nothing, apparently, since the non-teleological investigator, looking at conditions "as is," would discover that there were jobs for only seventy per cent of the labor force. Today we would say that the non-teleologist was as easily satisfied that he had seen the whole picture as was the teleologist that he had found the cause.

Of course, there is some soundness in Steinbeck's position. The critique of causality has a history two centuries old. And it is true that cause has sometimes meant blame: Greek *aitia* (first element in *aetiology*), for instance, has both meanings. The fact remains that Steinbeck and Ricketts set up a straw man. The "teleological" answers which they give to the model questions (e.g., "Why are some men taller than others?") are superficial, and yet they put these answers on the same level with the cause-effect sequences of physics. They have confused final causes, against which their case is good, with efficient causes, which we cannot eliminate from our thinking (nor did they). Physicists are as well aware as they of statistical methods and continuous processes, but physicists properly apply the term "cause" to that event or operation which must take place before another can. Whether we say "outgrowth" with Steinbeck or "result" with most scientists makes no difference. As for blame-thinking, Isaiah Berlin (in *Historical Inevitability*) has attacked the search for causality in history on the ground that it does not let us blame the malefactors of history.

Nothing would seem more rationalistic and non-religious than this positivistic philosophy, and yet it is purposely placed in the chapter concerned with the events of Easter Sunday. Non-teleology is a new gospel, properly proclaimed upon this day; it is "the 'new thing,' the Hegelian 'Christ-child'" (although Christmas would seem the more appropriate occasion for that). Steinbeck compares it "to the triangle, to the Christian ideas of trinity, to Hegel's dialectic, and to Swedenborg's metaphysic of divine love (feeling) and divine wisdom (thinking)." It amounts to a grand reconciliation: everybody—Jesus, Francis, Darwin, Einstein—has been saying the same thing in different vocabularies.

The ideas expressed in *Sea of Cortez*, although receiving complete articulation and formulation here for the first time, underlie all Steinbeck's novels of the thirties. *To a God Unknown* obviously expresses the same panpsychic view of the world: Joseph Wayne could have made the statement which Steinbeck attributes to an imaginary Gulf Indian: ". . . I am the whole thing, . . . I ought to know when I will rain." So does *The Grapes of Wrath* in Jim Casy's one big soul of which everybody is a part.

Stanley Hyman and other critics have seen a change in Steinbeck's social thinking from a kind of agrarian socialism in *The Grapes of Wrath* to an antisocial individualism in *Sea of Cortez*, in which he expresses a social Darwinism which Herbert Spencer would have heartily approved. He makes such statements as that a reservoir of unemployed is inevitable; that war is a diagnostic trait of human beings; that pain, sorrow, disease, hunger, are necessary conditioning factors, to keep us tough and prevent our becoming an easy prey to the stronger; that hope is illusory, a diagnostic trait useful only as a "therapeutic poultice" or shock-absorber, and the principal source of "iron teleologies." Again, man's present mutation, says Steinbeck, appears to be in the direction of greater collectivism and "there is no reason to suppose . . . [that this mutation] is for the better." For a collective state, like that of the Incas, becomes soft and corrupt: the aggressive, warlike Spaniards destroyed the Inca empire. Steinbeck may hedge a bit with an "It might be so" or a "viewing-point man" but this revised Spencerism is apparently the view which he accepts in *Sea of Cortez* as something like "the whole picture."

There is really no change in his views, for such convictions as these were expressed in his novels of the thirties. For example, Doc Burton of *In Dubious Battle* saw labor troubles, unemployment, and wars as afflictions and drives of the group animal. Doc Burton is Ed Ricketts, and his doctrine dominates *Sea of Cortez:* "When it seems that men may be kinder to men, that wars may not come again, we completely ignore the record of our species." In 1940 men were engaged in a war that nobody wanted (not even Hitler, it seems), says Steinbeck, any yet they had it, "a zombie war of sleep-walkers which nevertheless goes on out of all control of intelligence." As Doc Burton said, individual men formulate reasons and purposes for going to war, but the group animal merely wants war, and there is nothing that individual men can do about it. So these non-teleologists, telling us to look at the whole picture, to see what actually "is," direct us to the behavior of group organisms which are all part of the one world organism. We might suppose that we should study economic conditions, historical backgrounds, governmental policies, in order to arrive at the whole picture. But no, we must not "place the blame for killing and destroying on economic insecurity, on inequality, on injustice, . . ." In a somewhat dubious fashion, studying socio-economic conditions of war has become blaming them, and the living actions, decisions, oppressions, become three abstractions that can be dismissed at once. One begins to suspect that "the whole picture" is preconceived.

Steinbeck's non-teleological speculations are the foundation of his social Darwinism, organismic theory, and chain of being (the last in

striking agreement with Leibniz, whose philosophy is thoroughly teleological). These are uneasy bedfellows, since social Darwinism favors
aggression, go-getting, business success, heaping up of riches; whereas
the organismic and panpsychic ideas look toward cooperation, harmony, and the family virtues—there are reprehensible groups, but,
like bad individuals, they are out of tune. Hence Steinbeck finds an
ethical paradox, to which he recurs in *Cannery Row:* that though we
profess love "of wisdom, tolerance, kindliness, generosity, humility,"
and hate "of cruelty, greed, self-interest, graspingness, and rapacity,"
yet the approved "good qualities are invariable concomitants of failure, while the bad ones are the cornerstones of success." Men, he continues, secretly admire the bad qualities which bring success and
riches, and though they regard Jesus, Augustine, and Socrates with
love, they "would rather be successful than good." So if a biologist
objectively observed these phenomena in another species, he "would
replace the term 'good' with 'weak survival quotient' and the term
'bad' with 'strong survival quotient.'" Here Steinbeck puts his finger
on a conflict of moralities in our civilization, but he has lapsed into
the social-Darwinistic equation of survival with success in economic
competition (and overlooked the present reality, that competition no
longer accurately describes the economy), which means the acquisi-
tion of that property and wealth which cut one off from the "we."
Nevertheless, all the heroes of his novels for a decade illustrated the
good qualities of friendliness, generosity, humility (though not always honesty): his paisanos are healthy when they have nothing to
do with the values of property and business success and go into decline as soon as they acquire property. His point had been that these
values did not matter and that no real success was won in realizing
them. So he appears to express inconsistent views about viable qualities: the ruthless wealth-seeker has a "strong survival quotient," and
the poor but honest man has a healthier and more satisfactory way
of life. Steinbeck attempts to reconcile these views by pointing to a
"routine of changing domination." The successful rich become soft
in security and are replaced by men who had become strong in adversity; then the new dominants become soft in their turn. In *The
Grapes of Wrath,* Ma Joad told Tom that hardships make the people
tough: "Rich fellas come up an' they die, an' their kids ain't no good,
an' they die out. But, Tom, we keep a-comin'." And in interchapters
of that novel Steinbeck shows that property and too great security
have corrupted the owners, making them soft or dehumanizing them,

whereas the pickers gain strength in adversity. But the point of the dominance-cycle theory is that success, survival, is gained through the bad qualities which are its concomitants. That is, the unsuccessful good men, toughened by hardships, adopt the bad aggressive qualities and win. The Joads, however, moved in precisely the opposite direction, towards greater friendliness and generosity; for their contingent success lay in the direction of greater cooperation and union with other men. The truth is that Steinbeck (and Ricketts) did not think the question through. With his natural selection in human affairs and his group organism he had stopped with Herbert Spencer, who died in 1903.

Steinbeck's "agrarian socialism" is really Chestertonian Distributivism, a society of small-scale farmers working their own plots. First, the men who want land must be given some; second, the present owners must realize this or go under. In *The Grapes of Wrath* Steinbeck lectures the owners: "If you who own the things people must have could understand this, you might preserve yourself. . . . For the quality of owning freezes you forever into 'I,' and cuts you off forever from the 'we.'" That is, they do not recognize their human and cosmic identity, are no longer in harmony with nature, and are therefore vulnerable. Aroused by the migrants' problems, Steinbeck expressed his characteristic views in social terms and envisaged a cooperative society based on small landholdings. Despite this, the vision was fitful; *In Dubious Battle* and *The Grapes of Wrath* waver between optimism and doubt and end without coming to a conclusion. Shortly afterwards in the Gulf of California, as Steinbeck repeatedly tells us, world and national affairs became remote. A world war was going on, and the collecting party hardly gave it a thought.

With Chesterton I believe that the most important thing about a man is his view of the world, and when we know Steinbeck's philosophy the meaning of his novels becomes clearer. And since it is an inadequate philosophy for a novelist, the central theses of his novels are not likely to carry complete conviction, whatever his narrative and poetic skill. Here is the big fault. Great as Steinbeck's novels of the thirties are, and they are truly great, they fall short of eminence, simply because Steinbeck lacked a genuine theory of society; for the group organism will not do. He was constantly trying to put man in relation to the universe instead of to his fellows, like the Akkadian mythmaker who started from creation in order to define toothache's place in the world. One might almost say that Steinbeck's characters do not have social relations; certainly they do not have them as do the characters of Henry James, Dickens, George Eliot, Stendhal, or Faulkner.

One can learn something about marine zoology from Steinbeck's *Log* as well as from Ricketts' phyletic catalogue. The book is a contribution to zoological science both valuable and useful. A pleasant feature is Steinbeck's evident love of the work that he was doing and admiration for the creatures that he observed and collected.

Cannery Row: Steinbeck's Pastoral Poem

by Stanley Alexander

> Cannery Row in Monterey in California is a poem, a stink,
> a grating noise, a quality of light, a tone, a habit, a nostalgia,
> a dream.

When Malcolm Cowley called *Cannery Row* "a very poisoned cream-puff," he meant that the novel concealed its attack on modern American values in what appeared to be an insubstantial confection. In the twenty years since the best of Steinbeck's fiction was written, it has become a commonplace that his "poison" was brewed for the middle or commercial class values that are dominant in American life. In fact, almost every criticism of Steinbeck has concentrated on his ideas and not his art, on his "skill" as a writer and his sympathetic humaneness but not his remarkable adaptations of traditional literary forms. I hope to show that in the case of *Cannery Row* the form, Cowley's "cream-puff," is that literary confection known since late classical times as pastoral.

Now until William Empsom's *Some Versions of Pastoral* (1938) pastoral conventions in literature had been relegated to the realm of particularly conceitful artifice. Following *Some Versions* it has been widely recognized, however, that the "artificial" formalities and pretences of pastoral are the conventional literary signals of certain intellectual conventions. Pastoral is, in Empson's view, the primary literary convention which reflects the characteristic class relations of western society. Pastoral literature also constitutes a recognizable response to the process of Western civilization which removes men farther and farther away from nature and into the total city. It gets its particular form, sentiments, and aesthetic from the motive of unity which it expresses.

"*Cannery Row:* Steinbeck's Pastoral Poem" by Stanley Alexander. From *Western American Literature*, II (1968), 281–95. Copyright © 1968 by *Western American Literature*. Reprinted by permission of the publisher.

As is suggested above, pastoral motives accommodate the age-old need of oneness within humanity itself and oneness with the forces in nature. I agree with Empson, as I understand him, that these two sub-motives are interfused; they are strangely keyed to one another, with the result that pastoral literature typically brings together in rural or even wilderness scenes representatives of (relatively) exalted social classes and (relatively) low social classes. The key figure in such literature is, then, the low man in society, originally peasant, of whom it is felt that he combines in himself both essential humanity and brute nature. Its form can be seen most simply in a tableau: in the center stands the unsophisticated man; on one side of him is ranged the animal kingdom and the whole world of nature; on the near side stands the sophisticated man and, back of him, the city or world of civilized humanity.

Tortilla Flat and *Cannery Row* are very similar books, although I cannot agree with Woodburn O. Ross that *Cannery Row* is "merely a repetition of *Tortilla Flat* in everything except tone." [1] The earlier novel is also a version of pastoral, but the mock-heroic tone of *Tortilla Flat* got out of hand, producing an unwanted, ultimately confusing incongruity.[2] Insofar as *Cannery Row* covers the same ground as *Tortilla Flat*, the differences are owing to a superior conception of style and its appropriateness to content rather than to any basic change in the intensity of his hatred of artificiality in society. *Cannery Row* is still solidly in the comic vein of the pastoral tradition from whence comes the form of both novels, but it is obviously more thoughtful and much less a kind of literary joking. Its sentiments, one feels, are somehow deeper and more admirable.

In *Cannery Row* Steinbeck once again took as his subject the simple and direct, imputedly "natural" striving of men who, although they

---

[1] Woodburn O. Ross, "John Steinbeck: Earth and Stars," reprinted in *Steinbeck and His Critics*, ed. E. W. Tedlock, Jr., and C. V. Wicker (Albuquerque, 1957), p. 177. Ross anticipates my conclusions about *Cannery Row* in the following statement: ". . . the significance of Steinbeck's work may prove to be in the curious compromise which it effects. It accepts the intuitive, nonrational method of dealing with man's relation to the universe—the method of the contemporary mystics. But, unlike them, it accepts as the universe to which man must relate himself the modern, scientifically described cosmos." My interest here is in the formal means Steinbeck found available for such a compromise.

[2] In "The Conflict of Form in *Tortilla Flat*" (*American Literature*, XL [March 1968], 58–66), I have urged that as a result of this formal conflict, *Tortilla Flat* reveals a measure of social condescension which, although it suited readers when the novel was published, is unpleasant today.

are not "primitives" or peasants in the same degree as the paisanos of *Tortilla Flat* or the sharecroppers of *The Grapes of Wrath,* are deliberately primitive and pagan. The Palace Flophouse and Grill, a masculine institution located only a scant city block from Dora Flood's whorehouse, is a millennium away from Monterey, its woman-dominated society, its commercial values, and its pieties of decency, respectability, circumspection, and conformity. Mack and the boys work only for the necessities of life, narrowly conceived, and they are free for play, much as are the adult males of Polynesia and Africa. Thus, they are, by comparison with the dominant society on whose affluent fringes they have a quite comfortable marginal existence, relatively primitive.

That the form of *Cannery Row* so closely approximates Renaissance pastoral is owing to the presence of Doc, the marine biologist, fictional counterpart of Steinbeck's friend Ed Ricketts. This fictional presence is pastorally "from above," Doc (like Martin Arrowsmith in Sinclair Lewis's novel) representing not only the detached, truth-hungry scientist but also the secure, educated, powerful class from which he comes "down" to operate the Western Biological Laboratory. As in the conventional pastoral of Spenser, Sidney, and Shakespeare, this novel brings about a meeting between lofty and low, and the result is aesthetically, emotionally, and intellectually far different from any fiction which does not bring about this strategic sharing of scene. This form of pastoral appears very frequently in American fiction of the second quarter of the century. One thinks immediately of Fitzgerald's fascination with the difference between classes (pecuniary, but pastoral as well), of Hemingway's tendency to discover the pastorally beneficient relationship of the classes abroad and when at home to be moved by democratic uniformity toward the pure primitivism of "Big Two-Hearted River," and of Faulkner's "realistic" but no less pastoral social fabric of exalted Southern families and cultured townmen, and poor white farmers and Negroes. Despite the real and mythic uniformities of American democracy, the relations of the classes have exercised a strong pull on our art, although the force of the democratic reality and myth have rendered American pastoral rather more covert than explicit.

The pastoral tone of *Cannery Row* is established in the short interchapter where Steinbeck renders Monterey as a cosmos and indicates that the irregular orbits of Mack and the boys are more stable than those of the great world which lies behind Doc:

The Virtues, the Graces, the Beauties of the hurried mangled craziness of Monterey and the cosmic Monterey where men in fear and hunger destroy their stomachs in the fight to secure certain food, where men hungering for love destroy everything lovable about them. Mack and the boys are the Beauties, the Virtues, the Graces. In the world ruled by tigers with ulcers, rutted by strictured bulls, scavenged by blind jackals, Mack and the boys dine delicately with the tigers, fondle the frantic heifers, and wrap up the crumbs to feed the sea gulls of Cannery Row. What can it profit a man to gain the whole world and to come to his property with a gastric ulcer, a blown prostate, and bifocals? Mack and the boys avoid the trap, walk around the poison, step over the noose while a generation of trapped, poisoned, and trussed-up men scream at them and call them no-good, come-to-bad-ends, blots-on-the-town, thieves, rascals, bums. Our Father who art in nature, who has given the gift of survival to the coyote, the common brown rat, the English sparrow, the house fly and the moth, must have a great and overwhelming love for no-goods and blots-on-the-town and bums, and Mack and the boys. Virtues and graces and laziness and zest. Our Father who art in nature.[3]

There could scarcely be a more precise imaging of the master icon of the essential pastoral idea than this passage gives. By means of tone that might be called "mock-cosmic," Steinbeck achieves a sense of inclusiveness which serves brilliantly to contain his many and sometimes contradictory ideas concerning the multiform meaning of man's experience of his life. At one extreme of this inclusiveness, there is the vast and imponderable cosmos; at the other, the ecological demi-world of small animals. The "Peaceful World" image is evoked as being cosmically "right," and, at the same time that the naturalistic value of survival is affirmed, the large predations of the animals of the "human jungle" are shown to be "unnatural" and pathetic. The effect of these implied and explicit comparisons is to connect the multitudinous events of the world, great and small, with the primitivist-pastoral idea of "the natural." Nature is the great and final arbiter of right and good, overseeing and rewarding and punishing the actions of man and species. "There are three main ideas about Nature," Empson writes:

> putting her above, equal to, and below man. She is the work of God, or a god herself, and therefore a source of revelation; or she fits man, sympathizes with him, corresponds to his social order, has magical connections

[3] John Steinbeck, *Cannery Row* (New York, 1945), p. 10. All future references to this edition will be indicated in the body of the text by page number.

with him and so forth; or she is not morally responsible so that to contemplate her is a source of relief. . . .[4]

Mack and the boys are outcasts from a social world which has arrogantly and wrongfully denied its connectons with and dependence upon nature; they have relinquished, not their humanity, but their participation in an impious and destructive way of life whose adherents call it civilization. Mack's famous apology to Doc for wrecking his lab ("It don't do no good to say I'm sorry. I been sorry all my life. This ain't no new thing.") has been taken by many critics as indicating either a contradiction in Steinbeck's logic concerning the value of the life of renunciation which Mack and the boys live, or else a momentary admission that their life here is mere evidence of their failure in the larger world of decency and respectability. It is neither of these things, I think, but only a means of realistically accounting for the outcast-renunciate condition of these men. A few pages later Steinbeck has Doc describe in the bums one of the most basic attributes imputed to simple men by primitivist-pastoral convention: "Mack and the boys know everything that has ever happened in the world and possibly everything that will happen." And in the same conversation, a linking of this attribute with the actually primitive:

> "The things we admire in men, kindness and generosity, openness, honesty, understanding and feeling are the concomitants of failure in our system. And those traits we detest, sharpness, greed, acquisitiveness, meanness, egotism and self-interest are the traits of success. And while men admire the quality of the first they love the produce of the second."
>   "Who wants to be good if he has to be hungry too?" said Richard Frost.
>   "Oh, it isn't a matter of hunger. It's something quite different. The sale of souls to gain the whole world is completely voluntary and almost unanimous—but not quite. Everywhere in the world there are Mack and the boys. I've seen them in an ice cream seller in Mexico and in an Aleut in Alaska" (p. 131).

Mack and the boys are made to magically incorporate the whole world by holding it more or less passively as a complex but unified object of contemplation. This mystical inclusion of All in One (or more specifically, of the complex in the simple) is here connected with the primitivism of Mexican and Aleut and is placed in opposition to the obsession of participants in the "system" who, in Steinbeck's para-

---

[4] William Empson, *Some Versions of Pastoral* (New York, 1960), p. 179.

phrase of the New Testament, acquiesce in "The sale of souls to gain the whole world. . . ." The proper striving of mankind is after simple things; the most successful striving is that of simple men.[5]

Just as important as the naturalistic, primitivist and pastoral symbolism of the Cannery Row bums is the related symbolism of Doc, one of Steinbeck's most significant characters because he can be taken to represent certain conclusions the novelist reached during his years of association with the marine biologist Edward Ricketts. For this reason, *Sea of Cortez*, the book they produced together following a collecting voyage into the Gulf of California, is especially useful in the study of *Cannery Row*. Even so, it is necessary to guard against too easy and direct equation of Steinbeck's characters with the people—in this case, the person—of his experience. More than likely Doc is very much like the person that Steinbeck conceived Ricketts to be, but Doc is also very much the creature of Steinbeck's imagination and, as such, has his existence as far as we are concerned in the tradition to which imagination committed Steinbeck in *Cannery Row*.

Peter Lisca would make of Doc the "God" of Cannery Row, a kind of Buddha who has touched earth here and who is worshipped and served by Mack and the boys.[6] But Doc's role is merely more Western than such an interpretation would indicate, and he is surely more a man in search of truth and a soul in search of deity than he is Deity itself. Observe, he finds deity in Mack and the boys quite as much as they find it in him, and he locates it ultimately in the same generalized world of nature in which his speculations also place the Cannery Row bums. "Our Father who art in nature."

With his scientific training and the personal discipline it requires, and his appreciation of certain works of literature and music, Doc serves as the twentieth-century embodiment of the relatively exalted (noble or genteel) figure of conventional pastoral who, ostensibly for some definite purpose, comes away from castle or city and into the company of the lowly. The scene of this meeting in Cannery Row is

[5] Describing the pastoral formula which lies behind the convention of the wise fool in such works as Shakespeare's *As You Like It*, Empson could as well be writing of Mack and the boys or Danny and his friends: under this convention, "The simple man becomes a clumsy fool who yet has better 'sense' than his betters and can say things more fundamentally true; he is in 'contact with nature,' which the complex man needs to be . . . he is in contact with the mysterious forces of our own nature, so that the clown has the wit of the Unconscious; he can speak the truth because he has nothing to lose."

[6] Peter Lisca, *The Wide World of John Steinbeck* (New Brunswick, N.J., 1958), pp. 214–215.

very interesting. Steinbeck, as much as Faulkner, has given evidence in his writing of a fascination with what remains of pastoral locale. But the scene Doc shares with Mack and Dora and the rest is neither sylvan dale nor frontier ranch nor family farm; it is instead an industrial slum, and Steinbeck has moved the pastoral scene into an unlikely but appropriate twentieth-century locale. The ostensible reasons for Doc's presence in Cannery Row are quite realistic: his work of collecting and preparation requires that he live in or very near his laboratory, and his odd hours and the laboraory odors make him a bad neighbor for a suburban locale. But this is only fictional furniture; Doc is in Cannery Row because that is where he can satisfy these occupational requirements and, in terms of the literary convention this novel roughly approximates, share a scene with mock-pastoral bums and whores who in better days were swains and maids.

The world of nature which conventional pastoral required as scene is not *in* Cannery Row exactly, but it laps at the deserted wharves at the ends of its streets. It is of course the ocean and, ultimately, the Pacific tide pools where Doc goes to do his collecting. It is most curious to think that the tide pool, the extremely naturalistic scene which is the controlling metaphor of *Cannery Row,* could play a part in pastoral literature. But it seems to me plain that this is the case and that some of Steinbeck's ideas in *Sea of Cortez* are helpful in understanding the "music of the tide pool" chapter which is one of the most important of the book.

One of the central ideas in Steinbeck's non-teleology or "Is-thinking" is that, as Robert Frost has put it, "Nothing gold can stay." That is, the things and relationships to which men attach value and strive to maintain are by definition the very things which cannot be maintained. Certainly the most fragile of these things and relationships are those which are most insisted upon and identified with civilization itself. Steinbeck's statements about the California ranchers and vineyard owners in *The Grapes of Wrath* are examples of this. These men believe passionately, religiously, in their right to maintain absolute control over their property. This property will be taken from them by a new race of men, the horde of displaced tenant farmers from the now desolated folk-culture of the Southwestern plains. And, Steinbeck suggests, these invaders will, in their turn, be subject to rigidities of the same kind as those of the ranchers they displaced.

The principal metaphor of this thinking is, of course, biological. In *Sea of Cortez* Steinbeck many times dramatizes this idea in connection with his speculations concerning the ultimate mystery of organic ecology and his observation in some places of seeming balances of nature which were absent in others. The metaphor is historical as well, however, and Steinbeck frequently refers to occurrences in history which seem to him to represent in human terms the unpredictability and the mystery of natural organic selectivity. The formula for this kind of thinking seems to be inherently primitivistic. It seems to say, to advance as a universal principle, that the low, the presently downtrodden, the abused in civilized society will provide the next class which will hold power, exercise its particular variety of will, and dominate over other orders or classes in the timeless way of momentary supremacies. It is by definition the lower orders which possess those qualities which will give the next era its forms.

Steinbeck's basically biological and Marxist view of civilized history is one which, predictably, places emphasis on the irrational and non-rational. His variety of "brooding sympathy" is not markedly different from Dreiser's, the harshness of many of his treatments of individuals and classes being departures from and contradictions of his non-teleology. The contradictions of his view of history are readily apparent: to propose that the seeds of the next era of civilized history are present even now among the lowly, barbarian orders and classes, either biological or social, is surely a teleological and not a non-teleological view. Offsetting this kind of contradiction to some extent, however, is his vaguely oriental mysticism which seems to imply that the universe is an entity already designed and made and that the change which men and other organisms experience in it is simply an aspect of its unfolding. Certainly Steinbeck's view of the human mind is not markedly different from the speculative psychologies which have had such influence on twentieth-century literary thought. In *Sea of Cortez*, for example, he presents a view very like Gustav Jung's of the connection the mind has with a level of reality that, ultimately, cannot be known in the ordinary sense. Of the human unconsciousness, Steinbeck writes:

> We have often thought of this mass of sea-memory, or sea-thought, which lives deep in the mind. If one asks for a description of the unconscious, even the answer-symbol will usually be in terms of a dark water into which the light descends only a short distance. And we have thought how the human fetus has, at one stage of its development, vestigial gill-slits. If the gills are a component of the developing human, it is not unreasonable to suppose a parallel or concurrent mind or psyche develop-

ment. If there be a life-memory strong enough to leave its symbol in vestigial gills, the preponderantly aquatic symbols in the individual consciousness might well be indications of a group psyche-memory which is the foundation of the whole unconscious.[7]

He goes on to link this archetype with moon and tide and to speculate about the extent of the effects which lunar cycles and tidal pressures continue to have upon the higher animals and even upon man, whose civilization makes little or no allowance for such effects:

> There is tied up to the most primitive and powerful racial or collective instinct a rhythm sense or "memory" which affects everything and which in the past was probably more potent than it is now. It would at least be more plausible to attribute these profound effects to devastating and instinct-searing tidal influences active during the formative times of the early race-history of organisms; and whether or not any mechanism has been discovered or is discoverable to carry on this imprint through the germ plasms, the fact remains that the imprint is here. . . . The imprint lies heavily on our dreams and on the delicate threads of our nerves. . . . The harvest of symbols in our minds seems to have been planted in the soft rich soil of our pre-humanity. Symbol, the serpent, the sea, and the moon might well be only the signal light that the psycho-physiologic warp exists.[8]

This seems to align the non-teleological with the primitive unconscious mind and the teleological with the conscious, operational mind's superficial distinction between subject and object. The non-teleological unconscious is, we can gather from the above, operative through our dreaming and through our irrational, non-rational, more or less impulsive behavior. It is operative as well in the archetypal symbols which man seems to use, largely unconsciously, to achieve certain mental states. The justice of these remarks can be shown by tracing the symbolic and formal implications of Doc's pastoral role and examining the pastoral symbolism of the "music of the tide pool" scene (Chapter 18) in *Cannery Row*. For it is in this scene that Steinbeck achieves in Doc and in his readers a mental state of acquiescence in the naturalistic mergence of human and lower organic life.

Pastoral can be defined as a literary strategy of inclusion; the motive it serves is that of unity or harmony, achieved by encompassing in its typical scenes both the hierarchic distances in society and between art

---

[7] John Steinbeck and Edward F. Ricketts, *Sea of Cortez* (New York, 1941), p. 32.
[8] *Sea of Cortez*, p. 34.

and nature.[9] Characters can serve this symbolic strategy and its motive also, as in pastoral drama and narrative when noble or genteel characters masquerade as peasants or fools, or, as in romantic poetry when the persona of the poet sometimes communicates an all-encompassing breadth. Doc has the pastorally exalted function of recognizing the value of the two sub-worlds constituted by Cannery Row and the tide pool. That this is no merely fanciful interpretation is made clear in *Sea of Cortez* where Steinbeck observes that after a time the members of the collecting expedition no longer were avidly interested and goes on from this to speculate about the relation of the knower to what is known. The scientist, the teacher, or the ordinary man "may observe his own world narrowed down until interest and, with it, observation, flicker and go out." This may be, he says, "the same narrowing we observe in relation to ourselves and the tide pool—a man looking at reality brings his own limitations to the world." But, he continues:

> If he has strength and energy of mind the tide pool stretches both ways,
> digs back to electrons and leaps space into the universe and fights out of
> the moment into non-conceptual time. Then ecology has a synonym
> which is ALL.[10]

Doc's experience at the tide pool yields a complex image which supports the naturalistic connection between man and the lower forms of life but which, without incongruity, supports as well a cluster of pastoral ideas about the relation of man the knower to the nature that is known. He is, of course, the only character of the book who is capable of such knowledge, and this is true not simply because he is capable in the use of language nor merely because he is a scientist. Doc's true apotheosis is in the realm not of language or reason but of aesthetic perception. He is that pastoral figure who, so various are his attributes, has the breadth to encompass the social, cultural and organic distances within nature's All and to contain this All in a unified perception of beauty.

When we entertain the possibility of finding such elements of pastoral rationale in *Cannery Row*, what we principally see is the literary spectacle afforded by Doc, the nominally cultured member of the scientific nobility who goes "down" first to the Cannery Row community

---

[9] This is of course Empson's definition in *Some Versions of Pastoral*, one affirmed by Frank Kermode in his introduction of *English Pastoral Poetry* (New York, n. d.), p. 31.
[10] *Sea of Cortez*, p. 85.

of bums and misfits and then, in an ultimate descent, to the natural world of the tide pool. It is not difficult to see the similarity that I have been pointing out between Doc and Mack and the boys and their counterparts in more conventional pastoral literature. It is perhaps more difficult to see a formal similarity between the complex, emotionally and aesthetically charged dramatism of the conventional pastoral scene and the dramatism of the tide pool scene in *Cannery Row*. We are alerted to this possibility by the obvious and pointed analogy Steinbeck makes between Cannery Row and the tide pool. Doc's descent to A (Cannery Row) is consubstantial with his descent to B (the tide pool). Then if we are alert we are likely to perceive that the tone of this scene is a curious blend of gravity and glory of the kind we ordinarily associate with the aesthetic experience typical of pastoral. Take for example this description:

> The tide goes out imperceptibly. The boulders show and seem to rise up and the ocean recedes leaving little pools, leaving wet weed and moss and sponge, iridescence and brown and blue and China red. On the bottom lies the incredible refuse of the sea, shells broken and chipped and bits of skeleton, claws, the whole sea bottom a fantastic cemetery on which the living scamper and scramble (p. 99).

Here as elsewhere in Cannery Row there is the suggestion of analogy between the world of men and that of the lower organisms. The idea is complicated in this passage by the linking of death and beauty; not only do we have the "fantastic cemetery on which the living scamper and scramble," but a demonstration of the beauty of the whole which suggests not simply an intellectual, but a markedly *aesthetic* perception of the analogy between life in the cities of men and the tide pool's life and death and beauty. Observe how Steinbeck develops Doc's discovery of the dead girl at the outer barrier of the tide pood. He sees a flash of white and, investigating, looks down at the girl's face.

> The lips were slightly parted and the teeth showed and on the face was only comfort and rest. Just under water it was and the clear water made it very beautiful. It seemed to Doc that he looked at it for many minutes, and the face burned into his picture memory (p. 100).

The earlier image of small animals in a state of utter being, scampering (avid and energetic, even playful) and scrambling (hungry, hurried, fearful) is a veritable catalogue of archetypal symbols. This existence endures in time, generation after generation adding to the incredible—and beautiful—refuse of the ocean floor. We know this process;

it is the natural analogy of the process of city building and hence of civilization itself. Unlike civilized life, however, here is life whose only purpose is living; it possesses in itself no pathos or tragedy because it produces no mind capable of such feeling. As in conventional pastoral, the recognition of such possibilities must come from the human world above; we as readers respond to the beauty and gravity and glory of the process. The image of endless, violent, and unmourned death is somehow not disquieting at all but comforting. This exuberance of life, ordinarily beneath the notice of men, were "wasted on the desert air" except that, like Gray, we are aware of it and now it seems quite proper and in its place.

The pathos of the dead girl is, like that of the littered dead of the tide pool, felt momentarily and then, as before, dissolved in Doc's and our own perception of beauty. When Doc gathers his equipment and walks back toward the beach:

> . . . the girl's face went ahead of him. He sat down on the beach in the coarse dry sand and pulled off his boots. In the jar the little octopi were huddled up each keeping as far as possible from the others. Music sounded in Doc's ears, a high thin piercingly sweet flute carrying a melody he could never remember, and against this, a pounding surf-like wood-wind section. The flute went up into regions beyond the hearing range and even there it carried its unbelievable melody. Goose pimples came out on Doc's arms. He shivered and his eyes were wet the way they were in the focus of great beauty. The girl's eyes had been gray and clear and the dark hair floated, drifted lightly over the face. The picture was set for all time. He sat there while the first little spout of water came over the reef bringing the returning tide. He sat there hearing the music while the sea crept in again over the bouldery flat. His hand tapped out the rhythm, and the terrifying flute played in his brain. The eyes were gray and the mouth smiled a little or seemed to catch its breath in ecstasy (pp. 100–101).

I have quoted at length here in order that the reader may have before him all the essential elements of this remarkable piece of writing; it is some of Steinbeck's finest and it is, although not the climax of the novel, the aesthetic crisis of the version of pastoral in *Cannery Row*.

With this our perception of the disturbing linkage between tide pool and the city of men is given a unity, less intellectual than aesthetic, which it did not possess before. Symbolic (or analogical) connections have been made, first, between humanity's dead girl and the tide pool's unmourned dead and, second, between Doc (and through him the humanity of Cannery Row, Monterey and the wide world) and the expressions of life that scamper above that "fantastic cemetery." These symbolic linkages are now made to inhere in a single perception, the unearthly beauty of the music in Doc's mind. Even this perception is brief, for after Doc talks to a landsman who does not know of the octopi in the tide pools and, when told of the body, is only stimulated by the thought of reward, the music quickly fades from Doc's mind. But it does not fade from the reader's mind. There it plays on, giving *Cannery Row* an aesthetic climax that transcends the mock-pastoral, comic events which culminate in the party.

Under the terms of this approach, Cannery Row becomes the human, the tide pool the non-human symbols of human immersion in an ultimately unknowable nature. Insofar as I am correct in finding a roughly pastoral form in the novel, Doc's experience at the tide pool is a brief but undeniable containment of the meaning of ALL. That this containment is finally aesthetic rather than intellectual, reduced to the beauty of the symbolic music ("of the spheres" and "of the universe") which Doc hears, is all the more justification for our approach to Cannery Row in terms of pastoral. The primary strategy of pastoral inclusiveness is aesthetic.

The aesthetic strategy of the tide pool scene is essentially the same as that of the "green thought" stanza of Andrew Marvell's "The Garden":

> Meanwhile the mind, from pleasure less,
> Withdraws into its happiness;
> The mind, that ocean where each kind
> Does straight its own resemblance find;
> Yet it creates, transcending these,
> Far other worlds and other seas;
> Annihilating all that's made
> To a green thought in a green shade.[11]

[11] Empson's incomparably brilliant explication of this stanza provided me with a model for my approach to this important scene in *Cannery Row*. Although his discussion is too long to quote here, a brief excerpt will indicate the appropriateness of the model: "The sea if calm reflects everything near it; the mind as knower is a conscious mirror. Somewhere in the sea are sea-lions and -horses and everything else, though they are different from land ones; the unconscious is unplumbed and pathless, and there is no instinct so strange among the beasts that it lacks its fantastic echo in the mind. In the first version [of Marvell's poem] thoughts are

> Nor harsh, nor grating, though of ample power
> To chasten and subdue.

The same ideas, explicit here, are implicitly active in Steinbeck's scene. Doc, the displaced member of a middle-class intelligentsia and of the fairly exalted, almost aristocratic scientist class, is comfortable in the company of Mack and the others, but he finds his true pleasure and happiness in the loneliness of his own mind, a loneliness that is most fully achieved at the tide pool. It is at the tide pool where the powerful analogies of his speculation are at last fused into the unity of his own "green thought in a green shade," his own aesthetic perception of ALL in the music of the universe.

Doc's (and of course Steinbeck's) willing submissions to the doubled ecstasy of the music and the look of the dead girl's face are, no less than in Marvell, the annihilation of disparity and disunity between the fact of man's dreaming and "all that's made," the sometimes harsh and grating facts of the natural world.

---

shadows, in the second [like the green thought] they are as solid as what they image; and yet they still correspond to something in the outer world, so that the poet's intuition is comparable to pure knowledge."

The Pearl: Realism and Allegory

by Harry Morris

John Steinbeck has never been very far away from the alegorical method. Some of his earliest work—and among that, his best—shows involvement with elements of allegory. *The Grapes of Wrath* (1939) employs as a framework the journey, the most common of allegorical devices:

> Go thou to *Everyman,*
> And show him in my name
> A pilgrimage he must on him take
> Which he in no wise may escape.

Eight years later, Steinbeck displayed his perfect familiarity with *Everyman* by using a passage from the morality play as an epigraph for his own most complete allegory of the life-journey, *The Wayward Bus* (1947). *In Dubious Battle* (1936) has some things in common with the medieval psychomachia, the debate, the poetry of warfare between body and soul, between head and heart. The title itself comes from the opening book of *Paradise Lost* (I.104), where, shortly following, Milton presents his own great allegory of sin and death (II.648–814). Some episodes in *The Pastures of Heaven* (1932) and some stories in *The Long Valley* (1938) move into allegory frequently, although in the early fiction allegorical materials are so completely absorbed into the techniques of realism as to be almost undetectable.

But beginning in 1945 and through the years immediately following World War II, following the realistic works that belong to that war, Steinbeck wrote a series of novels that he proclaimed openly to be allegorical. In addition to the already mentioned *Wayward Bus* (1947) were *Burning Bright* (1950) and *East of Eden* (1952). Preceding these three was *The Pearl.* Peter Lisca, in *The Wide World of John Stein-*

"*The Pearl:* Realism and Allegory" by Harry Morris. From *English Journal* LII, no. 7 (October 1963), 487–95, 505. Copyright © 1963 by the National Council of Teachers of English. Reprinted by permission of the publisher and the author.

beck (1958), cites letters which Steinbeck wrote to Pascal Covici to show that *The Pearl* was completed by early February 1945. *Woman's Home Companion* in its December issue of the same year was the first publisher, presenting the short novel under the title *The Pearl of the World*. An earlier letter to Covici indicates that while the story was still in progress Steinbeck called it *The Pearl of La Paz*. When it was issued in book form in 1947 to coincide with its release as a motion picture by RKO, it had become simply *The Pearl*. A rehearsal of these variations in the title should not be considered pedantry, for nothing more clearly indicates the allegorical nature of the work as it developed in Steinbeck's mind from the beginning. Although the city of La Paz may be named appropriately in the title since the setting for the action is in and around that place, the Spanish word provides a neat additional bit of symbolism, if in some aspects ironic. In its working title, the novel tells the story of The Pearl of Peace. When this title was changed to *The Pearl of the World* for magazine publication, although the irony was partially lost, the allegorical implications were still present. But Steinbeck had apparently no fears that the nature of the tale would be mistaken when he reduced the title to merely *The Pearl,* for he could rely still upon the epigraph to warn his readers:

> If this story is a parable, perhaps everyone takes his own meaning from it and reads his own life into it.

STATUS OF ALLEGORY

But why should a critic labor to put the stamp of allegory on a modern novel? For almost two hundred years now such a mark has been almost equivalent to a seal of literary oblivion. Shakespeare, the greatest writer in the English language, had eschewed allegory. One of the next best, Chaucer, turned an early hand to translating *The Romance of the Rose,* but after a few more false starts, found his genius in narrative and satire and produced his two masterpieces, *Troilus and Criseyde* and *The Canterbury Tales.* But it was Coleridge who downgraded allegory in a series of critical pronouncements and then became the master and model of a hundred and fifty years of literary criticism. His influence has been such that I have heard one of America's foremost poets and one of the major figures in what has long been called the "New Criticism" say, "I simply cannot read Spenser," by which he meant he could not abide allegory. Steinbeck's *Pearl* has come also under this interdict. Wher first published, it was reviewed by Maxwell

Geismar, who wrote, ". . . the quality that has marked Steinbeck's
work as a whole is . . . the sense of black and white things and good
and bad things—that is to say, the sense of a fabulist or a propagandist
rather than the insight of an artist. . . ." The fabulist as Geismar describes him is neither more nor less than the allegorist. We see how far
distaste for allegory has come. The writer who employs the mode is
read out of the ranks of the artist; the fabulist lacks insight.

It is doubtful that Coleridge ever intended his sometime-mentioned
disapproval of allegory to be taken as strong aversion. His lecture on
Spenser seemed to equate allegory with a one-to-one relationship between story and underlying meaning:

> No one can appreciate Spenser without some reflection on the nature of
> allegorical writing. The mere etymological meaning of the word, allegory,
> —to talk of one thing and thereby convey another,—is too wide. The true
> sense is this,—the employment of one set of agents and images to convey
> in disguise a moral meaning.

The unfortunate suggestion that moral meanings have to be disguised
is also present. But the more famous and more severe disavowal is in
Coleridge's *Statesman's Manual:*

> Now an allegory is but a translation of abstract notions into a picture-
> language which is itself nothing but an abstraction from objects of the
> senses; the principal being more worthless even than its phantom proxy,
> both alike unsubstantial, and the former shapeless to boot.

But elsewhere Coleridge found exceptions to his general censure: the
allegory of Cupid and Psyche, the Sin and Death episode in *Paradise
Lost,* and the first part of *Pilgrim's Progress.*

Nevertheless, Coleridge had done almost irreparable damage. Only
recently have there been signs that allegory has been given a false
character. Rosemond Tuve has shown that the first mistake is to imag-
ine that medieval and Renaissance allegory could ever be compre-
hended as a one-to-one relationship of story and second meaning. Allegory in Spenser's hand is as rich in its multiplicity of meaning as is
symbolism, the most highly admired literary device both of Coleridge
and of modern criticism. Parable in the New Testament and medieval
commentary on the Old Testament gave rise to the rich legacy that we
call the fourfold manner of Scriptural interpretation, of which Dante
wrote, "although [three of] these mystical meanings are called by various names, they may all be called in general allegorical, since they
differ from the literal." No literary figure can ever quite ignore that

Christ chose to talk in parables; none can ever forget that *The Divine Comedy* is one of the most complex allegories ever written. Great allegory, even in its purest forms—in so medieval a work as the anonymous *Pearl* of the fourteenth century—carries all the exciting allusiveness of the most complex symbolism. Our own age is rediscovering this fact, and much fine literature is being produced in the allegorical mode, from the serious attempts of Steinbeck already mentioned and including such important novels as Orwell's *Animal Farm*, Faulkner's *A Fable*, and Katherine Anne Porter's *Ship of Fools* all the way to the intellectualized comic strips of Schulz and Walt Kelly. Of course, allegory has never been completely dead in the modern novel, for in their ways Conrad's *Heart of Darkness*, Mann's *Magic Mountain*, and Joyce's *Ulysses* carry an allegorical burden. It has become fashionable to call them mythopoeic—reworkings of old or inventions of new myths—but the myths themselves are true allegories.

STEINBECK'S METHOD

In reading *The Pearl*, we encounter the work of a professed parabolist, and we must assert, and so reject Geismar's explicit objections to *The Pearl*, that the fable is an art form and that the fabulist as artist has never lacked insight. We cannot evaluate Steinbeck's performance with the criteria employed for judgment of the realistic novel. We cannot condemn *The Pearl* because as Geismar says it is all black and white, all good and bad. Such was Steinbeck's intention:

And because the story has been told so often, it has taken root in every man's mind. And as with all retold tales that are in people's hearts, there are only good and bad things and black and white things and good and evil things and no in-between anywhere.

Writing about its composition, Steinbeck said elsewhere, "I tried to write it as folklore, to give it that set-aside, raised-up feeling that all folk stories have." He was telling us again that *The Pearl* is not totally in the realistic tradition.

But Steinbeck knew that the modern fabulist could write neither a medieval *Pearl* nor a classical Aesopian Fox and Grapes story. It was essential to overlay his primary media of parable and folklore with a coat of realism, and this was one of his chief problems. Realism as a technique requires two basic elements: credible people and situations on the one hand and recognizable evocation of the world of nature and of things on the other. Steinbeck succeeds brilliantly in the second of these tasks but perhaps does not come off quite so well in the first. In supplying realistic detail, he is a master, trained by his long and productive journeyman days at work on the proletarian novels of the thirties and the war pieces of the early forties. His description of the natural world is so handled as to do double and treble duty in enrichment of both symbolism and allegory. Many critics have observed Steinbeck's use of animal imagery that pervades this novel with the realistic detail that is also one of its strengths:

> Kino awakened in the near dark. The stars shone and the day had drawn only a pale wash of light in the lower sky to the east. The roosters had been crowing for some time, and the early pigs were already beginning their ceaseless turning of twigs and bits of wood to see whether anything to eat had been overlooked. Outside the brush house in the tuna clump, a covey of little birds chittered and flurried their wings.

Kino is identified symbolically with low animal orders: he must rise early and he must root in the earth for sustenance; but the simple, pastoral life has the beauty of the stars, the dawn, and the singing, happy birds. Yet provided also is a realistic description of village life on the fringe of La Paz. Finally, we should observe that the allegory too has begun. The first sentence—"Kino awakened in the near dark" —is a statement of multiple allegorical significance. Kino is what modern sociologists are fond of calling a primitive. As such, he comes from a society that is in its infancy; or, to paraphrase Steinbeck, it is in the dark or the near-dark intellectually, politically, theologically, and sociologically. But the third sentence tells us that the roosters have been crowing for some time, and we are to understand that Kino has heard the cock of progress crow. He will begin to question the institutions that have kept him primitive: medicine, the church, the pearl industry, the government. The allegory operates then locally, dealing at first with one person, Kino, and then with his people, the Mexican peasants of Lower California. But the allegory works also universally, and Kino is Everyman. The darkness in which he awakes is one of the spirit. The cock crow is one of warning that the spirit must awake to its own dangers. The allegorical journey has often been called the way into the dark night of the soul, in which the darkness stands for despair or hopelessness. We cannot describe Kino or his people as in despair, for they have never known any life other than the one they lead; neither are they in hopelessness, for they are not aware that there is anything for which to hope. In a social parable, then, the darkness is in-justice and helplessness in the face of it; in the allegory of the spirit, darkness concerns the opacity of the moral substance in man.

The social element is developed rapidly through the episode of Coyotito's scorpion bite and the doctor's refusal to treat a child whose father cannot pay a substantial fee. Kino's helplessness is conveyed by the fist he crushes into a split and bleeding mass against the doctor's gate. This theme of helplessness reaches its peak in the pearl-selling at-tempt. When Kino says to his incredulous brother, Juan Thomás, that perhaps all three buyers set a price amongst themselves before Kino's arrival, Juan Thomás answers, "If that is so, then all of us have been cheated all of our lives." And of course they have been.

Kino is, then, in the near dark; and, as his misfortunes develop, he descends deeper and deeper into the dark night of the soul. The jour-ney that the soul makes as well as the journey that the living Kino makes—in terms of the good and evil that invest the one and the op-pression and freedom that come to the other—provides the allegorical statement of the novel.

DIFFICULTIES OF THE METHOD

In the attempt to achieve believable situations, create three-dimen-sional characters, Steinbeck met greater difficulties that he did not en-tirely overcome. The germ-anecdote out of which he constructed his story gave him little more than the bare elements of myth:

An event which happened at La Paz in recent years is typical of such places. An Indian boy by accident found a pearl of great size, an unbe-lievable pearl. He knew its value was so great that he need never work again. In his one pearl he had the ability to be drunk as long as he wished, to marry any one of a number of girls, and to make many more a little happy too. In his great pearl lay salvation, for he could in advance purchase masses sufficient to pop him out of Purgatory like a squeezed watermelon seed. In addition he could shift a number of dead relatives a little nearer Paradise. He went to La Paz with his pearl in his hand and his future clear into eternity in his heart. He took his pearl to a broker and was offered so little that he grew angry, for he knew he was cheated. Then he carried his pearl to another broker and was offered the same amount. After a few more visits he came to know that he could not sell his pearl for more. He took it to the beach and hid it under a stone, and that night he was clubbed into unconsciousness and his clothing was searched. The next night he slept at the house of a friend and his friend

and he were injured and bound and the whole house searched. Then he
went inland to lose his pursuers and he was waylaid and tortured. But
he was very angry now and he knew what he must do. Hurt as he was he
crept back to La Paz in the night and he skulked like a hunted fox to the
beach and took out his pearl from under the stone. Then he cursed it
and threw it as far as he could into the channel. He was a free man again
with his soul in danger and his food and shelter insecure. And he laughed
a great deal about it.

Steinbeck recorded this sketch in *The Sea of Cortez* (1941), where he
noted also how difficult it would be for anyone to believe:

> This seems to be a true story, but it is so much like a parable that it
> almost can't be true. The Indian boy is too heroic, too wise. He knows
> too much and acts on his knowledge. In every way, he goes contrary to
> human direction. The story is probably true, but we don't believe it; it
> is far too reasonable to be true.

We see in Steinbeck's source all the major elements of his expanded
version: the Mexican peasant, the discovered pearl, the belief that the
pearl will make the finder free, the corrupt brokers, the attacks, the
flight, the return, and the disposal of the pearl. But there are also
additions and alterations. The episodes of the doctor and the priest
are added; the motives for retaining the pearl are changed. While the
additions add perhaps some realism at the same time that they increase
the impact of the allegory, the alterations tend to diminish the realistic
aspects of the hero. Kino becomes almost unbelievably sophisticated.
The boy wants only to be drunk forever; Kino wants his son educated.
The boy wants to buy prayers for his own soul and for the souls of his
relatives in Purgatory; Kino distrusts the priest who asks that the
church be remembered when the pearl is sold, closes his fist only more
tightly about the pearl, determined instead to buy a rifle. The boy's
desires are primitive; they are consonant with his origins and his intel-
lect, crafty and wise as he may be. Kino's wants are sophisticated; he
sees in the pearl not the objects that can be bought, but beyond.
Coyotito's education will make the Indians free, a social, political,
and economic sophistication; new clothes and a church wedding will
give Kino and Juana position and respectability, again a social sophistication; the rifle will give Kino power, an intellectual sophistication.
With the rifle all other things were possible: "It was the rifle that broke
down the barriers. This was an impossibility, and if he could think
of having a rifle whole horizons were burst and he could rush on."

Later, ironically, all that the rifle gives to Kino is the power to destroy human life; and in this irony, the symbolic import of the pearl-rifle fusion gives to the allegory the very complication that Geismar (and even Steinbeck himself) says is lacking. The pearl is not clearly good or evil, black or white.

DIMINISHED REALISM

In these alterations, employed perhaps to add reality to a fable, Steinbeck has diminished realism. Narrative detail alone supplies this element. The opening of chapter three, like the beginning paragraph of the book, is descriptive:

> A town is a thing like a colonial animal. A town has a nervous system and a head and shoulders and feet. A town is a thing separate from all other towns, so that there are no two towns alike. And a town has a whole emotion.

Animal imagery again dominates the human scene, but this passage is only the first half of a statement that is concluded midway through the chapter:

> Out in the estuary a tight woven school of small fishes glittered and broke water to escape a school of great fishes that drove in to eat them. And in the houses the people could hear the swish of the small ones and the bouncing splash of the great ones as the slaughter went on. . . . And the night mice crept about on the ground and the little night hawks hunted them silently.

Symbol, allegory, and realistic detail are again woven satisfactorily together. The large fish and the hawks symbolize the doctor, the priest, the brokers, and the man behind the brokers, in fact all enemies of the village people from time prehistoric. Allegorically these predatory animals are all the snares that beset the journeying soul and the hungering body. Realistically these scenes can be observed in any coastal town where water, fowl, and animal ecology provide these specific denizens.

Somewhere in every chapter Steinbeck adds a similar touch: the tidepool description that opens chapter two, the pearl-buyer with his sleight-of-hand coin manipulation midway in chapter four, the great winds passages at the end of chapter five, and the wasteland imagery a third of the way into chapter six. All these passages operate symbolically as well as realistically, and some of them work even allegorically.

INTERPRETATION OF THE ALLEGORY

One of the major charges against allegory is obscurantism. Why does the author not say what he means outright? Is it not too easy to derive two or more entirely separate and frequently contradictory meanings from a single allegory? These are the terms in which Coleridge first objected. Being told what a poet intended by his allegory, he responded:

> Apollo be praised! not a thought like it would ever enter of its own accord into any mortal mind; and what is an additional good feature, when put there, it will not stay, having the very opposite quality that snakes have—they come out of their holes into open view at the sound of sweet music, while the allegoric meaning slinks off at the very first notes, and lurks in murkiest oblivion—and utter invisibility.

Such is the reaction to *The Pearl* of Warren French in *John Steinbeck* (1961), who finds Kino's disposal of the pearl capable of contradictory interpretations: it may be seen as "noble renunciation," but it can also be read as "defeatism." *The Pearl* is most commonly understood as a rejection of materialism. Peter Lisca accepts the theme of anti-materialism but suggests a second layer of allegory which creates a "pattern of man's search for his soul." Others think *The Pearl*, like many another Steinbeck novel, to be a search for values, something like Odysseus' ten-year wanderings in the Homeric epic.

I often wonder at the ability of the anti-allegorists to read any piece of literature. Like Coleridge, allegory-haters are usually symbolism-lovers. How do they find any more certainty in the meaning of the evasive symbol than in "obscure" allegory? How do they respond to the "negative capability" of Shakespeare and Keats? What is their reaction first to Christ's parables or Dante's *Paradiso* and then to the mountains of commentary on both that indicate there is very little certainty in any interpretation? We might say to them (since allegory deals almost always with the ways toward faith) that their faith is weak and urge that they ask in order to be given, seek in order to find, and knock in order to have opened.

But even the interpreters who have dealt with and accepted the allegory of *The Pearl* have been disturbingly vague. What are the results of Kino's particular search, we ask? What is the nature of Kino's soul? its disposition? in grace? in reprobation? What set of values did he arrive at? What is the precise nature of the materialism which he rejected?

Let us consider the general implications of any allegorical journey. Either it chronicles the transition of the soul from its captivity in the body and this mortality to liberation in Paradise and eternal life, or it records simply man's passing from a state of sin to one of grace. Quite often both these things happen at the same time. In *The Divine Comedy*, for example, Dante the pilgrim passes from this world into the existence of the afterworld; yet the entire journey is also one man's moral regeneration from error to rectitude, an object lesson that instructs the traveler in the nature of sin and the terrors of its punishment as opposed to the beatitude of salvation and the glories of its rewards.

But one thing always remains at the end of an allegorical journey. The traveler of the literal journey is still alive, still mortal, still in this world, and still to make the true journey from the corruption of this earth to the crystal bowers of heaven or sulphurous pits of hell that is undergone only after death.

KINO'S JOURNEYS

Kino's flight may be seen as a double journey, with a third still to be made. The journey is one half spiritual—the route to salvation of the soul—and one half physical—the way to freedom from bodily want. The second half is obvious; it is the theme of most of the early Steinbeck works; it is delineated in the list of things Kino will buy with the pearl. The first half may not be obvious, since for a long time now critics have been calling Steinbeck's writing non-teleological, by which they mean it does not concern itself with end-products, with what might be, what should be, or what could be, but only with what is. Especially is he unconcerned with eschatology. This view has long seemed to me mistaken. An allegorist with no teleology, no eschatology is almost a contradiction in terms. How this view of Steinbeck came into being is easy to see. His early novels such as *In Dubious Battle* and *The Grapes of Wrath* are a-Christian. No set of characters ever swore by Christ's name or cried out their disbelief in the church more often than those in *In Dubious Battle*. Mac says to Jim Nolan, "You got no vices, have you. And you're not a Christer either." But these are early works. In Steinbeck's latest novel, *The Winter of Our Discontent* (1961) the central character, Ethan Allen Hawley, is a regular member of the Episcopal Church; his problems are oriented about morality in a Christian framework, and much of the incidental symbolism is sacramental. Perhaps we have witnessed in Steinbeck himself an orthodox conversion, which, once witnessed, gives us cause to look for signs of it in previous writings. *The Pearl* is one of the first in which I detect a change; Juan Chicoy's bargains with the Virgin of Guadalupe in *The Wayward Bus* may be reluctant religion, but they represent at least a willingness to sit at the arbitration table with what used to be the enemy. *East of Eden,* in my view, among other things is an allegory of redemption through grace.

One of Kino's journeys then is the search for salvation. The forces that necessitate the literal journey, the flight, are cloaked in mystery and darkness:

> "I was attacked in the dark," said Kino. "And in the fight I have killed a man."
> "Who?" asked Juan Thomás quickly.
> "I do not know. It is all darkness—all darkness and shape of darkness."
> "It is the pearl," said Juan Thomás. "There is a devil in this pearl. You should have sold it and passed on the devil."

We are reminded of the formlessness of Milton's allegorical Death. Juan Thomás, torn like Kino by desires for a better life but concerned for his brother's safety, both blesses the journey and argues against it:

> "Go with God," he said, and it was like a death.
> "You will not give up the pearl?"
> "This pearl has become my soul," said Kino.
> "If I give it up I shall lose my soul."

Already almost overburdened with multiple symbolic equivalences—it stands for greed, for beauty, for materialism, for freedom from want, for evil, for good, for effete society, degenerate religion, and unethical medicine, for the strength and virtue of primitive societies—the pearl, with these words of Kino, stands also for Kino's soul.

The Indian boy of the germ-story had quite falsely identified his hold on the pearl with a firm grasp on salvation, a salvation absolutely assured while he still went about enveloped in flesh and mortality: "he could in advance purchase masses sufficient to pop him out of Purgatory like a squeezed watermelon seed." Kino also holds the pearl in his hand and equates it with freedom from want and then, mystically, also with freedom from damnation: "If I give it up I shall lose my soul." But he too has mistaken the pearl. The chances are very much more likely that with freedom from want his soul will be all the more in danger from sin. The Indian boy becomes free only when he throws the pearl away, only when he is "again with his soul in danger and his food and shelter insecure." The full significance of Kino's throwing the pearl back into the sea now becomes clear: the act represents his willingness to accept the third journey, the journey still to be made, the journey that Dante had still to make even after rising out of Hell to Purgatory and Paradise, the journey that any fictional character has still to make after his dream-vision allegory is over. Kino, Dante, Everyman have been given nothing more than instruction. They must apply their new knowledge and win their way to eternal salvation, which can come only with their actual deaths.

KINO'S TRIUMPH

It is difficult to understand how Warren French can interpret the "gesture [of flinging the pearl back into the sea] . . . as defeatism," how French can say that Kino "slips back not just half a step, but toboggans to the very bottom of the heap, for his boat smashed, his baby dead, and the pearl cast into the sea, he has less when the story is over than he had when it started." Kino is not defeated. He has in a sense triumphed over his enemy, over the chief of the pearl buyers, who neither gets the pearl nor kills Kino to keep him from talking. Kino has rid himself of his pursuers; he has a clear road to the cities of the north, to the capital, where indeed he may be cheated again, but where he has infinitely more opportunity to escape his destiny as a hut-dwelling peasant on the edge of La Paz. He has proved that he cannot be cheated nor detroyed. But his real triumph, his real gain, the heights to which he has risen rather than the depths to which he has slipped back is the immense knowledge that he has gained about good and evil. This knowledge is the tool that he needs to help him on the final journey, the inescapable journey that everyman must take.

A final note should be added concerning some parallels between Steinbeck's novel and the anonymous fourteenth century *Pearl*. The Pearl Poet tells the story, in dream-vision and allegory, of the personal grief of a loving father who has lost his daughter, a child dead before she had lived "two years in our land." As the poem opens, the narrator returns to a place where a "pearl of great price" has dropped from his hand to the ground. He falls asleep over the spot; a young maiden appears whose garments are covered with pearls; and the narrator speaks to the girl, now identified with the pearl he has lost and whom he believes to be his daughter in heaven, grown in stature and wisdom:

> O Pearl, quoth I, in pearls bedight,
> Art thou my pearl that I have 'plain'd?

She lectures him about the ways to salvation. He struggles to cross a stream that separates him from her and from the heavenly city—the new Jerusalem—which is her abode. The effort awakens him, and he rises from the ground with new spiritual strength.

Steinbeck's familiarity with medieval English literature is easy to document. His general interest in allegory indicates a steeping in the tradition. The epigraph to *The Wayward Bus* establishes his close reading of *Everyman;* and two quotations from Old English in *The Winter of Our Discontent* (one of them significantly from the poetic *Genesis* in the Junius MS., ll. 897–899) show not only wide reading but also study in the original Anglo–Saxon.

The importance of the medieval *Pearl* for a reading of Steinbeck's novel is centered in the role of the children in each. Coyotito can, in several ways, be identified with Kino's "pearl of great value." The pearl from the sea is only a means by which Coyotito will be given an education. For the doctor, who at first refused to treat Coyotito, the child becomes his means to the pearl, i.e. the child is the pearl to him. But more important than these tenuous relationships is the fact that with the death of Coyotito the pearl no longer has any significance. The moment the pursuer with the rifle fires, Kino kills him. Kino then kills the two trackers who led the assassin to him and who were unshakable. This act gives Kino and his family unhindered passage to the cities of the north, where either the pearl might be sold or a new life begun. But the chance shot has killed Coyotito, and though Kino and Juana are now free, they return to the village near La Paz and throw the pearl back into the sea. Thus the sole act that has altered Kino's determination to keep the pearl which has become his soul is the death of his child; and, as I read the allegory, Kino and Juana turn from the waterside with new spiritual strength, regenerated even as the father in the medieval *Pearl*.

Much has been made of the *leitmotif* of music in *The Pearl:* the song of the family, the song of the enemy, etc. The suggestion for this musical background, interlaced as it is with Steinbeck's chief themes (cleaning of the soul, new wealth, complete well-being), may have come from the second stanza of the medieval poem:

Oft have I watched, wishing for that wealth
That was wont for a while to make nought of my sin,
And exalt my fortune and my entire well-being—

. . . .

Yet never imagined I so sweet a song
As a quiet hour let steal to me;
Indeed many drifted to me there.

And, finally, the medieval *Pearl* ends on the same note of renunciation that is the crux of Steinbeck's fable:

Upon this hill this destiny I grasped,
Prostrate in sorrow for my pearl.
And afterward to God I gave it up.

(modernizations of *The Pearl* by
Sister Mary Vincent Hillmann)

However, I do not think that anything overmuch should be made of these similarities. Possibly the mere title of Steinbeck's allegory brought memories to his mind of the fourteenth century poem. He may have gone back to look at it again, but he may have satisfied himself with distant evocations only. For myself, whatever likenesses I find between the two works serve only to emphasize the continuing tradition of true allegory and the modern writer's strong links with the past.

John Steinbeck: The Fitful Daemon

by R. W. B. Lewis

Steinbeck's literary reputation is not very high at the moment and I see few reasons why it should grow greater in the future. It has declined a good deal since its peak during the war years. Following the publication of his most determined novel, *The Grapes of Wrath*, in 1939, it declined in America, where Steinbeck had for some years exerted a strong but as it were non-literary, and hence non-durable, appeal. And it declined in Europe, where he had been confusedly but advantageously associated with writers like Hemingway and Faulkner, with whom Steinbeck has little in common, and with writers like Dos Passos and Thomas Wolfe, whom he has at times perhaps superficially resembled. The prestige of that entire hydra-headed beast, the American novelist, has diminished notably in Europe, and the Steinbeck-head of it as much as any.

At the same time, Steinbeck is no doubt in some vague way established as a novelist. I see that a university press is bringing out a doctoral dissertation on Steinbeck's fiction, and a volume of critical essays about him by several hands has made its appearance. Thus he has been accorded the respectful burial which is our contemporary American way of honouring living writers whom we have pretty well decided not to read any longer. The decision is perhaps unfortunate and even unfair, but it is not altogether unreasonable. There is a sense of promise unfulfilled in Steinbeck's writing over the past decade and a half. His career is something of a casualty, and a casualty I think in this particular case of an unlucky wedding between art and rebellion which developed into a fatal marital hostility between the poetic and the political impulse. His career to date has the shape of a suggestive, a representative, and a completely honourable failure.

"John Steinbeck: The Fitful Daemon" by R. W. B. Lewis. From *The Young Rebel in American Literature*, ed. Carl Bode (London: William Heinemann Ltd., 1959), pp. 121–41. Copyright © 1959 by Carl Bode. Reprinted by permission of the author and the publisher.

If, as Faulkner has rather perversely contended, a writer is to be measured these days by the extent and quality of his failure, Steinbeck must inevitably be reckoned among our most sizeable novelists. Steinbeck's failure is great, and it is incomparably more interesting and valuable than the successes of nine-tenths of his contemporaries. For where Steinbeck has failed is in an effort to engage, with the resources of fiction, the complex realities, the evolving motifs, the outlines and images of things, the very sense of life which make up the matter truly, if deeply and almost invisibly, available to an American novelist of his generation. I am not cheaply hinting that Steinbeck deserves, as the schoolboy saying goes, 'E' for effort. I am saying that because of his effort and even because of its failure he has made more visible for the rest of us the existence, indeed the precise character, of the realities and themes and images he has not finally succeeded in engaging. This is the kind of failure which is, in the end, almost indistinguishable from success, though we may not be sure where to catalogue it; whether, for example, under the heading of literature or of criticism, of art or of history.

Amidst the larger failure of Steinbeck there are smaller units of undeniable achievement. At least one of these comprises a whole brief story; more usually the achievement is partial—a passage, a character, or perhaps merely an aspect. *Of Mice and Men* (1937) seems on a rereading to stand up remarkably well, to stand up whole and intact. It skirts breathtakingly close to disastrous sentimentality; stock minor characters (especially the villain and the villainess) move woodenly through it; the deliberate stage technique gives one the cramps; and there is an unpersuasive quality of contrivance about the episode—the mercy-shooting of an aged dog—which prepares by analogy for the climax—the mercy-shooting of the animal-child, Lennie. Yet the entire action of the story moves to its own rhythm, rescued and redeemed by a sort of wistful toughness, a sense not of realism but of reality. The end is an authentic purgation of feeling, pity if not terror, and the end crowns the whole.

Of Mice and Men is probably the only one of Steinbeck's works which is satisfying as a whole, and it is a short novel or *novella*. His longer and thicker writings may be differentiated by the moment and degree of wreckage, and they have culminated in *East of Eden* (1952), professedly Steinbeck's most ambitious novel. "Nearly everything I have is in it," he said. I am afraid it is a very bad novel of a very special and revealing badness which can most quickly be described by saying that it would have been greatly admired by the late H. G. Wells, who referred to Steinbeck as "that amazing genius."

The badness of *East of Eden* is a basic premise in this paper and I must return to it, but meanwhile a couple of observations of a less negative kind. The sheer bulk of Steinbeck's work is impressive, for one thing, and marks him clearly as a professional of sorts: twenty-three volumes, some of them no doubt slim ones, in the twenty-six years following his first book, *The Cup of Gold*, in 1929. Bulk is not the first attribute of artistic achievement, but it is *an* attribute, and we note again the courage and resiliency which are part of Steinbeck's temperament, which set him apart from the 'signers-off' of contemporary fiction, with their tender brevities and their lamentations about the plight of the artist, and which permit him to continue in the face of what must surely be for Steinbeck periodic frustration.

More important, and secondly, in the longer novels (*To a God Unknown*, 1933, *In Dubious Battle*, 1936, *The Grapes of Wrath*, 1939, and *East of Eden*) we come upon electrifying passages, sudden and tragically short-lived moments of vision, little spurts of verbal energy; momentary manifestations, as it were, of a trapped and imprisoned artistic daemon struggling to get out and on to the page and into the language, and to dwell there for ever. We come upon an occasional character too who lights up for us the adventure he is engaged in: normally not the hero—not Joseph Wayne or Tom Joad or Jim Nolan or Adam Trask—but the Steinbeck sage, the renegade doctor or renegade minister or renegade philosopher, whose puzzled involvement with the action helps to give the action such force and meaning as it may possess.

More largely yet, through these swift moments of light and these infrequent bearers of light, we dimly detect in these novels the effective presence and the design of the realities, motifs and images I have mentioned earlier. I distinguish here two kinds of motif in the fiction of John Steinbeck. The first may be called the American motif: a celebrational sense of *life*, a sense of promise and possibility and of as yet unspoiled novelty in man and his habitation, a mystical sympathy both for the individual and for what Whitman called the "en-masse." In short, a vision, if that is not too rarefied and romantic a word for it, which was of New England and the American east in its nineteenth-century origins and which Steinbeck has—I think very properly—naturalised in his native California and translated into its idiom.

The second is the contemporary motif: something so close in substance to the American motif that it can be seen as growing organically out of it, and yet which also appears as a dominant motif in the fiction of other contemporary languages and countries. It appears in the fiction, for example, of Silone in Italy, of Malraux and Camus in France, and to some extent of Graham Greene in England. This motif springs from the tragic awareness, which in Steinbeck's case is sometimes only an intensely pathetic awareness, of the fateful division between man and man; and of that division as a central feature of the mutilated life it is the novelist's business to give a direct impression.

The sense of division leads naturally to the political theme. It leads, that is, to the intuition that the form which the human struggle currently assumes, the representative plot of contemporary experience and the soul of its tragedy, is political in design. The political theme consists of a revolt against the forces that keep men separated, and its heart tends to beat to the formula of Albert Camus: I rebel, therefore we are. Or it pulses yet more movingly to the rhythm suggested by Ignazio Silone: "What determined my rebellion was the choice of companions."

Steinbeck has made his contribution to the theme and its heart-beat, especially in *The Grapes of Wrath*. "This is the beginning," he says there, flatly, in his own voice, "from 'I' to 'we'." But the relation between the elements—the felt division, the rebellion, and the ordering power of art—is extremely complex. It is partly Steinbeck's habit of over-simplifying both life and art that has kept him from seeing and taking hold of the complex entirety. The elements rarely fuse in his fiction; they tend rather to jar against each other. The same may be said of the two leading motifs. The evolution of what I have named the contemporary motif from the American motif may be seen within the development of American literature itself, in the movement from Thoreau and Emerson to Hawthorne and from all of them to Henry James; a movement from the happy evocation of "the simple separate person" and the sturdy conviction that the world was, or could be seen as, young and uncorrupted, to the gradual sense of self-isolation, of darkness and bewilderment. And thence to the ensuing perception that the form of human experience was exactly the strenuous, perhaps desperate, need and effort of separated individuals to draw close to one another, to enjoy an experience of life by means of a human relationship, in what Henry James was to call "the great greasy sea" of the anarchic modern world.

There is no such coherent and meaningful evolution in Steinbeck's work, though he began reasonably enough in the recognisably American vein and has gone on to identify, and respond boldly to, the contemporary challenge. The motifs have not so much met together as collided, in a struggle, as it were, between poetry and politics. For Steinbeck's poetry, the truly creative side of him, has remained American while his engrossing theme has become contemporary and political. As it turns out it has been the poetry which has suffered, which is simply a way of referring again to Šteinbeck's intermittent novelistic achievement. Maybe the sacrifice was beneficial. Steinbeck's gallant effort and his honourable defeat can remind us how huge an enterprise it is to make known the results of seeking.

The American theme announces itself regularly in Steinbeck's stories in a recurring image of a sort of *Drang nach Westen*—or perhaps *Drang nach* California. Steinbeck's first novel, *To a God Unknown,* begins with the departure of Joseph Wayne, the book's indistinctly godlike hero, from the family home in New England, near Pittsford, Vermont, to the green hills of California. "I've been reading about the West and the good cheap land there," he tells his father; "I've a hunger for the land, sir." "It's not just restlessness," his father replies. "You may go to the West. You are finished here with me." The process is repeated, through dialogue rather less stagey, in *East of Eden,* when Adam Trask leaves his Connecticut home and heads for California. "It's nice there, sun all the time and beautiful." And the Joad family in *The Grapes of Wrath,* though starting much farther west, in Oklahoma, similarly sets off for the Pacific coast not only to find work and a place to live but to find a new world of hope and opportunity after the hideous destruction of their old world.

Steinbeck's instinct at these initial moments was altogether sound; he was knowingly possessing himself of a native theme and a native resource, a resource both of history and of literature. It is the traditional American impulse to withdraw into the terrain of freedom in order to find or re-find one's identity and one's purpose as a human being; to dissociate from the given, the orthodox, the habitual, from whatever passes at the time for civilisation. "Aunt Polly she's going to . . . civilise me, and I can't stand it. I been there before," Huck Finn says on the last page of his memoirs. He determines accordingly to "light out for the territories." The same impulse, of course, received its most eloquent treatment in the recorded withdrawal of Henry David Thoreau from the quiet desperation of civilised Concord to the unfallen nature and fertile solitude of Walden Pond, a few miles away.

But we remember also Cooper's Natty Bumppo lighting out for the uncomplicated forest from the oppressive society of the town of Templeton, and Herman Melville, in fact and fiction, jumping ship to reflect unfavourably upon the evils of civilisation from the Eden-atmosphere of the Taipi valley in the South Seas. Such was the form that rebellion originally took in American literature.

But in seeing his native Salinas Valley in California as a new Eden, the scene of a new chance for man and for men, and in transporting his heroes thither from the exhausted East, Steinbeck is not only continuing in an American tradition, enacting again an old American dream. He is also suggesting that the dream itself has moved west and has settled there, that it is now California which stimulates in its inhabitants the intoxicating sense of fresh beginnings and untroubled potentialities which the eastern scene once stimulated in Emerson, in Thoreau, in Whitman. This is the point and purpose of the prefatory incantations of *East of Eden,* where the local California countryside is observed and named as though by the first man at the dawn of time.

Much of the best and no little of the worst can be found in Steinbeck's work, and most apparently in the work of the early thirties— *The Pastures of Heaven, To a God Unknown,* and *Tortilla Flat—* where there are many parallels and continuities linking him to the age of Emerson and its cultural predispositions. Steinbeck really did, for example, write about those subjects Emerson urged on his contemporaries, when he suggested the range of native materials and the unsophisticated but robust activities ready to be celebrated: "Our log-rolling, our stumps and their politics, our fisheries, our Negroes and Indians, our boasts and our repudiations, the wrath of rogues and the pusillanimity of honest men, the northern trade, the southern planting, the western clearing, Oregon and Texas, are yet unsung." And in translating these persons and places and occupations into narrative, Steinbeck managed to shed over all of it a warm, in fact a slightly sweaty, haze of trustful moral purity. Innocent are these early writings, and he who wrote them; innocent in the manner of Emerson and Thoreau; innocent in the manner of Whitman, detecting or claiming to detect beauty and purity amidst the lowliest squalor. There is no vice in the inhabitants of the heavenly pastures; its liars and lunatics and killers and prostitutes are merely well-intentioned eccentrics.

Joseph Wayne, in *To a God Unknown,* is so thickly enveloped in mythological fog that he scarcely seems to arrive at humanity at all. *To a God Unknown,* for all its artificial loftiness, is perhaps the most promising of these early books, but it has the severe literary—that is, novelistic—defect of a protagonist who is so primal a figure that he never takes on the burden of becoming human, never enters into or is affected by the maturing pressures of time.

Joseph Wayne is a representative character, for the fact is that most of these early creations are morally pure because they are morally as yet unborn. Joseph is physically vigorous and his eyes have seen the glory. With his vague, mystical far-sightedness, he is a sort of buckskin Bronson Alcott, but he shares with the antic trouble-makers of the other books the quality—in them often very attractive—of pre-moral sensibility. None of these persons has yet arrived at the condition of conscience, at the human condition, and with luck none of them ever will. Joseph's pre-moral, pre-historical profile seems an act of will. Following a traditional American pattern, Joseph has abandoned a closed or closing society. He has withdrawn westwards to commune in solitude with untainted nature and to listen for its secret. That, to repeat, is the form the rebellious impulse has so often taken in America —not a direct assault from within upon an intolerable social order or disorder, but a removal of the self with the aim of experiencing again the graceful simplicity by which society may be measured and from which society has gravely, but perhaps not hopelessly or irretrievably, fallen. It is a matter of tasting once more of the tree of ignorance and the interest of the story lies in what the refreshed hero can later make out of his wilderness adventure. For the next phase, in American litera- ture, has customarily been the return into society to testify amidst its betrayals and denials to the lessons learned in solitude. Joseph Wayne does not live to make that return journey, but it is a sign of John Steinbeck's development that the role of the returned witness is exactly the one assigned, in *The Grapes of Wrath,* to Jim Casy, the one time preacher who abruptly quits his vocation—"an' went off by myself an' give her a damn good thinkin' about"—and who has now come back to counsel Tom Joad and his family, and finally to die for the new faith that his good thinking had produced.

One of the favourite images by which American writers have tradi- tionally sought both to describe and to comment on the process I have mentioned is the image of Adam. Such is the case with John Steinbeck and *East of Eden,* his longest novel, in which the author put "nearly everything I have . . . pain and excitement . . . and feeling good or bad and evil thoughts and good thoughts—the pleasure of design and some despair and the indescribable joy of creation." This is a novel whose allegorical framework is indicated not only in its title but in its hero, whose Christian name is Adam. This is a novel which introduces us not only to a new Adam, but to a new Lilith and even to a new Cain and Abel—called Cal and Aron—with the former again responsible, if indirectly, for the death of the latter. And this is a novel whose characters spend many hours arguing the meaning of the Genesis story —"the best-known story in the world," as one of them says, "because it is everybody's story . . . the symbol story of the human soul."

Here, then, is the book in which Steinbeck has presented the whole of his experience of America. Although it has been a huge economic success, it is, unhappily, a literary disaster, and of such proportions that it sheds a very disturbing light on the career that has allegedly culminated in it. Either Steinbeck has not understood the original story of Adam or he has failed to grasp its profound relevance to experience in America: which is not to understand America itself. The story of Adam is the story of the fall of man. There are many mysteries about it, but there is no questioning the fact that it is a story about sin, about the encounter with evil and the corruption of human nature by an act of its own will and an expression of its pride. It is indeed the story of human nature *becoming* human, of someone less than or more than or other than human taking upon himself the tainted, paradoxical, tragic, and hopeful burden of authentic humanity; it is therefore about what it means to be human. It is a story about death, and a story which has always appealed to the characteristic dark humour of the American novelist. For its content is so well suited to suggest the maturing calamities which can befall the American Adam, neglectful of sin and evil, uninterested in paradox and impatient with tragedy, which he too often confuses with gloom.

Little of that old story remains in *East of Eden* and nothing of its inner essence. Adam Trask grows up in the East, some ninety years ago, marries a purportedly very bad woman named Cathy, takes her to California, where she leaves him and sets up as a madam in a bordello —after giving Adam twin boys. He engages in various enterprises, among them long and instructive conversations with his philosophical Chinese servant, and grows old among an assortment of family tribulations.

The biblical allegory is the more intrusive throughout this jumbled tale because the allegory has remained unfleshed. Failing to represent the case, Steinbeck has attempted to name it. This gives rise to a pervasive sense of contrivance and we are conscious everywhere not of a sense of life but of an abstraction from it. The Bible story is about evil and in few novels has the word "evil" been invoked as frequently as it is in *East of Eden*, but that itself is an evil sign. Moreover, Cathy, the alleged embodiment of evil, is revealingly defined as a moral freak, a preposterous deviation from human nature, rather than an aggravated and disturbing instance of its congenital tendencies. She strikes us at last as altogether unreal, a very naughty girl in some fable or ballad, the little girl, perhaps, who gave her father forty whacks.

There is no great image of human experience in *East of Eden* though a great one was intended, and not only because there is no sense of life but even more because there is no sense of death in it. Death is almost always the end of experience in Steinbeck, and the end of his characteristic fictions; it is almost never a beginning, never a dying into life. The fact is that Steinbeck does not really believe in his Biblical story. It is as though Emerson had written the book, and all that remains when the abstractions and monsters have been cleared away is the old Emersonian material and the old Emersonian tone: "the northern trade, the southern planting, the western clearing," and so on.

But the calamity which is *East of Eden* is partly explained by what had happened to Steinbeck's subject-matter and his attitude towards it in the years between those earlier and funnier and more cheerful works and the decision, say around 1950, to tackle the Adamic allegory. These were the years of observed human misery, of protest and rebellion, of *The Grapes of Wrath*.

Steinbeck's editor, Pascal Covici, has accurately noted in Steinbeck "an expression of the joy of living." It should be remembered here that by communicating that joy Steinbeck has given very many people a great deal of pleasure, revived in them perhaps some lost sense of the sheer excitement of being alive. And I cannot resist adding personally that behind his stories I detect a figure who is to me altogether sympathetic; a person of zest and humour and nervous anger, and with an uncommonly large fund of humanity. The difficulty with Steinbeck's peculiar brand of joyfulness is not so much that it can easily turn fuzzy or mawkish (a kind of melting process observable in the development, or the decline, from *Tortilla Flat* to *Cannery Row* and *Sweet Thursday*). The difficulty is rather that it is constitutionally unequipped to deal with the more sombre reality a man must come up against, in these times or in any times, if he is honest and alert.

Steinbeck was up against a part of that reality during the years between 1936 and 1942 when he was writing *In Dubious Battle, The Grapes of Wrath* and *The Moon is Down,* and when he was also writing the one work in which his trapped daemon did squirm out and get almost completely into the language—*Of Mice and Men.* With the important exception of the latter, the work of those years is characterised among other things by a seeming refusal, or perhaps an inability, to confront tragic truth. The result of having done so might have been a considerable enlargement of Steinbeck's art; the transformation, for instance, of the earlier earthy humour into what Hawthorne once called "the tragic power of laughter."

But the work of those years was characterised, too, by a relatively superficial analysis and a makeshift solution of the case, whether it be social injustice or Fascist invasion and oppression. To have looked more searchingly into those ugly phenomena would have been to have discovered their tragic implications for the nature of man—the proper concern, I venture, of the artist if not of the politician or the sociologist. *The Moon is Down,* for example, is intended as a consoling image of heroism—that of a number of European villagers in a town occupied by the Nazi forces. But it is woefully limited by the absence of anything but the slightest hint that the fault, the guilt, the very Fascism, is a manifestation of the human heart, and so detectable on all sides of the conflict. Steinbeck typically permits a portion of goodness to modify the badness of some of the invaders—especially the commanding officer, the book's one interesting characterisation—but none of the invaders' badness is reflected in the hearts of the staunch and faithful villagers. Be good, sweet maids and men, Steinbeck seems to be telling them, and let who will be Fascist.

I am not now raising the somewhat tired issue of the artist's responsibility. I am sure that responsibility is a great one, but I am talking about the form it can most suitably and effectively take—and that is the prophetic form, penetrating to hidden realities and not combing up appearances. Neither *The Grapes of Wrath* nor *In Dubious Battle,* the novels where Steinbeck's rebellious sympathy for the wretched and the luckless is most evident, succeeds in arriving at that form; and in the absence of the prophetic we are left with the merely political. There are many fine, pungent and moving things in each of these books, and Steinbeck has given *The Grapes of Wrath* momentum, an inner drive, which in its generation only Faulkner—and he only a few times—has equalled. It also has a sweetness which never once goes sticky. Yet neither book quite touches bottom, quite manages to expose beneath the particular miseries and misfortunes the existence of what used to be called fate, what now is called the human condition—that twist or flaw in the very nature of things which Steinbeck has himself laid poetic hold of and expressed in the very similar phrases which conclude *The Red Pony* and *Of Mice and Men,* and which refer to two very similar acts of destruction: "I had to do it—had to" and "You hadda, George, I swear you hadda." *In Dubious Battle* and *The Grapes of Wrath* have, as it were, everything but that simple acknowledgement of the secret cause of our suffering and our violence. The secret cause is the ally of the poetic impulse, but these novels reach only as deep as the political cause, and politics in its usual meaning is the enemy of poetry, or anyhow of Steinbeck's poetry.

The Grapes of Wrath does not manage to transcend its political theme because the question "What is man?" was not really accepted by Steinbeck as the root question. He could not bring himself to believe that there was anything really wrong with the human heart, so that the causes of the wrongs observed must be other—practical, even mechanical; political, in short. The point here is that the application of Steinbeck's special and happy-natured poetry to his newly-discovered and unhappy historical materials could only result in a defeat of the poetry. It would have taken a different brand of poetry, something with a more tragic thrust to it, to have survived. *The Grapes of Wrath* remains with the political answer, the same political theme—unity—of *In Dubious Battle,* but what it does is to expand on that theme.

To the story of Tom Joad and his family—their long, rickety journey westward, their exhausted efforts to make a living in California, and the bitter resistance they encounter among the rich, frightened, and greedy land owners—Steinbeck has added a large sky-blue vision of things which is not only like the vision of Emerson, it is straight out of Emerson. It is his notion of the over-soul, the world-soul of which each individual has his modest and particular share. Jim Casy, the former preacher and future martyr, pronounces this idea: "Maybe all men got one big soul and everybody's a part of it." He had come to this vision during his retirement into the hills: "There was the hills, an' there was me, an' we wasn't separate no more. We was one big thing. An' that one thing was holy. That's the Holy Spirit—the human spirit—the whole shebang. An' it on'y got unholy when one mis'able little fella got the bit in his teeth, an' run off his own way . . . Fella like that bust the holiness."

The doctrine of the whole shebang is the warrant for all the des-

perate organisational efforts, the violence and the heroism which follow
later; they are all efforts to reconstruct the busted holiness, to mend
once more the unity of the one soul of mankind. That doctrine also
is the philosophical basis for the famous speech that Tom Joad makes
to his mother after Casy has been killed—those words which rang
bravely and beautifully in 1939 but which, if you will forgive me, seem
to have lost a little of their glow since. Tom Joad is about to leave, to
continue the whole struggle in hiding. His mother asks:

"How'm I gonna know about you? They might kill ya an' I wouldn't
know."

Tom laughed uneasily. "Well, maybe like Casy says, a fella ain't got
a soul of his own, but on'y a piece of a big one—an' then . . . then it
don't matter. Then I'll be all aroun' in the dark. I'll be ever'where—
wherever you look. Wherever they's a fight so hungry people can eat.
I'll be there. Wherever they's a cop beatin' up a guy, I'll be there. If
Casy knowed, why, I'll be in the way guys yell when they're mad an'—
I'll be in the way kids laugh when they're hungry an' they know supper's
ready. An' when our folks eat the stuff they raise an' live in the houses
they build—why, I'll be there. See?"

What does get lost amidst the genuinely lyrical flow of that passage
and in its infectious hopefulness is the element on which not only the
social struggle but the art of narrative depend—the image of the
sharply outlined, resolutely differentiated, concrete individual personality. The political movements of the 1930s did tend to submerge
the individual in the group, whether or not at the behest of the oversoul, but in reflecting that fact in his fiction Steinbeck has again yielded
up his poetry to his politics. And his poetry is not saved by adding
above that political tendency a metaphysical principle which (even if
true, as most probably it is not) is totally unsuited for the craft of
fiction. Fiction deals with individuals, however intimately related. The
relationship, in turn, which both fiction and politics were seeking,
and are seeking, must be composed of inviolable and separate persons.
A modern philosopher has wisely said that relationship depends upon
distance. What seems to be needed, both for society and for art, is not
unity, which dissolves the individuals within it, but community, which
is a sharing among distinct human persons. What is needed is not
group-men but companions. Steinbeck has always had trouble focusing
on individuals, and he has always known it. "You have never known
a person," Joseph Wayne's sister-in-law says to him; and we feel it is
Steinbeck admonishing himself. "You aren't aware of persons, Joseph;

only people. You can't see units, Joseph, only the whole." Therefore it is heartening as well as a trifle surprising to come at last and in *East of Eden* upon the long awaited awareness, the long delayed perception; to arrive in Steinbeck's pages at the revelation withheld from Joseph Wayne and even from Doc Burton and Jim Casy. And this occurs in a passage not wholly justified by the immediate context, but erupting with a fierceness of feeling reminiscent of the explosive and superficially irrelevant ode to democracy which pops up in the early pages of *Moby Dick*. "And this I believe," Steinbeck's voice suddenly announces to us:

> And this I believe. That the free, exploring mind of the individual human is the most valuable thing in the world. And this I would fight for: the freedom of the mind to take any direction it wishes, undirected. And this I must fight against: an idea, religion or government which limits or destroys the individual. This is what I am and what I am about. I can understand why a system built on a pattern must try to destroy the free mind, for this is the one thing which can by inspection destroy such a system. Surely I can understand this, and I hate it and I will fight against it to preserve the one thing that separates us from the uncreative beasts. If the glory can be killed, we are lost.

It can no doubt be explained that such a belief and the passion behind it have been generated by revolt against the peculiar misbehaviours, the conformist pressures, of the 1950s, just as the emphasis on unity and the world-soul were stimulated by the ruggedly destructive individualism of the 1930s. But this time Steinbeck's rebellious impulse has produced a theme which goes beyond politics; which is, very simply and very greatly, human; which is the actual stuff of the art of narrative. *East of Eden* itself does not, as a novel, demonstrate this new and potentially happier wedding. But in the passage quoted Steinbeck's familiar daemon leapt out at us for an instant, and some day he will emerge to stay.

Chronology of Important Dates

1902   Born February 27, in Salinas, California, third of four children and only son of John Ernst Steinbeck, Sr., and Olive Hamilton.

1919   Graduates from Salinas High School.

1920–25 Sporadic attendance at Stanford University, works as laborer. First publications in *Stanford Spectator*.

1925   To New York, working as laborer and as reporter for the *American*.

1926–29 Living in California, writing stories and novels and publishing one story, various unskilled labor.

1929   *Cup of Gold,* his first novel.

1930   Marries Carol Henning and settles in Pacific Grove, where he meets Edward Ricketts.

1932   *The Pastures of Heaven.* Moves to Los Angeles.

1933   *To a God Unknown.* Returns to Monterey area.

1934   Steinbeck's mother dies. "The Murder" wins O. Henry Prize.

1935   *Tortilla Flat,* his first successful novel, wins Commonwealth Club of California Gold Medal.

1936   Steinbeck's father dies. *In Dubious Battle* wins another Commonwealth Club medal. "The Harvest Gypsies," series on migrant workers, published in *San Francisco News.* Trip to Mexico.

1937   *Of Mice and Men* successful as novel and, as play, wins Drama Critics' Circle Silver Plaque. *The Red Pony,* in three parts. Trip to Europe and later from Oklahoma to California with migrants.

1938   *The Long Valley.* Pamphlet version of *News* articles, *Their Blood Is Strong.*

1939 *The Grapes of Wrath.* Becomes a member of the National Institute of Arts and Letters.

1940 Pulitzer Prize for *The Grapes of Wrath.* Collecting trip to the Gulf of California with Ricketts. Films "The Forgotten Village" in Mexico. Film versions made of *The Grapes of Wrath* and *Of Mice and Men.*

1941 With Ricketts, publishes *Sea of Cortez.*

1942 *The Moon Is Down,* novel and play. *Bombs Away,* written for the Army Air Corps. Divorces Carol Henning. Film of *Tortilla Flat.*

1943 Marries Gwyndolen Conger (Verdon) and moves to New York. To Europe as war correspondent for the *New York Herald Tribune.* Film of *The Moon Is Down.*

1944 Writes script for Alfred Hitchcock's *Lifeboat.* First son, Thomas, born.

1945 *Cannery Row. The Red Pony,* in four parts. "The Pearl of the World" in *Woman's Home Companion.* Coauthors script of *A Medal for Benny.*

1946 Son John born.

1947 *The Wayward Bus* and *The Pearl.* Trip to Russia with photographer Robert Capa.

1948 *A Russian Journal.* Divorced from Gwyndolen Conger. Ed Ricketts dies after car-train collision. Elected to American Academy of Letters. Film of *The Pearl.*

1949 Film of *The Red Pony.*

1950 *Burning Bright,* novel and play. Writes script for *Viva Zapata!* Marries Elaine Scott.

1951 *Log from the Sea of Cortez,* with preface on Ricketts.

1952 *East of Eden.* Articles from Europe for *Colliers.*

1954 *Sweet Thursday.*

1955 *Pipe Dream,* Rodgers and Hammerstein musical based on *Sweet Thursday.* Film of *East of Eden.*

1957 *The Short Reign of Pippin IV.* Film of *The Wayward Bus.*

1958 *Once There Was a War,* collection of war dispatches.

1961 *The Winter of Our Discontent.*

1962   *Travels with Charley.* Wins Nobel Prize for literature.

1964   Wins Press Medal of Freedom and United States Medal of Freedom.

1965   Columns for *Newsday,* including reports from Vietnam.

1966   *America and Americans.*

1968   Televised versions of *Travels with Charley, Of Mice and Men,* scenes from *The Grapes of Wrath.* "Here's Where I Belong," musical based on *East of Eden,* closes after one performance. Dies December 20, buried in Salinas.

1969   *Journal of a Novel: The "East of Eden" Letters.*

1970   Opera based on *Of Mice and Men* produced in Seattle.

Notes on the Editor and Contributors

ROBERT MURRAY DAVIS, editor of this volume, is associate professor of English at the University of Oklahoma, editor of *The Novel: Modern Essays in Criticism, Modern British Short Novels,* and *Evelyn Waugh,* and author of essays on fictional theory and on modern British and American fiction.

FREEMAN CHAMPNEY has been active in university and commercial press work since 1937, was a founding editor of *Antioch Review,* and has published *Art and Glory: The Story of Elbert Hubbard.* The essay reprinted in this collection was written in Pacific Grove after a social evening with Ed Ricketts and his wife.

ARTHUR F. KINNEY, JR., associate professor of English at the University of Massachusetts, is coeditor of *Bear, Man, and God,* editor of *Symposium* and of the journal *English Literary Renaissance.*

ANDRÉ GIDE (1869–1951), French novelist and man of letters, won the Nobel Prize for Literature in 1947.

HOWARD LEVANT, chairman of the department of English at Hartwick College, has published several articles on modern poetry and on American culture.

WARREN FRENCH, chairman of the department of English at the Indianapolis branch of Indiana University–Purdue University, is the author of *John Steinbeck* and of many other volumes on American fiction.

ARNOLD L. GOLDSMITH, professor of English at Wayne State University, has published *Modern American Literary Criticism, 1905–1965,* and essays on nineteenth- and twentieth-century American fiction.

PETER LISCA is professor of English at the University of Florida and has published articles on modern American fiction in addition to *The Wide World of John Steinbeck* and a critical edition of *The Grapes of Wrath.*

GEORGE BLUESTONE, formerly of the University of Washington and now free-lance film writer and producer, is author of *Novel into Film, The Private World of Cully Powers,* and *The Send-Off.*

JOSEPH FONTENROSE, professor of Classics at the University of California, Berkeley, has written *Python: A Study of Delphic Myth and Its Origins, The*

Cult and Myth of Pyrros [sic.] *at Delphi, The Ritual Theory of Myth,* and *John Steinbeck.*

STANLEY G. ALEXANDER, professor of English at Stephen F. Austin State College, is author of *George Sessions Perry* and editor of the journal *Re: Arts and Letters.*

HARRY MORRIS, professor of English at Florida State University, is the author of *Richard Barnfield* and *Sorrowful City.*

R. W. B. LEWIS, professor of English and American Studies at Yale and editor of the Malraux volume in this series, is the author of *The American Adam, The Picaresque Saint,* and *Trials of the Word.*

Selected Bibliography

Bibliography

Hayashi, Tetsumaro. *John Steinbeck: A Concise Bibliography (1930–1965)*. Metuchen, N.J.: Scarecrow Press, 1967. Repetitious and poorly proofread, but the most thorough list of primary and secondary material.

Beebe, Maurice, and Jackson R. Bryer. "Criticism of John Steinbeck: A Selected Checklist." *Modern Fiction Studies*, XI (Spring 1965), 90–103. Within obvious limitations, more usable than Hayashi's bibliography.

French, Warren. "John Steinbeck." In *Fifteen Modern American Authors: A Survey of Research and Criticism*, Jackson R. Bryer, ed. Durham: Duke University Press, 1969. An excellent survey and evaluation of Steinbeck criticism.

The Steinbeck Quarterly, edited by Hayashi, publishes bibliographical and critical articles.

Books

Donohue, Agnes McNeill. *A Casebook on "The Grapes of Wrath."* New York: Thomas Y. Crowell Company, 1968.

Fontenrose, Joseph. *John Steinbeck: An Introduction and Interpretation.* New York: Holt, Rinehart & Winston, Inc., 1963. In the "American Authors and Critics Series."

French, Warren. *John Steinbeck.* New York: Twayne, 1961. In the "United States Authors Series."

———. *A Companion to "The Grapes of Wrath."* New York: The Viking Press, 1963. Like Donohue's book, a collection of critical and historical material, although the two overlap very little.

Hayashi, Tetsumaro, and Richard Astro. *Steinbeck: The Man and His Work.* Corvallis: Oregon State University Press, 1971.

Lisca, Peter. *The Wide World of John Steinbeck.* New Brunswick, N.J.: Rutgers University Press, 1958. The most thorough and by far the best book on Steinbeck.

Marks, Lester Jay. *Thematic Design in the Novels of John Steinbeck.* New York: Humanities Press, 1969. Originally published as No. IX in "Studies in American Literature," The Hague: Mouton, 1969.

Moore, Harry T. *The Novels of John Steinbeck: A First Critical Study.* Chicago: Normandie House, 1939. Second edition, "With a Contemporary Epilogue," Port Washington, N.Y.: Kennikat Press, 1968. The epilogue recants Moore's earlier interest in Steinbeck as a novelist.

Tedlock, E. W., Jr., and C. V. Wicker, eds. *Steinbeck and His Critics: A Record of Twenty-Five Years.* Albuquerque: University of New Mexico Press, 1957. A good selection of previously published material.

Watt, F. W. *John Steinbeck.* New York: Grove Press, Inc., 1962. In the "Writers and Critics Series."

Essays

Aaron, Daniel. "Radical Humanism of John Steinbeck: *The Grapes of Wrath* Thirty Years Later." *Saturday Review,* LI (September 23, 1968), 26–27, 55–56.

Alexander, Stanley. "The Conflict of Form in *Tortilla Flat.*" *American Literature,* XL (March 1968), 58–66.

Beach, Joseph Warren. "John Steinbeck: Journeyman Artist," pp. 309–24; "John Steinbeck: Art and Propaganda," pp. 327–47. *American Fiction, 1920–1940.* New York: The Macmillan Company, 1942.

Fairley, Barker. "John Steinbeck and the Coming Literature." *Sewanee Review,* L (April 1942), 145–61. Historically important for its emphasis on vernacular speech and epic breadth.

Hyman, Stanley Edgar. "Some Notes on John Steinbeck." *Antioch Review,* II (Summer 1942), 185–200.

Jones, Lawrence William. " 'A Little Play in Your Head': Parable Form in John Steinbeck's Postwar Fiction." *Genne,* LLI (March 1970), 55–63. Explains what Steinbeck was doing but not the works' aesthetic value.

Levant, Howard. "*Tortilla Flat:* The Shape of John Steinbeck's Career." *PMLA,* LXXXV (October 1970), 1087–95. Denies relevance of parallels to Malory.

Levidova, I. "The Postwar Books of John Steinbeck." *Soviet Review,* IV (Summer 1963), 3–13.

Richards, Edmund C. "The Challenge of John Steinbeck." *North American Review,* CCXLIII (Summer 1937), 406–13. Sympathetic and competent early praise.

Whipple, T. K. "Steinbeck: Through a Glass, Though Brightly." In *Study*

Out the Land. Berkeley: University of California Press, 1945. Originally published in *New Republic,* XCVI (October 12, 1938), 274–75.

Wilson, Edmund. "John Steinbeck." In *Classics and Commercials: A Literary Chronicle of the Forties.* New York: Farrar, Straus & Giroux, Inc., 1950.

"John Steinbeck Special Number." *Modern Fiction Studies,* XI (Spring 1965). Besides the two essays reprinted in this collection, includes work by Lisca and French dealing with Steinbeck's later work, excellent discussions of the short stories "The Chrysanthemums" and "Flight," and four other essays.